China Business

Navigating the Maze that is China!

Saba Joseph

ISBN-13: 978-1463699994

ISBN-10: 1463699999

Printed in USA

CONTENTS

PREFACE

China Business closely follows my personal experience and that of my family during a three year assignment. I moved to Mainland China to help launch a U.S. based Fortune 100 Company's Personal Cleansing Business there. During my three year assignment, the business grew at breakneck speed from $40 million in annual sales to over $500 million.

Before going much farther, I would like to provide some historical perspective and context on what China was like during the time period when the events in this book took place.

I moved to Mainland China during a period of intense and rapid change. At that time, Deng Xiaoping, China's Supreme Leader, was still alive and China was in the early stages of opening up to business and the West. During my assignment, Deng Xiaoping, passed away and Jiang Zemin became the new Supreme Leader.

Deng Xiaoping was responsible for moving China toward economic reforms that began in 1978 and occurred in two stages.

The first stage, in the late 1970s and early 1980s, involved the de-collectivization of agriculture, opening up of the country to foreign investment, and giving permission to entrepreneurs to start businesses. However, during this stage, most industry remained state-owned, inefficient and acted as a drag on economic growth.

The second stage of reform, in the late 1980s and 1990s, involved the privatization of much of the state-owned industry and the lifting of price controls, protectionist policies, and regulations. However, state monopolies in sectors such as banking and petroleum remained untouched by those reforms. The private sector grew remarkably as a result of those reforms.

The events in this book took place in the mid to late 1990's, during the second stage of Deng Xiaping's economic reforms. Allowing foreign investors to form Joint Ventures (JV's) with local businesses that were owned and operated by the various bureaus was the approach that the Communist Party preferred to use and was typical of how most foreign companies were able to break into the Chinese market.

Up to this point in China's recent history, a large number of companies were a burden on the Chinese economy. The Communist Party's "Iron rice bowl" policy provided people in the military, civil service and employees of state run enterprises an occupation with guaranteed job security, steady income and benefits. The government had to subsidize and prop up those companies in order to keep people employed. Typically, manufacturing plants had dormitories, where employees and their families lived, and cafeterias, where they ate 3 meals a day.

The formation of JV's transformed state owned enterprises from being a cost burden on the Chinese economy to becoming profitable contributor's to China's exploding export economy and, with that, the decades of having to subsidize a very broad range of industries was coming to an end.

Clearly, this was a clever approach by the Communist Party since it allowed China to get the best of all worlds. The government was able to maintain part ownership in those companies as it shifted the cost and responsibility for modernizing its antiquated industrial base to their new JV Partners. Regardless of one's perspective, in many ways, this was a "marriage" made in heaven ... on the one hand, China needed to get out from under the weight of carrying tens of thousands of antiquated and unprofitable manufacturing plants and, on the other hand, there was an endless line of eager foreign investors that desperately wanted to get in on the ground floor and have free access to Chinese consumers …. So, voilà, just like magic, the new age of JV's was born.

The way things worked (at least for the most part) was that a foreign company would buy an equity position in a manufacturing facility and become a Joint Venture Partner. This would soon be followed by an injection of capital from the foreign Partners to replace virtually worthless and antiquated technology with modern and sometimes state of the art technology. Western style management would replace existing command and control management structures.

For the foreign JV Partners, there were two major benefits. The first is that they had instant access to the Chinese market with potentially over 1 billion consumers. The second benefit was that they were setting up a manufacturing facility with instant and ready access to one of the cheapest and most plentiful sources of labor on the planet with relatively low barriers to entry.

Expatriate housing was filled to capacity and, in many cases, the only choice of living accommodations available to foreigners was at hotels, but companies paid the exorbitant prices that were being charged and chocked it up as the cost of doing business.

In writing this book, I aimed to achieve two main objectives. The first was to write an entertaining novel about the trials and tribulations that expatriates go through when they move to mainland China. Here I tried to describe real life experiences that would be both entertaining and educational. The second objective was to provide a balanced and realistic view of what it is like to start, run or do business in China by providing as many insights as I could into Chinese Culture, the way people think, interact and behave towards foreigners and, just as important, I tried to explain why they do what they do.

Understanding Chinese culture and keeping an open mind are basic prerequisites that can easily mean the difference between a generally pleasant assignment and a painful one.

As you read this book, I hope that you will find it both entertaining and educational as you learn about Chinese culture, how to build a robust business strategy, the challenges and rewards of taking an expatriate assignment, the importance of maintaining a positive outlook, how to deal with daunting bureaucracy and finally, how to achieve superb results despite the absence of an experienced management team.

I hope you enjoy reading this book as much as I enjoyed writing it.

ACKNOWLEDGMENTS

I would like to thank my wife Nancy who was always by my side every step of my career. While I was busy with my job, she managed the family affairs and raised our children to become very nice and responsible human beings. Through the years she became an expert at managing our household through eight relocation's and was always there through thick and thin ... from teachers conferences to greeting the kids when they came home from school.

The bamboo painting on the cover and opposite page is one of hundreds she did since studying watercolor painting in Tianjin, China. In 1998, she was recognized by the Tianjin Artists Association and won an award for 'best painting by a foreigner' when, unbeknownst to her, her teacher Mr. Zhao Yingbin, a famous Chinese artist and poet, entered her paintings in a competition. Her work was displayed in an art exhibit, featured on local television stations and, more recently, on greeting cards.

I would also like to thank my son John and daughter Elizabeth for their insights and support both for this book and beyond. Over the years, they transitioned from simply being my children to becoming trusted friends.

I would also like to thank the many professional people I had the privilege of working with over the years. I was fortunate enough to have so many people help me at important junctures in my career. Some were coaches, others simply listened and all were dear and precious friends. I always tried and will continue to try to pay their kindness forward. They know who they are.

I would also like to remember a dear friend and colleague that was instrumental in helping me learn and better understand Chinese culture, the late Marie Sun. whose passing after a car accident prematurely extinguished a young and vibrant life much before its time. Her kindness and eagerness to help me learn and adjust to life in China will always be remembered.

Finally, I want to acknowledge my parents, brother and two sisters. They always believed in me and were always there for me. My father always worked very hard and set the example I tried to follow in my personal and professional lives. As for my mother, she was an extraordinary woman. I still remember the day she insisted that I apply for admission to M.I.T. while we were on a tour of Cambridge, Massachusetts. At the time, I did not think I could get into M.I.T. let alone afford it. But she insisted and I had to listen. To my surprise, I was accepted and managed to sign on to do breakthrough research sponsored by the National Science Foundation which paid for my tuition. Once completed, my research became the new technical standard for identifying organic pollutants in air and water. Who knows what turn my life might have taken without her grabbing my arm and insisting that I walk into M.I.T.'s admissions office that afternoon. May she rest in peace!

This simple maze, designed by my son John, who has spent several years studying Mandarin and Chinese culture, aims to symbolize the dichotomy of doing business in China.

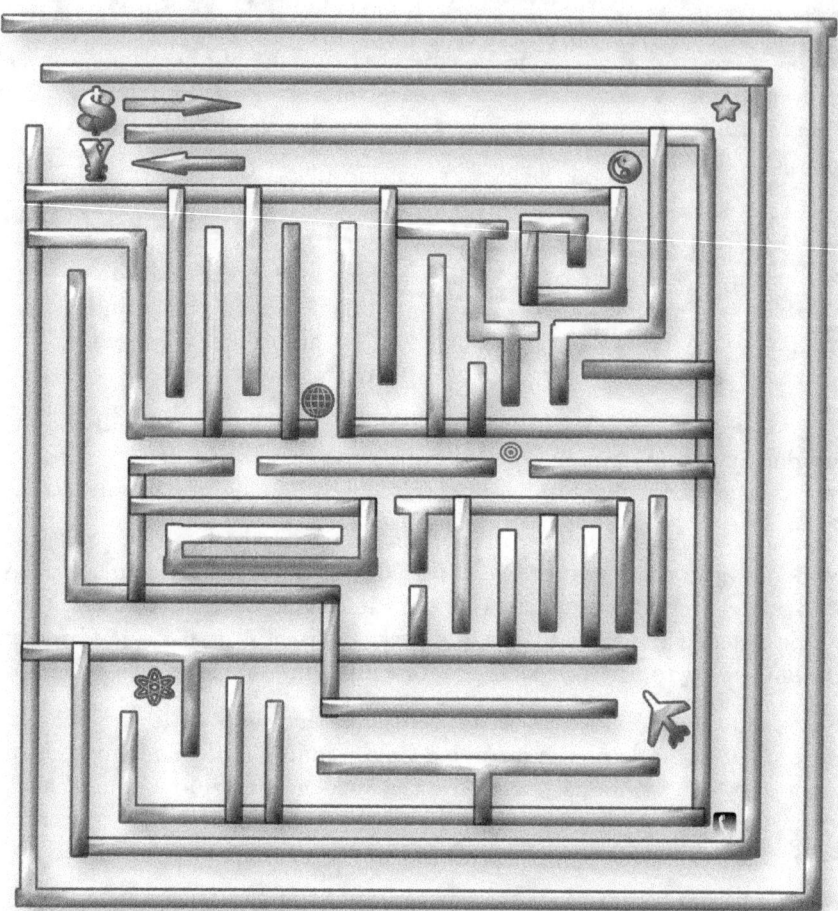

One side of this dichotomy represents the complexities foreigners face when they try to get anything done. That would be the equivalent of trying to navigate this maze without the help of the arrows and guiding symbols. Without the right relationships and Guang Xi, the arrows and symbols would be invisible and navigating the maze would be much more complex..

The opposite side of this dichotomy is the equivalent of navigating this maze with the help of the arrows and the symbols. Those symbolize what understanding Chinese culture and building relationships, Guang Xi, can do for those who invest the time and energy necessary to build relationships and learn how to navigate through the maze of China.

1

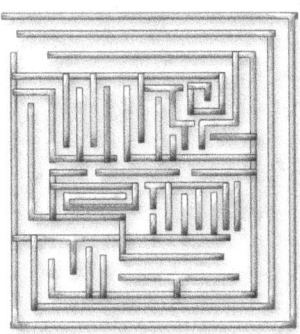

THE LOOK-SEE TRIP

The Captain announced over the intercom that we were on our final descent into Hong Kong. We are a long way from Cincinnati. Peter had said it was entirely up to me to decide if I wanted to take the assignment in Tianjin. A thousand thoughts were lingering in my head. Will Nancy and the kids be able to adjust? What do I know about running a business in China or the Chinese culture? Sure I read some books in anticipation of the look-see trip, but really, what do I know?

The pilot skillfully maneuvered the plane towards Hong Kong's Kai Tak International Airport's single runway which is infamous for its difficult landings. I was surprised at how close the plane was to skyscrapers and mountains. Out of my window, I could see people on apartment balconies and objects through their apartment windows. The plane touched down and slowly taxied along the runway which juts out over Victoria Harbor.

Soon we were in line to clear immigration. That went smoothly and we were greeted by a driver who worked for the New World Harbor View Hotel. The baggage was collected and minutes later we were in the back seat of a plush Mercedes limo.

The driver deftly maneuvered his way through the heavy rush hour traffic and had us to the hotel within fifteen minutes. The hotel lobby was sophisticated. It was richly appointed with granite and marble floors and mahogany wood accents were everywhere. The scent of fresh lilies greeted us as we walked past a quaint European-style flower shop adjacent to the reception desk. The receptionist, efficiently checked us in and within minutes we were walking towards the elevator. The smell of linseed oil on the mahogany wood that lined the elevator walls, mingled with the scent of lilies, permeated the air as we ascended to our room for a much needed rest.

The next day, I briefly met with Jack, who would be my new boss. A serious, medium built man with salt and pepper hair, green eyes and a thick mustache. Jack informed me that he was planning to fly with us to Tianjin later that morning. For the rest of the morning, we met with Laura from Human Resources to get information about schooling for our teenage kids, medical and other basic information about living and working in China. Laura is a petite woman, who was originally from Minneapolis. She was new with the company and much of her knowledge was from information she read and not based on firsthand experience. The meetings were quick and two hours later we were on our way with Jack to catch the two and a half hour flight to Tianjin, China.

I couldn't wait to see the plant the company just purchased, but my curiosity has to wait until tomorrow. The company has high hopes for this plant. It was bought with the expectation that it will allow the company to quickly launch the bar soap business in China. The expectations are very high indeed. Tomorrow, I will be meeting Rick, the General Manager that I will be replacing, to get a firsthand look at the plant and review the plans to launch and build the business.

For the rest of the day, Nancy and I will spend the evening with Jack and enjoy a nice dinner. Two American ex-pats, Ed and his wife Sharon will also be joining us to help give us a feel for what it would be like to live and work in China.

As the driver took us from the airport to the Hyatt hotel, I couldn't help but be amazed by the sea of humanity on bicycles all around us. It was quite an amazing sight. People were everywhere. There were cars and thousands of bicycles going in every direction. To me it looked like there was absolutely no order or logic to the way people moved. I did not see accidents or cars and bicycles colliding as I might have expected to see if this traffic pattern happened in New York or LA. Somehow it all worked.

"How big a city is Tianjin?" I asked Jack

"About eleven million" he said "I believe it is the third largest city in China after Shanghai and Beijing."

"For the life of me" I said "I can't understand the traffic movement. People seem to drive or cycle into incoming traffic without hesitating or even looking in both direction and yet I am not seeing crashes as I would expect if I was driving in any major city in the US or anywhere else I've been."

"It is amazing" he said "I don't get it either, but somehow it works over here. By the way, if you accept this assignment, you will not be allowed to drive. The company will assign you a car and driver."

"Given time, I am sure I can figure out how to drive around here" I said and then I started to laugh as I looked at Nancy's face and quickly added "I better take that back. I must have lost my mind for a second to think that I can possibly drive safely over here."

"You don't understand" Jack said "it is not a choice in this particular case. The company policy clearly says that ex-pats are not allowed to drive in China even though you can get a legal license to drive."

"I don't understand why we have such a policy" I said "not that I am eager to drive in this insanity"

"The way things get settled here are by the side of the road. The company does not want the liability. If a foreigner gets into an accident and someone is hurt, the general rule of thumb is that the foreigner will be financially responsible for that person and their family from that point on."

"I understand that it can be a big deal to be stuck in a situation like that" I said.

"Yes, and from what I hear, sometimes the family can quickly become quite extended, especially if an ex-pat is involved" he said "which is why the company has a policy that provides a car and local driver for executives and reimburses lower level ex-pats for their cab costs and other transportation expenses."

The car pulled to the front of the Tianjin Hyatt Hotel. The bags were collected by the bell boys and we were quickly checked in. Before going to our room to freshen up for dinner, I called Ed and Sharon's room to let them know that we arrived and to agree on a time to meet for dinner. The call went to the answering machine, so I left them a message.

Ed and Sharon had lived in Tianjin for six months. Ed is one of the engineers sent to Tianjin as part of the initial study team charged with developing plans for expanding the plant's capacity. They were going to join us for dinner and help answer our questions about the challenges expatriates face in their every day life in China.

Unfortunately, to our surprise, Ed and Sharon never showed up that evening and the questions we had for them had to go unanswered for the time being. Since Jack was stationed in Hong Kong and had an office in Guangzhou, he had limited knowledge about Tianjin; however, since Ed and Sharon did not show, it gave me more time to get to know Jack a little better and get a feel for how I might like working for him. After dinner, Nancy and I retired to our room.

Just as we were about to get into bed, the phone rang. It was Ed.

"I am sorry" he started. "I just got your message, but no one told me that Sharon and I were supposed to meet you and your wife for dinner. The voice mail you left me was the first I heard about this".

I was trying to think of what I could possibly say to that. We had all those questions and little time to make our decision and then something like this happens, but we can't blame Ed for this. How can he be at a dinner he did not know about?

"Sorry to hear that" I said "Nancy and I were so looking forward to meeting the two of you and learning about what it is like to live in Tianjin."

"It is a little late now to get together, but if you and Nancy are up to it, why don't you come up to our place. We are in room 912." Ed said.

"Let me talk to Nancy and see if she is still up to it. The flights were brutal."

A few minutes later we were at 912 and finally met Ed and Sharon. Ed is six feet tall with graying hair. He had a very gentle and friendly demeanor while Sharon is a slim woman with a wide and welcoming smile. As it turned out, Ed and Sharon are very nice people and we immediately liked both of them.

They shared stories with us about daily life and Sharon offered to take Nancy the next morning and show her around Tianjin, including all the good shops. I could see that the two of them were off to a good start. At least, for tomorrow, I can focus on the plant and business and not have to worry about what Nancy will be doing. But first, Nancy and I are scheduled to go to the Tianjin International School to see where the kids will be going to school if I accept this assignment.

The next morning, Jack, Nancy and I met for breakfast. Lydia, from Human Resources arrived a few minutes later to accompany us to the School. Jack left shortly after that and we agreed to meet at the plant after Nancy and I tour the school.

The school tour was interesting. The school was housed at the same location as a Chinese elementary school. The local government made this space available to the International school as a way to encourage foreign investment in the area. The premise was simply that if foreign companies can't convince ex-pats to accept assignments in Tianjin, then the rate at which investment can be made in the city will be limited. By facilitating the presence of an

International School, the city made it easier for ex-pats to accept assignments there and move their families with them.

The classrooms were very basic but the space was clean. Since it was summer when we were there, we were able to meet with the principal only. Most of the teachers were on summer break visiting family back home.

While the school was not perfect, it was a pass and both Nancy and I agreed that it could work.

Lydia and Nancy went back to the hotel while I went on to the plant to catch up with Jack and meet Rick. Rick and Jack had just finished their meeting as I arrived. Rick, as it turned out, was from the company's UK Division. He was slightly balding with mostly grey hair and a ready smile.

He had the type of personality that made him instantly likeable. He and his wife Maureen had accepted an international assignment for the last 2 years of Rick's career before retirement and they enjoyed traveling. They lived in Beijing and he commuted for two hours to get to Tianjin every morning and another two hours to get back at night. When he had to work late or the weather was bad, he would stay at the Hyatt hotel for the night.

Rick introduced me to Julie, a young Chinese woman with short trimmed hair. She was his assistant and also doubled as his translator. Her English was very good. She was somewhat shy but quite capable. Next he introduced me to Mr. Tian. An older, slightly built man of about five feet who could not have weighed more than 100 pounds even after a big meal. He had a big smile that exposed a front right silver tooth that sparkled in the sunlight coming through the window.

"Mr. Tian is one of two Deputy General Managers" Rick explained. "He was assigned to the Joint Venture by BOLI, the Bureau of Light Industry".

BOLI is the official arm of the local government bureau that oversees industry in the Tianjin area for the Communist Party. I later found out that until his reassignment to the Joint Venture, Mr. Tian had worked for the Tianjin Toilet Soap Factory (TTSF) which happened to also make bar soap and was literally located across the street from our plant. Mr. Tian was soft spoken and appeared to be shy.

Next, Rick introduced me to the other key managers including Lou, who was the second Deputy General Manager. Lou was assigned by the Company as required by the Joint Venture agreement. He is in charge of the day to day running of the operation. Both Deputy General Managers will be reporting to me if I accept this assignment and take over from Rick as the General Manager.

After all the introductions, it was time to take a tour of the plant and learn about the business plans and strategies. The tour was at once both shocking and fascinating. Rick explained that the company purchased 90% ownership in the plant from the Tianjin BOLI. This particular factory was originally built to make sewing machines. Over time, demand for sewing machines dropped and the Communist Party decided to convert it from a sewing machine factory to one that makes bar soap.

"Sewing machines and making soap technology have very little in common" I said scratching my head.

"I agree" said Rick "but when there was no work for those employed by the factory because they could not sell many sewing machines, the communist party had to find a way to keep the workers productively employed, so they decided to convert the factory figuring that people can always use soap"

"Yes, but you told me when you introduced me to Mr. Tian that he had worked for a soap factory that was located across the street from us. So they decided to have two soap factories located across the street from each other?"

"Yes, that is true. Both factories were run and coordinated as one to the extent possible under a central planning system." Rick said "unfortunately, the one they were willing to sell us was the converted one. The other one was built as a kettle soap making factory. It would have been a better acquisition … at least it was designed to make soap" He chuckled and said "one of the few challenges you will have to work through if you take this job".

"Thanks a lot, you are a real pal" I said as I wearily chuckled.

Rick went on to tell me that when the company took over the factory. It employed over 800 people and, in typical communist style, had dormitories that housed workers and their families. Food was provided by the company at a cafeteria and, generally, the factory was a place where people worked, lived and raised their families.

The technology they were using to make Soap was ancient. Kettle soap making was an "art" that was practically forgotten in the West. As a Chemical Engineer, I was fascinated to see Soap being made using kettles. It reminded me of a time when the kids were little and Nancy and I took them to Old Sturbridge Pioneer Village in Massachusetts where they showed us how the pilgrims made their soap.

While I was standing by the window reflecting on the pioneer village visit, I spotted a mule drawn cart transporting some barrels, pulling in through the main gate. It stopped at one of the buildings.

"What have we here?" I asked Rick pointing at the carriage.

"Oh, this is a delivery of pig fat or lard. The lard is collected from butchers in the local area and delivered to the factory." he said. The Chinese do not eat a lot of beef and don't have a lot of coconut trees" he added, "Much of the local soap is made from lard instead of beef tallow as its primary ingredient."

The men by now were unloading the drums and tipping them over small open pits. He went on to explain that steam is used to melt the lard which is then pumped to the kettles where it is made into soap.

As we climbed to the third floor of the building, my mind was racing. The company wants me to take over a business that may have been technologically obsolete a hundred years ago. Lard makes inferior quality soap. This is insane. I thought back to my university days and wondered what my professors or classmates would say if they could see me now. I shook my head and smiled.

On the third floor, I saw some signs of relief. A somewhat modern series of columns pumps and gauges with some controls that were about 20 years old, but at least from this century. I turned to Rick with excitement and said "you have been holding out on me. You had me scared until we got here".

"Don't get too excited" he said as he laughed "this unit was purchased from an Italian Vendor but they have never been able to make it work here. My best guess is that when it was started up, the material balance was wrong and when it was shut down, it was not cleared. So what you likely have is a giant bar of bad quality soap that has solidified inside each piece of machinery. If we can make this unit operational, it is designed to produce six tons of soap an hour. Not enough capacity, but certainly a big improvement over what we have at the moment."

"Does anyone here know how to run it?" I asked

"There are a few who were trained by the vendor, but I would say, we are seriously short on experience" he said as he ushered me to the next part of the building that housed the soap making kettles. The kettle soap making was a very basic operation with no new surprises.

Finally, we walked up to the fourth floor where the packaging room was located. An army of close to three hundred women was clustered in groups of 8 around long tables with trays of soap and stacks of small boxes all around them. All packaging was done by hand. The packers skillfully formed the cartons, applied glue on one end with their finger, picked a bar of soap, inserted it into the box and glued the other end. I was fascinated and thoroughly impressed by the speed they were able to form, fill and glue those soap boxes. Rick told me that they are paid by the piece and are very motivated by the rewards of their productivity.

Next we started to head back towards the office. "Let me show you the boiler house and where our environmental treatment plant will be located" Rick said.

The boiler house, where the steam was generated, used coal as its source of energy. Next to it was a big yard where the coal was stored. On the other side of the coal yard was a construction site where two huge "swimming" pools that were part of a new water treatment plant were under construction. Beyond that, a large building was also under construction. Rick said that this was the building that will house the glycerin refining facility.

Glycerin is a byproduct of making soap. Once it is refined, it can be used in food products, cosmetics and as an ingredient in many industrial, consumer and pharmaceutical products. Rick went on to tell me that for the time being, the glycerin we produce is sold to the Tianjin Toilet Soap Factory (TTSF) across the street.

By the time we got back to the office, it was getting late and Jack needed to head back to the airport to catch his flight back to Hong Kong. So we said our goodbyes and Jack asked me to let him know sometime next week if I am interested in taking this assignment.

Rick packed his desk and we headed to the Hyatt hotel to pick up Nancy before departing for Beijing. The plan was for Nancy and me to spend 2 days in Beijing as tourists before flying back to Cincinnati. Nancy was already waiting for us. We said good bye to Sharon as Rick's Driver, Mr. Zhang, put our bags in the trunk and we were off to Beijing.

As we started our two hour drive to Beijing, I asked Nancy how her day went and what she thought so far.

"Sharon is a great lady" she said.

I looked at her waiting to hear more.

"By that" she continued "I mean she is a generous and caring human being. She visits the orphanage in Tianjin daily and is an integral part of their organization. When you consider her sincere concern for people on top of the time she had spent living in Tianjin, it is easy to understand why the company asks her to be the 'look-see' companion and guide for potential transferees for the company."

"I agree" I said "she is a very nice lady."

"She took me to the street markets" she continued "its funny, but they looked like the produce section of any small town grocery store display with one big exception. The produce was on the street, not on tables or stands, but literally in clumps on the ground stacked on top of newspapers or burlap. The vegetables were glorious --- shiny skinned eggplants, small and round not large and oval. Fresh tomatoes, plump, with flawless skins. Carrots, potatoes, onions, scallions, ginger, peppers or whatever the local farmers had in season, was there. Everything looked extra fresh, but cleanliness would be an issue."

"After that, she took me back to the school for a second look." She paused for a second before continuing "the school tour was enlightening. An eye opener I would say."

She turned to Rick and asked "did you ever go to the school?"

"No" Rick answered "since I am way past the age of having to worry about school age kids, I never took the time. What did you think?"

"Different" she said "very different from what I am used to. It has large metal entrance doors that are painted a pale blue. Inside, the floors and stairwells are all raw cement. The classrooms, however, are normal looking, with desks that seem current. during the morning visit, we only met the principal; but when I went back with Sharon, we ran into two of the teachers. They were very typical of the teachers I met in the US, and seemed to really love their work, and also seemed to really enjoy living in Tianjin. They both remarked that moving back now, would feel 'foreign' as they have made friends here, and have a routine that they feel rivals any they would have had back home. They told me that most teachers were from the US, I think there is one teacher from England, but I did not meet her."

"The Math and Science books" she continued "seem to be on par with the kids' current ones. So far, except for the fact that there is no air conditioning and it was a bit hot, I think it will be fine for John and Liz. We also stopped back and talked to the principal for a few moments. He had more encouraging things to say about their curriculum and the extra-curricular activities the school offers. Those include field trips to other cities in China. I think this could work just fine. Everyone speaks English, and inside the classrooms it looks a lot like the US schools. I think once the kids see it, they will be fine."

"I am glad you had a chance to go back and revisit the school" I said. The time we spent there together was a little rushed. This makes me feel better."

"Yes, me too" she said and continued "we also toured the Friendship Store. It reminded me of pictures I'd seen of older department stores in some of the rural towns in the U.S. 50 or 60 years ago .... only a bit rougher. At all the door entrances there were many hanging vertical strips of heavy plastic. Something like what you might see in the freezer section in some supermarkets. The floors were a mix of linoleum and tile, some pieces broken or missing and scatter mats covering the more treacherous parts. The merchandise was new and quality good; although not as fashionable as what we have at home. I bought some table linens and a couple of scarves that were labeled silk, but I knew had to be polyester.

From there, Sharon took me to Isetan, the other department store in Tianjin, which is owned by a Japanese company. It was like being in the US present day, but with a sense of something different. It was clean and had escalators and perfectly tiled floors. Large sized ones that had been polished. All the make-up lines and latest perfumes were there: Estee Lauder, Lancôme, all familiar names and I felt "at home". We spent just enough time to make a quick tour of each floor and then it was back in the taxi to the hotel. We agreed to have lunch together at the Hyatt, which has fantastic Western/European food. After seeing those places, I felt that this could be manageable for three years" she concluded.

It took about forty five minutes to get to the main highway from the city. We drove through endless rows of single story houses, that house several families each, and hundreds of neighborhoods with their own small stores, street vendors, street barbers and groups of men on the side of the street sitting around small tables on the sidewalks and playing mahjong or simply visiting with each other.

Of course, there was also the ever present sea of humanity moving around the neighborhoods on bicycles along with the local mode of trucking, the tricycle. Chinese tricycles are full size with the front of a regular bicycle complemented with what looks like a mini truck bed in the back that sits on what looks like two regular bicycle wheels. Tricycles are usually man powered and are used in place of "mini trucks". They are loaded up to the hilt with anything that needs to be transported short distances. Furniture, vegetable and even material collected for recycling or garbage.

I was puzzled by how long it took to get to the highway from the center of Tianjin.

"Is it my imagination or did we just drive forever to get to the Tianjin/Beijing Highway?" I asked Rick.

"No, it's not your imagination" he said "what you need to know is that Tianjin is also a port city. The port of Tianjin is a gateway to China's Northeast and vast Western region. It is located at the estuary of the Hai He River along the western edge of the Bo Hai Bay in the Pacific Ocean. While you and most people would think the Beijing-Tianjin highway is designed to conveniently and efficiently link those two cities; in reality, that was not the case when this highway was constructed. The real objective of building this highway was to provide Beijing with direct access to the Port of Tianjin since the Port is used for shipping millions of tons of exports . It also provides a very important naval access point for the Chinese military.

Granted, the port has played an integral role in Tianjin's development as a manufacturing and export center in the Bo Hai region, which encompasses He bei and Shandong. The planners had a mission. The convenience of the people of Tianjin was not part of that mission. Things are of course improving all the time, but as a general rule, during Mao Tse Tung's rule, Beijing was the center of the universe and in many ways that has not changed much."

"This sounds like the Chinese equivalent to the old saying about 'all roads lead to Rome' that was coined about the glory days of the Roman Empire" I said "in this case, all roads lead to Beijing, and the most direct way between the Port and Beijing is what we are driving on right now."

Ahead in the distance, we started to see the lights of the city of Beijing. As we approached, it was impressive to see all the modern looking high-rises in every direction. The lights were brilliant with a lot of neon lights like one might see on the strip in Las Vegas. Again, there was that sea of humanity. People riding their bicycles everywhere I looked and the same orderly chaos that I observed in Tianjin. The streets of Beijing were wider than streets in Tianjin and there was even more cars competing for space on the road with the now familiar bicycle traffic.

Rick dropped us at the Kempinski Hotel in the Beijing Lufthansa Center and said that his wife Maureen will pick us up in the morning around 10:00 AM to show us around. We thanked him and said goodbye.

The Kempinski Hotel is a five star Joint Venture of German, Chinese and Korean investors. It has an expansive lobby with a glass dome roof that houses the reception area as well as lots of wall hangings, contemporary art and bamboo features. It is part of the same complex that houses a convention center and one of Beijing's biggest malls. Within a short walk, one can find a replica of the more famous Silk Street and a wide range of art and craft shops.

We checked in and found our way to one of the restaurants to get a bite to eat. The food was mostly foreign fare similar to what you might expect in any US or European hotel restaurant. We ordered salad, entrées and some wine and started to debrief about our day now that we were finally alone.

As Nancy started to tell me about her impressions, three men, whom we later found out were originally from the Philippines, started playing guitars and singing mostly familiar romantic songs. They were making the rounds to the tables and asking guests for their requests. When it was our turn, we asked them to play 'Bésame Mucho', an old Spanish song written in 1940 by Mexican songwriter Consuelo Velázquez, a favorite of ours. We sat back and enjoyed our dinner, the wine and music.

Afterward, we decided to go out for a walk and enjoy the rest of our evening together. Outside the hotel, we saw something that we did not see in Tianjin, there were people who looked like they lived on the street and a few small children who were begging. We felt sad. Later we found out that, in China, people are not free to move from city or locality to another without permission from the central government. However; since the big cities, especially Beijing, offered the opportunity to work and make higher wages than people can make in the rural areas, many people come to the cities illegally. Since they are illegal, it is difficult and risky for them to try and find permanent housing, so they live on the street. However, in contrast to other third world countries, in China, beggars and obvious homelessness is rare.

We saw a lot of interesting items and Nancy decided that there was no time like the present to start shopping for gifts. Since, at that point, I was not yet 100% sure that I would be accepting this assignment, I decided to join her and our gift buying frenzy was on.

After both of us were loaded up and we could not possibly carry any more bags, Nancy turned to me and asked "so what did you think about the plant and the business? Do you think you are interested in taking this assignment?"

"I am not sure" I said "it is both exciting and scary"

She looked at me and waited for me to elaborate. "To start with, the plant is a mess. I don't know what people where thinking when they decided to buy it instead of building a new one from the ground up. They don't have the raw materials we need, the technology is ancient, and the plant is also home for many employees and their families."

"The only modern technology, and I am using the word 'modern' very loosely here, is at least 20 years old and no one has figured out how to use it and make it work. They receive material on mule drawn carriages … need I say more?" I said "not to mention the pollution problems with the use of coal for making steam. As best as I can tell, the controls to minimize pollution and clean the air are nonexistent or minimal."

"On the positive side" I continued "the company needs me to take this assignment. I have the experience and the background that is needed to make things work, but I don't really know the size of the challenge that I would have to face in adapting to the culture and trying to do business in China."

"Throughout my career, I never shied away from taking on a challenge" I continued "however, I have the distinct feeling that this takes the meaning of accepting a challenge beyond anything I have experienced in my professional life before."

Nancy finally said "very interesting. It sounds like a huge challenge and lots and lots of work" then she turned to me and said "if you accept the position, how will this assignment affect your career?"

"Like everything else, if I do a good job, it will help my career, otherwise, it could kill it" I said as I contemplated that point more deeply. "On the positive side, I can't imagine that I or even a monkey, if put in charge, can screw this plant any more than where it is right now. So the downside is limited. The upside, on the other hand is unlimited."

She looked me in the eyes and said "there you have it. But before we get ahead of ourselves, what is the downside of saying no to this?"

"When I talked to Peter back in Cincinnati, he told me several times that there is no penalty for saying no. He said that if I decide not to take this position, I should consider this as a vacation for the two of us. 'A gift to the two of us from the company for a job well done' was how he put it. He was emphatic that I should not accept this position unless I really wanted it. It was completely our choice." As I reflected on that I added "I trust Peter. He is a man of his word."

"Good" she said "we need to think about what this means for John and Elizabeth. As I told you in the car, Sharon took me back to see the Tianjin International School this afternoon for a second look. I am not one hundred percent sure about this, but I think it should work out. So we can rule schooling out as a major obstacle for now."

I turned to her and said "how do you feel about moving to China?"

She was silent for a few seconds. She turned to me and said "if you want to do it, I will support you."

I then heard her laugh out loud. "Boy" she said "this is as far as things can get from a nice little house with a white picket fence. It is funny how things turn out. As I was growing up, all I wanted was to have a simple life, live in a simple house with a white picket fence. But I can tell you this much, if you decide to accept this assignment, things will certainly be very interesting!"

I turned to her again and said "we don't have to do this you know!"

"I know" she said "I know. As long as you are sure you want to do this, I am fine. I also think it would be good for the kids. They can benefit from living outside the country and from being exposed to new and different cultures. It would be an adventure." With that, we arrived back at the hotel. The bell boys saw us carrying all those bags and ran over to help us get them to the room.

The next morning at ten sharp Maureen walked into the hotel lobby. We introduced ourselves and soon were on our way to take a guided tour of Beijing. First she took us to Silk Street. Nancy was in heaven. She was like a kid in a candy store as she discovered all those bargains and some interesting and unique pieces that she could not find at a mall in Cincinnati.

To my surprise, even I was getting into this shopping business. Even though my idea of shopping typically consists of going to a store, picking up exactly what I went there to buy, pay and leave. In and out in less than 10 minutes suits me just fine. But not today, it was different. I was really getting into what I came to think of as 'the sport of bargaining with Chinese street vendors'; particularly after receiving a quick lesson from Maureen that morning. After this mini adventure, we went to the Swiss Hotel for a leisurely late lunch.

Next Maureen said she was going to take us to visit the Temple of Heaven. It was spectacular. We were told that it was larger than the Forbidden City with an area of over two and a half million square meters. It was built in 1420 A.D. during the Ming Dynasty to offer sacrifice to Heaven. The Temple is enclosed with a long wall. The northern part is semicircular and is built on higher ground symbolizing Heaven while the Southern part is square and built on lower ground symbolizing earth. This reflected ancient Chinese thought that Heaven was round and earth was square.

The most magnificent buildings are The Circular Mound Altar (Yuanqiutan), Imperial Vault of Heaven (Huangqiongyu) and Hall of Prayer for Good Harvest (Qiniandian).

The Circular Altar has three layered terraces with white marble and was where the Emperors would offer Sacrifice as thanks to Heaven and hope for good things for the future.

The Hall of Prayer for Good Harvest is a big palace with a round roof and three layers of eaves. Inside the Hall are 28 huge posts. The four posts along the inner circle represent four seasons-spring, summer, autumn and winter; the 12 posts along the middle circle represent the 12 months; and 12 posts along the outer circle represent 12 Shichen (Shichen is a means of counting time in ancient China. One Shichen in the past equaled two hours and a whole day was divided into 12 Shichens). The roof is covered with black, yellow and green colored glaze representing the heavens, the earth and everything on earth.

Another important building in the Temple of Heaven is the Imperial Vault of Heaven. If you look at it from far away, you will see that the Vault is like a blue umbrella with a golden head. The structure is like that of the Hall of Prayer for Good Harvest, but smaller in size. The structure is made of bricks and timber. The Vault was used to place memorial tablets of Gods. White marble railings surround the vault.

Finally, the Three Echo Stones is outside of the gate of the Imperial Vault of Heaven. If you speak facing the Vault while standing on the first stone, you will hear one echo; standing on the second and then the third stone, you will hear two and three echoes respectively.

Another interesting and famous place is called Echo Wall. The wall encloses the Imperial Vault of Heaven. Its perimeter is 193 meters. If two people stand at the east and west roots of the wall respectively, a whisper can be heard clearly on the other end.

I thought that it was very interesting that the Chinese civilization was advanced enough to know about the physics and mathematics of sound waves in 1420 and yet, when I reflect back on my plant tour yesterday, I couldn't help but wonder about this dichotomy.

"That was fascinating" Nancy said as we got back in the car and headed to Maureen and Rick's place for cocktails before going out to dinner. Their apartment was very nice and we were almost finished with our drinks when Rick arrived back from his daily commute to Tianjin.

Dinner was at one of the better Chinese restaurants in Beijing. The food was very good and was typical of what foreigners order in a Chinese restaurant. We talked some more about what it was like to live in China and Rick filled me in on some of the key people he deals with outside the plant including many people that I would have to get to know well if I accepted this assignment.

Soon it was time to say good night to our host and hostess. In the morning we were scheduled to go to tour the Beijing International School before heading for the airport and our flight back home to Cincinnati. Rick and Maureen dropped us at the hotel and went back to their apartment.

The long days and the 12 hour time difference was taking its toll on us and we quickly went to sleep.

The alarm went off way too soon.

"Rise and shine" I said, but Nancy simply gave me her 'are you kidding me?' look.

"How can you be cheery" she asked "I feel like I am dead to the world".

A knock on the door announced that the strong coffee had arrived. We both needed it. We quickly showered and got dressed. We only had about half an hour before Sonya, a part time HR person that worked for the company in Beijing, picks us up to go the International School.

The Beijing International School looked like any private US School. It catered to the children of all the diplomats stationed in Beijing and we knew that the school would work for both John and Elizabeth. It was a relief to know that there was a backup option for the kids schooling if all else fails.

Sonya dropped us back at the hotel where we had arranged for a taxi to pick us up and take us to the Airport.

A few hours later, we were on a Canadian Airlines flight bound for Vancouver, B.C. The flight was long but uneventful, we had a chance to catch up on our sleep and still had time to watch a movie, eat and talk. The food and service on Business Class was very good. After finishing our dessert and coffee, Nancy finally asked her open ended question "so, what are you thinking?"

I was trying to delay this conversation as long as I could because I knew this was as far as we can get from 'a little house with a white picket fence' life.

"Just like you, I am concerned about the kids schooling and how well they will adapt to such a big change. Everyday life in China appears to be much more difficult than what we are used to. It certainly reinforces how fortunate we all are to live in the US." I said.

"Even if I was to put all those concerns aside, the plant is a mess and my first reaction was that I would have to be at least a little crazy or slightly insane to accept this assignment."

"So you are leaning towards saying no?" she asked.

"Yes" I said "but the professional challenge of being able to take this business from where it is today to what I think the potential for it is, makes this a very difficult decision."

"What is so difficult about it" she prodded me on.

"From a professional point of view, an opportunity to make such a big impact on a company like mine, let alone getting in at the startup stage of building a business doesn't come around too often in a career." I said "as a matter of fact, very few of my peers will ever be offered an opportunity to take on such a challenge. To be honest, I am not sure if I should be feeling honored or insulted at being offered this opportunity"

Nancy looked at me inquisitively "what do you mean?" she said.

"When I look at all the negative, I wonder if the company thinks I am a fool to accept this assignment. But when I consider the positives and the size of the opportunity, I feel honored to be the one asked to take on such a huge challenge." I said and then added, "But I know Peter. He is honest and straight forward. He had repeatedly said that he thought this was a great opportunity to make a big impact on the business but was quick to let me know that I should not feel any pressure to accept it. So, here we are, it is up to us."

"Like I said before, this is not what I would choose to do. But if you really want this assignment and think it would be good for your career, then I will be there by your side." She said.

"Besides, in a way, while I have my doubts about the schools and how the kids will react, I think it would be good for them in the long run to experience living in a totally new and different culture. In Cincinnati, life may be a little too traditional and they don't get any exposure to people that are different from them."

The captain came on the intercom and announced that we are descending and should be at the gate in 15 minutes. We had six hours before our connecting flight so we decided to go to downtown Vancouver to have a late lunch. After all, Vancouver restaurants serve some of the best wild caught Pacific salmon dishes in the world. It would be a shame to just sit at the airport for six hours and pass up a trip to the city. We rented a car and drove to the Stanley Park area where we took in the views. We decided to circle the park because time was short and after that we headed to Gastown where we walked around Powell Street and onto the cobbled walkways past an array of interesting little stores on Water Street before finally settling on a restaurant.

Lunch was excellent. We enjoyed a glass of white wine, fresh greens and vegetables with our salmon. It was a sunny afternoon and the scenery was breathtaking but unfortunately, it was time to head back to the airport and catch our connecting flight.

We mostly slept through the next flight and at 9:00 pm, we were at the airport garage picking up the car and arrived home twenty five minutes later. John, Elizabeth and my sister, Mary, who flew from California to stay with the kids, greeted us at the door.

2

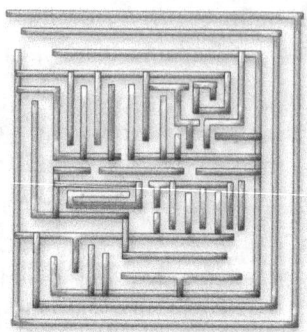

THE DECISION

Monday morning came around a little too fast. I was still a little jetlagged, but was starting to feel more human. My meeting with Peter was at 11:30 AM and we were scheduled to have lunch together after that.

I arrived a few minutes early. Peter's office door was open and he invited me to come right in. I said hi to Linda, his assistant and went in.

"Are you over the jetlag yet?" he asked.

"Barely" I said "but I do feel 200% better than I did Saturday morning."

"It usually takes me three to four days to get back to normal when I travel to Asia" he said "you and Nancy still have a couple of days to go" he added laughing.

"What did you and Nancy think about Tianjin and China?" he asked.

"It is not a simple answer" I said "but, at the risk of stating the obvious, we both thought that China is a very interesting country to visit. It has such a deep rich culture. As you know, very few people speak English, so daily life would be tough. Driving, from what Jack told me, was out of the question. To be honest, I am relieved that I will not have the option to drive over there. Based on what I observed first hand, I don't think many westerners would survive an assignment if they had to drive over there." I added.

Peter laughed and shook his head "I know, I was never able to figure out the logic with all the bicycles and cars going in every direction, but somehow, it works for them."

"What did you think of the plant?" Peter brought the conversation back to topic.

"Were you able to tour the plant when you visited China?" I asked him

"No, we were in the middle of sensitive negotiations to purchase it at the time and our people there did not think it would be a good idea to show too much interest by touring senior managers at that time" he said.

"In that case, let me tell you what I saw" I said and went on to describe the old buildings, the mule drawn carriages delivering raw materials, the army of women hand packing soap, the non-functioning continuous soap plant that no one knew how to run, the old kettles, coal fired power plant and environmental challenges. Then I described the people who are still living in the dormitories with their families at the plant and the challenge we will face in turning this plant into a typical company plant. "This should give you a rough idea of what you missed" I concluded about five minutes later.

"Sounds pretty bad" he said "but, as I understood things, this was about the only plant that was available for us to buy that allowed us to launch the soap business in China quickly. At least, it offered enough for us to run test markets and develop plans while we built our capacity. I was also told that it was in the best shape when compared to other plants that were available. From what you are telling me, though, it sounds like it will take a year or more for us to make this plant operational at a level that would bring it up to our standards."

"I agree with your assessment" I said "it may have been smarter for us to have started with a green field site and put in the latest technology. But we are where we are and we are going to have to find a way to make this work for us and fast."

"What did Nancy think about the schools and the possibility of living in China for three years?" he asked.

As I reflected on Peter's question, I thought back about yesterday afternoon when I accidentally overheard Nancy talking on the phone with her friend. While I was not trying to eavesdrop on her conversation, I could not help but overhear it since I was sitting in the family room going through some paperwork. She thought I was out in the back yard when her friend asked her if she had lost her mind to be lugging herself and the kids all the way to China.

"The prospect of living in China was never on my A list, B list, or even C list" she had said "but when he talks about it, I can sense his excitement at taking on such a big challenge. It's as if he is about to embark on a journey to discover the New World. I just had to get on board. Yes, I suppose I can stay in the comfort of our home in Cincinnati with John and Elizabeth and have him come home every month or two, but, the more I think about it, the more I realize it would be a bad idea to stay here and send him by himself. Besides, this can be an adventure of a lifetime for all of us ... he would get to do what he wants to do and I think it will be very good for his career. It will be a big challenge for all of us, but I have decided to embrace it and keep an open mind."

I noticed that Peter was looking at me and waiting for an answer to his question.

"Nancy has always been a trooper" I said "I can tell you that she has many reservations but when all is said and done, she said she will support my decision."

"If I wanted the job, she would be fine with me accepting the assignment."

"I don't envy you your position" he said "it is all up to you" he chuckled as he pressed on asking "so what do you think?"

"In all honesty, I am a little torn" I said "on the negative side; I know this will be tough on the family. But Nancy and I were thinking that it may be good for the kids to experience other cultures and it will make us come even closer as a family. The plant is a mess and there is a lot of building and fixing that needs to be done. No question, very challenging work and, at least on the surface, it looks like things can only go up from where things are today."

"On the positive side, I like the idea of being it" I continued "I don't know if you knew this, but, aside from my company reporting lines and Manufacturing responsibilities, I will also be the General Manager of the Joint Venture with full P&L responsibilities and will be reporting to the Chairman of the Board of Directors of the Joint Venture directly. If this isn't enough to keep me busy, I will also have broader Supply Chain responsibility for the Personal Cleansing Category as Product Supply Manager for Greater China responsible for Mainland China, Taiwan and Hong Kong."

"As you know" I said "those responsibilities would be held by two and most likely three people in the US organization and not just one person as I understand this role to be."

Peter looked surprised and said "no, I did not know about the extra responsibilities. The role sounds challenging and exciting; but I agree with you, they add up to a lot of responsibility for just one person. Do you want me to intervene?"

"Absolutely not" I said "to the contrary, the breadth of the role and level of responsibility is what attracts me to the role. When I put it all in the balance, I feel that I can't walk away from this. It is a great opportunity to make a big difference for the business at a critical point in the company's expansion into virgin territory."

I paused for a few seconds before I continued reflectively "it almost seems as if all the different assignments I had to date were designed to prepare me to take on such a major challenge and now, here it is, staring me in the face."

I paused again for a brief second before concluding "the company needs me to put all this experience to work Peter. You can count on me."

"I am delighted to hear this" Peter said "I meant it when I said that it was completely your choice and there was no downside if you said no. But I am glad you are saying yes. You have the right technical and leadership skills to lead this business to the next level. Let's talk over lunch about how you recommend we transition your current responsibilities and what timing we should look at for your move."

After ordering lunch, we worked the details of transitioning my responsibilities over the next four weeks. I told Peter that I felt I could not afford to take too long before I got there since the Engineers, in Tianjin, were already making decisions that will dictate the direction of the business for years to come. I wanted to be there as soon as I can to influence and participate in those decisions. We agreed on the announcements that needed to be made so that transition plans can be kicked into action. The target was to be there by early August including us taking our usual summer vacation with the kids in July.

Before heading back to my office, I called Nancy and gave her the name of the contact in Human Resources who will be working with us on the move. There was so much to do and we needed to start the process of listing our house and working all the details.

With that, the decision to take the assignment and move to China was made.

3

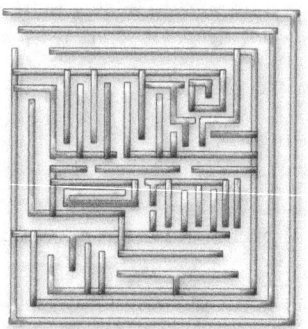

GETTING READY

We met with the realtor to work out the details of listing our home. It was a sad thing for us since we loved our home. It was the builder's model home when we bought it. Like most model homes, it was very tastefully decorated with a lot of upgraded features. The decision to sell it; however, had to be made. We could not imagine ourselves getting comfortable with the idea of holding on to it for the next three years and renting it out. After a lot of deliberations, we decided we did not want to be landlords and felt that trying to manage the situation from half way across the globe would be more than we were willing to take on.

Within the next few days, the "for sale" sign went up in the front lawn and the neighbors that had not yet heard from us directly started to call to find out what was going on. Things were moving very quickly. The date for our departure was set and so was the date for when packers from the moving company would come to start packing our belongings to get them ready to go into long term storage.

We were told by Paula, our HR contact, that we would not need our home furnishings since our new accommodations will be furnished. She also told us that it was very important that all the personal items that we absolutely had to have need to go with us on the plane because it was impossible to predict exactly how long it would take to clear our shipment through customs once it arrives in China. As a minimum, she suggested that we take things like medication and any clothing and personal items that we think we will need in the first six to eight weeks.

Not only did we have to sell the house, both cars also had to be sold. We agreed that storing cars for three years would not be a smart move.

As we packed what we thought were the 'essentials', we ended up with a total of thirteen suitcases. The thought of traveling with thirteen suitcases was intimidating, but it had to be done.

We decided to take our vacation on our way to China. As Nancy and I talked it over, we decided to make two stops. Spend three days in Las Vegas and Seven Days in Hawaii. We had been planning to go to Hawaii at some point and this was as good a time as any. It would be fun and making the two stops will break the trip into shorter flights making it a little easier on us. Besides, we can enjoy being together as a family and have fun with the kids before they have to start thinking about school again.

About four weeks before departure, I got home from work and Nancy was distraught. I asked her what was going on.

"Did you know that we are not allowed to take Terry and Cookie with us?" she asked through tears referring to our Jack Russell Terrier mix and Beagle dogs.

"What are you talking about?" I asked "of course we can take them with us. There must be some mistake."

"No, there is no mistake" she said "Paula broke the news to me today when I was trying to work the details of moving the dogs with her"

"I will see what I can do tomorrow" I said "there has to be a way to be able to take the dogs with us."

"Don't bother" she said "even if you could, I would not want you to do it."

I was puzzled and looked at her inquisitively.

"I am confused" I said "you don't want to take Terry and Cookie with us to China?"

"Of course I do" she said "but we can't because it would be cruel."

She paused for a second to take a deep breath before continuing "to start with, the dogs would have to be quarantined for six months once they arrive in China to make sure they are not carrying any diseases" she said

"Six months is way too long" I said "I can't imagine leaving them in a Chinese pound for 6 months."

"That is the good news" she continued.

"It gets worse?" I asked incredulously

"Much worse" she said "people in china eat dog meat." She started to sob "Cookie is about the size of a turkey" she added as she looked at Cookie wagging her tail and broke into tears again.

"Honey" I said, as a chill ran up my spine "I now see why you are so upset. I agree with you. We can't take them with us. I wish someone told us while we were still weighing all the facts and before making our decision" I whispered knowing how much the dogs meant to all of us.

"Do the kids know this?" I asked.

"I told them. They are upset but appear to be taking it a little better than I thought they might" she said "I think they are too busy being angry about your decision to accept this stupid assignment in the first place. What's another setback?" she asked.

"That hurt" I said "I thought we were all in this together"

"We are, but this one is going to take some time" she warned me.

While Terry was supposed to have been John's dog when we first adopted him from the pound about seven years earlier, he had clearly become Nancy's dog. She was very attached to him. Last year we decided that it would be nice to get a companion for Terry and that is when Cookie came into our lives.

Terry was very smart with a lot of personality. Nancy used to tell me that she knew when I was coming home because Terry would go to the window about five minutes before I arrived and would dutifully sit there waiting. Five minutes later, almost to the second, I would pull into the driveway. My office was a five minute drive from home and we suspected that somehow, Terry was able to hear me start my car. While we will never know, we came to believe that this was the case because it was consistent and predictable.

I thought about the times we would be calling John or Elizabeth to come down for dinner. If they did not come down quickly, we would turn to Terry and say go get the kids. Terry would run straight up to their rooms and soon we will have everyone at the dinner table. I was convinced that he knew exactly what we said to him. During the summer, Nancy would take him to the groomer to shave his hair. When he got home, we would say that he looked handsome; he would strut around proudly wagging his tail.

Cookie, on the other hand, was the prettiest beagle we ever laid eyes on, but she was dumb as a stump. She loved to strut around and look pretty and get everyone's attention. Teaching her anything was extremely tough. I remember when we went to pick her as an eight week old puppy from the run down old farm where her breeder lived. The woman asked us if we wanted her for hunting. I thought that was an odd question at the time, but I said no, I don't hunt. She said, that's good and we both left it at that.

Later, I came to find out that Cookie drops to the ground whenever she hears a loud bang. No wonder the woman was relieved that I was not buying Cookie as a hunting dog.

Later on, we decided to buy an invisible fence because Cookie kept dashing into the street. We often would hear cars braking and the street in front of our house was starting to look like skid mark alley after we had her for a few months because she would dash into the middle of traffic. One evening she came home limping with tread marks on her. Nancy had to rush her to the vet and thankfully, while she was badly bruised, she had sustained only relatively minor injuries. She had some internal bleeding but did not have any broken bones.

Funny, after that I thought that she would have learned not to dash into the street. But no such luck. While the invisible fence was supposed to help save Cookie's life, we later found out, that instead of keeping her in the yard as it did for Terry, Cookie would dash towards the street at full speed. When she felt the shock from the fence, she would yelp, but instead of retreating away from the fence, she would keep going. Unfortunately, when she wanted to come back, the memory of the shock would still be fresh in her mind and she would remember the fence. As things turned out, the fence was keeping her out instead of in and we would often have to look for her all over the neighborhood.

"I talked to my sister Jodie after talking to Paula" Nancy said "and she generously offered to take both Terry and Cookie and keep them for us while we are in China.

"That is a relief" I said "they would have a lot of fun at Jodie's farm.

The door opened and John and Elizabeth walked in. Our neighbor dropped them off after spending the afternoon at the community pool. It was clear they were not interested in talking to me. I guess in my eagerness to take on a big professional challenge, I misjudged what this all meant to the kids.

"Ok everyone, let's go" I said as I picked up the car keys and opened the door to the garage. The kids and Nancy looked at me "we are going to the Montgomery Inn for the best ribs in Cincinnati" I said.

Nancy looked at the stove where the food she cooked for dinner was ready to serve. Then she stood up and said "come on kids, I can't wait" as she turned the stove off and we all headed for the car.

The ride to the restaurant was a little too quiet, I thought.

"So where do you all want to go for vacation?" I asked

"I thought we were going back to Litchfield by the Sea" said Elizabeth and John added "I thought we already booked the same suite at the hotel where we always stay."

"Yes, we have" I said "but we can cancel as long as we give them 48 hour notice. Mom and I were talking about going somewhere different this year."

"Let's go to Las Vegas" Elizabeth jumped in "we have never been there. My friend from school went there with her family and they got to see the Pirate show at Treasure Island and had a lot of fun. She said there was so much to do there" John added "that sounds like a great idea, I also heard a lot of great things about Las Vegas. I agree with Liz."

I looked at Nancy and she nodded to let me know she was okay with the Las Vegas idea.

"Sounds like a great idea" I said "I am not sure that Las Vegas is the best place for young people to visit, but I agree there is so much to do and I am sure we can have a good time there."

After the waitress took our orders, we continued to talk about what kinds of things lay ahead for all of us. We also agreed that spending a few days in Hawaii would be a good idea and would break the trip to shorter segments.

And so the plans for our vacation were set and I felt that some of the anger was dissipating and starting to shift into excitement. However, I had to caution myself not to be overly optimistic. After all, the kids and Nancy's life was being turned upside down. The good news here is that I don't have time to second guess my decision or have worries of my own.

The week before departure, we sold one of the cars and were still working on selling the second one. Nancy received a call from someone who was interested in looking at the car. This turned out to be one of the scariest experiences we had anywhere. The guy came over and was insisting that Nancy and Elizabeth go in the car with him while he test drove it. Nancy was uncomfortable and told him he can take the car and go by himself. In the meantime, Elizabeth was in the driveway and looked inside his car and she saw a shovel, a rope, a bucket and a tarp in the back. So she started to signal her mom not to go in the car with him. Nancy told the man that she was expecting me to be home any minute now and could not leave. What was strange was that he decided not to take the test drive and left once he heard that I could be home any minute and that Nancy and Elizabeth were not getting in the car with him.

A few minutes later, I arrived. Nancy and Elizabeth were still shaken by their encounter as they proceeded to tell me about it. Sadly, three days later, we heard on the news that police captured a man who had raped a woman and tried to kill her. When his picture was flashed on TV, Nancy froze. It was a picture of the same man. We said a prayer for the woman who was attacked and were thankful for Nancy's and Elizabeth's safety.

Four days before our departure date, an army of packers arrived at the house. They spent the whole day working under Nancy's direction putting all of our belongings into boxes. We had to segregate everything into two groupings. Items that will go into long term storage and those that will be shipped to China. We also had to separate the items going with us into two groups. Items that we will need right away and those that we can wait for a couple of months before we receive them. The first group would accompany us on the airplane while the rest would be shipped via ocean freight to China to arrive at some future date.

The next day, the movers arrived bright and early to pick up our belongings and take them to the long term storage facility. This included all the furniture and heavy items, electronics, etc.

Two days before our departure date, the international shipping company arrived and picked up the items that were going via ocean freight.

Later that day, we had to drive Terry and Cookie to the airport to put them on a flight to Boston's Logan Airport where Jodie would be picking them up. It was a tough afternoon for all of us; but it was easier to accept because we knew that we would be seeing the dogs when we come back for Christmas and we knew that we would be reuniting with them when we return from the China assignment.

That evening, after returning from the airport, we drove the second car to a used car dealership and sold it for a little below market price but at least we were done with it.

The next day, I had one final piece of business to conclude before our departure. I was scheduled to meet with an expert for my Security briefing. He was responsible for the security of company executives both in the US and internationally. The objective was to educate me on the dos and don'ts with emphasis on company assets and intellectual property.

We spent about two hours discussing various aspects of personal and business security.

"The bottom line is this" he said "you have to be careful at all times and always" and for emphasis, he repeated the word always again three times "assume that anything you do or say will be heard by others and most likely even watched" then he added, "whenever in doubt, I want you to remember that, in China, the walls have eyes and ears." He went on to inform me that "e-mails, faxes and telephone conversations are not private or secure."

"What about the latest encryption technology we read about?" I asked "doesn't the company have the latest software protecting the confidentiality of our communications?"

"Absolutely" he said "but that can protect us up to a point. You have to assume that governments are able to break the encryptions and in China, all security is run by the government."

"You paint a grim picture" I said "what am I supposed to do if I have some sensitive information that I need to get input on or share with people in Cincinnati?" I asked.

"It is very simple, you hop on an airplane to Hong Kong or Singapore and you call, e-mail or fax that information from there" he answered.

"Taking a two and a half hour flight to Hong Kong or a six hour flight to Singapore seems a little too extreme" I said

"Of course it is" he said "you would have to use your best judgment. I wanted to emphasize the importance and seriousness of the key guidelines. In reality, you would not have been asked to take on this responsibility if the company did not have faith in you and your judgment. The point is for you to never hesitate or think twice about going to those extremes if you feel you need to."

"I understand the importance and sensitivity" I said getting up from my chair "I am going to try very hard not to become paranoid" I said laughing.

"You will understand this much better once you spend a little time over there. Having said that, I want you to know that I think everything is going to be fine. If you have any questions or need to contact me, feel free to do that any time day or night" he said as he handed me contact information and stood up to shake my hand, wish me luck and say goodbye.

When I arrived home, Nancy had finished packing for the most part.

"How many taxis do you think we need to get us to the airport?" she asked "I booked two. One for us and one for the thirteen bags. That should do it. Don't you think?"

"Yes" I said "I would think so. In any case, tonight, we will find out for sure when cabs take us to the hotel."

It turned out to be a challenge. We and the bags fit into the two taxis, but only barely.

This was repeated the next morning and off we were on our way to China and our new life for the next three years.

4

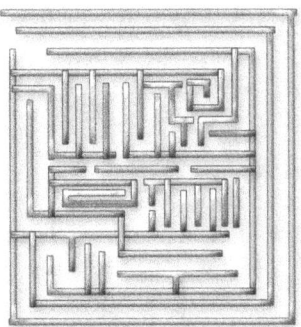

GETTING THERE

Las Vegas was an experience. To start with, if you can help it, don't travel with 13 bags. We had to rent a van plus a taxi to get us to the hotel.

The thirteen bags aside, we had a good time with the kids. We took them to several shows, watched the water and light show at the Bellagio Hotel, the pirates battling on the ships outside Treasure Island hotel and casino and enjoyed the good food and fun that Las Vegas has to offer. At one point, they chased us out of the gambling area because of the kids' age, but all in all, everyone had a good time.

Hawaii was more family friendly and we enjoyed the 'touristy' stuff and spent time on the beach. We spent three days in Honolulu where we went to a traditional luau. The last 4 days we traveled to Oahu where we stayed at another hotel by the beach and enjoyed the peaceful beauty of that island. Aside from having to deal with the bags as we hopped Islands, we had a great time and agreed that it would be worth another trip some day.

Now we were on our flight from Honolulu to Hong Kong with about one hour left before touchdown. The hotel knew that we had 13 bags with us and were sending a limo plus a van to pick us up. After the plane landed, we went through Immigration and customs without delay and soon were on our way to the New World Harbor View hotel on the Hong Kong side of Victoria Bay.

"Wow, this hotel is fancy" Johnny said as we entered the lobby.

"I know. Hotels in Asia appear to be more luxurious than we are used to back home. I think that they are more luxurious than the ones I have stayed at in Europe also" I said as we arrived at the front desk.

We gave the young clerk our passports and soon she handed us keys to our two adjacent rooms. There was a door between the two rooms which was convenient.

We were all tired from the trip but it was still early. We decided to have a quick bite at the hotel restaurant and then walk to the adjacent market to buy a new video camera. The food was very good. We had a table that looked out onto Victoria Bay. We could see all the hustle and bustle with ships of all sizes, some with exotic shapes, traveling the waters outside the hotel.

After eating, we walked out to the market area which was very interesting. Hong Kong feels like it has a pulse. The same feeling that one gets when visiting Manhattan. It gave us a sense of feeling alive and full of excitement which seemed to make us forget how tired we were. We walked from shop to shop looking at all the dazzling electronics and hundreds of video cameras. The choices were amazing and we saw models that we did not see back home. Prices were comparable to what we would pay in the US, but the technology and options seemed to be more advanced. We finally picked a JVC model that had all the bells and whistles and most important, one that Johnny, my technical adviser, thought was the best one to get. We walked around and did a little more shopping but had to keep ourselves in check because I was adamant that we were not going to have to buy a fourteenth suitcase.

The next morning, we met with Laura from HR.

She told us that we would have to stay at temporary living accommodations at the Sheraton Hotel in Tianjin since all the other locations that were available to house foreigners were already taken.

"The only place we were able to find was at the Sheraton" she said "we had to lean on them because they do not like to tie up the Presidential Suite for more than a few days at a time. They try to keep it available for when visiting dignitaries come to town."

"The Presidential Suite sounds nice" I said "but that means we will have to move again soon. In any case, it sounds like that is the only option available."

"The Crystal Palace has some openings still" she said "but you and Nancy ruled that out during your look-see visit."

Nancy jumped in to remind me that the Crystal Palace was the hotel that had the feel of 'an institution', and not a very good one at that.

"Ok, then it is settled" I agreed.

Laura went on to give names of contacts at the Bank of Hong Kong. She went on to explain that I will be paid in Hong Kong dollars and my paycheck will be deposited at the Bank in Hong Kong once a month. She explained that this arrangement was necessary since banking is still restricted in Mainland China and people are not allowed to legally exchange foreign currency there except through official channels controlled by the government. Laura went on to explain that we would have to travel to Hong Kong to do our banking.

"What do we do in the event we need money in an emergency?" I asked.

"Most people stock up on cash. They keep it in Hong Kong dollars in a safe until they need it. People usually exchange dollars to RMB's as they need the money" she said adding "in the event of a real emergency, money can be advanced from the local company and then we can figure out how to reimburse the company after the emergency is over."

"Part of the reason for the R&R budget that the company gives ex-pats in China is to allow for the cost of travel to Hong Kong for a weekend per month to do banking" Laura added "it also gives ex-pats a chance to get a break from the pressures of living there continuously. Many ex-pats use the trip to stock up on hard to find items while in Hong Kong."

She went on to tell us that the company has recently modified its policy to allow ex-pats more freedom in how to use their R&R funds. "After a few months, some ex-pats start to travel to other places like Bangkok, Singapore, Seoul or Kuala Lumpur for their R&R breaks." She said.

Laura went on to give us contact information for doctors and dentists who were western educated and practiced western medicine. We were scheduled to get more shots. Some of the immunization that we had to get required two or more shots. Some were 1 week apart; others were supposed to be 1 month apart. Nancy was keeping track for all of us and we were scheduled to take the second shot for some of those inoculations. They were timed to coincide with our arrival in Hong Kong. For the third shot, we needed to get back to Hong Kong in another month to finish the regiment.

We soon wrapped up our meeting with Laura and went to the bank to set up our new accounts. Hong Kong Bank is customer friendly and setting up the accounts was a breeze.

After the bank, we had a free afternoon. Nancy and the kids wanted to go shopping before dinner. The consensus was for us to go to the Times Square Mall. The Mall turned out to be eighty four thousand square meters (over nine hundred thousand square feet) of shopping space spread over nine floors. With Hong Kong being a small piece of land packed with millions of people, they tend to build upwards and hence, the proliferation of high rises. Shopping malls were no exception and Times Square was the first vertical shopping mall of its kind in Hong Kong.

We decided to try the sub-way which turned out to be much more efficient than any subway I used in the US. It was several stories below street level. There was hardly any wait before a train picked us up. A few minutes later we were at the Mall. Very impressive! Nancy and the kids managed to buy more things and I decided to stop fighting it and joined in. On the way out, as we started to head back to the hotel to freshen up, I decided to buy our fourteenth bag to accommodate the items we just bought.

"Tomorrow morning we go to see the doctor to get our shots" I reminded everyone as the cab was pulling to the hotel entrance" then we head to the airport and catch our flight to Tianjin, so we need to pack up as much as we can tonight."

Once we were back in our rooms, I turned on the TV to listen to some news while Nancy freshened up. The announcer was talking about a typhoon heading towards Hong Kong that was supposed to hit land in early afternoon the next day. I called the front desk and asked the attendant what we should do. She reassured me that there is no reason to be concerned. She told me that they get Typhoons on a regular basis in Hong Kong and that I had nothing to worry about.

"What you have to be careful about is falling windows or construction materials that may be flying around" she said "especially during the heavy rain. In any event, if there is a reason to take extra precautions, we will inform all of our guests" she added before we hung up.

I decided that since I had never been in a typhoon before, I felt uncomfortable taking a flight that leaves around the time the typhoon is supposed to hit, so I called a quick family meeting and we agreed to stay put in Hong Kong and delay our flight by one day.

After rescheduling our flight, I called the Tianjin Sheraton to inform them that we will not be arriving tomorrow. Instead, we will be on the same flight the next day. They were planning to pick us up with a hotel taxi and a van for the bags. I also informed the front desk that we will be staying an extra night and rescheduled our ride to the airport.

By then, everyone was ready and we headed out for dinner at a local Chinese restaurant where we enjoyed tiger shrimp and a variety of dishes.

The next morning, it was raining. We ventured to Times Square Mall again and the shopping spree continued. In the early afternoon, we went back to the hotel and decided to stay in while the typhoon hit. I was concerned since the hotel had an almost all glass facing and we could see the downpour. The wind was picking up speed and getting stronger. I decided to call the front desk and get reassurance that we did not need to go to a shelter.

"No sir" the clerk answered "we will be informing guests if the situation changes, but, for now, please stay indoors."

We decided that since we are stuck at the hotel, we might as well have some fun. So we went down to the lobby bar. We found that they were serving high tea and there was live music. A piano, violin, a guitar and a singer were at one side of the lobby bar playing a wide range of songs, but mostly all time soft music favorites. We enjoyed all the little morsels that were served as part of high tea. When the musicians took a break they sat at the table next to us.

"Where are you guys from?" I asked

"The Island of Cebu" was the answer.

"Please excuse my ignorance, but where is Cebu?" I asked

"It is an island in the Philippines" he answered

"What is it like over there?" I asked

"It is very beautiful" he answered "the beaches are beautiful. The island is famous for guitars. They make some of the best guitars in the world there, but most people know it for its natural beauty and come to enjoy the serenity the island offers. We get a lot of tourists there that come to relax, enjoy music, or enjoy water activities like boating, fishing, snorkeling or scuba diving."

"It sounds very nice." I said "What made you leave Cebu and come to work in Hong Kong?" I asked.

"Better job opportunities" he said "In Cebu there are so many good musicians and competition is very tough. In Hong Kong, there is demand for musicians from the Philippines because most of us can speak and perform in English, French and Spanish. Most local Hong Kong musicians tend to have trouble with languages other than Cantonese" he added as they started to get ready to go back and start playing music.

"Interesting" I said "can you play for us your most favorite Filipino song? I would love to hear it"

"You got it" he said "the name of the song is Anak. It was written by Filipino folk-singer Freddie Aguilar. It was a finalist for the inaugural 1977 Metro pop Song Festival held in Manila and has been translated to over a hundred local and international languages."

"Fascinating" I said "what is it about?" I asked.

"It is actually Freddie Aguilar's personal story. It is the story of a family where the parents have great joy when they have and raise their son. When the child becomes a teenager however; he becomes rebellious, loses his way and leaves home. Eventually, he grows up, becomes a man and falls in love, marries and has a child of his own. He starts to experience the same joys his parents experienced before he lost his way and realizes that his parents were right" he said "as I said, the inspiration for the song was Freddie Aguilar's life story. He left his family before he finished school at the age of 18. His father, who had wanted him to be a lawyer, was disappointed. Freddie traveled with his guitar to far-away places. With no one to guide him, he got into gambling. Realizing and regretting his mistakes five years later, Freddie composed Anak, a remorse song expressing apology to his parents. He went back home and asked for forgiveness from his parents who welcomed him with open arms. After his father read the lyrics of Anak, the two became closer than ever. The homecoming proved timely because soon after, his father passed away" he added as he walked over to where he had left his guitar."

The band started playing Anak. While I could not understand the words, I was touched by the beauty of the tune. At that moment, I decided to visit Cebu on one of our future R&R trips.

The afternoon and evening were pleasant. Going down to the lobby bar turned out to be a good idea and it made the time go by without us focusing on the typhoon. The rain was still coming down hard in the evening, but not with the same intensity as when we last looked. After dinner, we went back to our rooms and packed bag number 14 with all the new shopping.

Next morning, we had a late breakfast and got ready for our departure to Tianjin.

The Air China flight touched down at the Tianjin International Airport and taxied to the terminal. Before long, we were standing in the immigration line. This was our first official entry into Mainland China and since we were moving there for an extended period, there was some paperwork to complete. It went smoothly and we proceeded to pick up our luggage and clear customs. To our surprise, it was a non-event, although they put the baggage through an x-ray machine before allowing us to go through the "green" isle.

As we exited, we were greeted by a very nicely dressed young Chinese woman from the Sheraton Hotel.

"Welcome to Tianjin" she said "I am Julia from the Sheraton hotel. We are so happy to have you with us."

"Hi Julia" I said "it is nice to finally meet you in person" as I extended my hand to shake hers and continued "I want to thank you for all the help you gave me when I called you over the phone. We really appreciate your assistance in making the Presidential suite available for us. I know your General Manager likes to keep it open for when dignitaries visit the city."

"It is my pleasure" she said "as you had requested, we have a taxi and a van for the luggage. Let me tell the drivers to load your luggage."

She spoke to the drivers in Chinese and they started to collect the luggage and load it into the van. In the meantime, Julia ushered us to the taxi and said she would see us back at the hotel.

Julia, as it turned out, was our primary contact at the Sheraton. I had talked to her over the phone and she was instrumental in getting approval for us to stay at the only remaining open space at the hotel. During our time in China, we got to know Julia quite well and she became a lifeline for us whenever we needed help.

Unlike Beijing, Tianjin was not equipped to house ex-pats. Several major companies had decided to establish operations in Tianjin at the same time which put a huge strain on the infrastructure. While the local government was trying to put the needed infrastructure in place, it was going to take a few years for it to catch up with the influx of foreigners. Since the Communist Party did not want foreigners to be too immersed with the local population, the choice of places where foreigners can live was very limited, and of course, as more foreigners arrived, the availability was diminishing quickly.

The cost of housing was outrageous. The few places where people can live took full advantage of the fact that the demand outstripped the supply. The cost of the accommodations for us was going to be thirteen thousand US dollar per month. Outrageous, I thought, but what other choice did we have?

As we were getting closer to the hotel, we saw a lot of bicycles and cars. The kids, who were seeing this for the first time, were amazed. A few times, Elizabeth and John would cover their eyes since it looked like we were headed for a sure collision. Nancy and I were old hands at this from our look-see visit and we half laughed. In part still thinking it is not safe, but mostly knowing that this is how traffic moves in China.

When we arrived at the hotel, we received the royal treatment. We were greeted by the General and Deputy General Managers. The General Manager, Mr. Chao, was a Canadian who was originally from Hong Kong while Tyler, the Deputy General Manager, was from Australia. Right behind us was Julia who expediently checked us in making copies of our passports and walking us to our Suite.

The Suite was very spacious. The double doors led into the living room. We could see that they had put 2 single beds in the living room next to the sitting area. To the left was a dining room with a large table that can seat eight to twelve people and next to it was a small kitchen. To the right, there was a Master bedroom with a large luxurious bathroom. It was very nice and luxurious, but it was small compared to what we were used to and the kids were used to having their own separate rooms.

"What do you think?" Julia asked.

"It is very nice" I said "I see why it is called the Presidential suite" I added. "There is only one concern" I continued "we thought the kids would each have their own bedroom. I see that they would have to share the living room. They can share the living room for a day or two, but that won't work much longer than that."

"I was afraid of that" Julia said "let me see what I can do for you. It may take me a day of two to work out the details, but we should be able to do something."

The bags arrived, Julia left and with that we were officially at our new home in Tianjin, China.

5

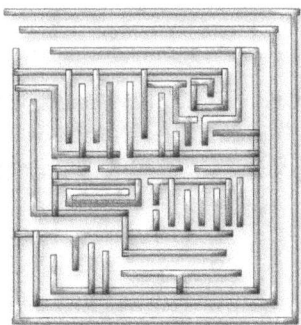

THE WORK BEGINS

I took a taxi from the Hotel on Monday morning. Rick was there to greet me.

"I sure am glad to see you" he said.

"I am glad to finally be here" I said "how is Maureen doing?"

"She is doing fine, thank you" he said and started to laugh adding "but she will be doing great soon."

I looked at him inquisitively

"This morning she said, I had to call her and let her know as soon as you arrive."

"That is very sweet of her" I said still wondering what Rick was getting at.

Still laughing, he went on "she may not be as sweet as you think. She figures that if you actually show up, she will know for sure that we will soon move to Hong Kong for my next and final assignment before we retire to the South of France."

I laughed and said "I see what you mean. You are right, she has her own agenda. Still Nancy and I are crazy about her. I guess we will have to visit you when we go to Hong Kong on R&R."

Julie peeked through the door to welcome me.

"I am getting some tea for Rick. Would you like some tea also or do you prefer coffee like the American Engineers?"

"I prefer coffee. Any kind of coffee will do. The stronger the better" I said as she exited.

"Let's adjourn to the conference room" Rick said "I plan to move out of the office and use the conference room for the next three weeks while we transition responsibilities."

Julie walked in with Rick's tea and my instant coffee.

"I will order coffee to make sure we have enough for you. I had to borrow some from the engineers because Rick likes to drink regular English tea most of the time, but I have gotten him used to drinking some of the Chinese tea and he says he likes it."

"Thank you Julie" I said adding "you are a life saver."

"It is my pleasure" she said and then turned to Rick and said "don't forget, all the managers will be in the big conference room in 15 minutes" as she walked out and closed the door behind her.

"I have called an all management meeting to introduce you to everyone" Rick said "they are all curious about you and would like to hear your thoughts and plans. This will help alleviate some of their anxiety. For many of them, I am the most senior manager they have met since joining the company."

"Great idea, I was going to suggest an all management meeting but I'm glad you already set one up" I said "getting back to you moving to the conference room, I don't think that would be necessary. You can stay in the office and I will use the Conference room" I said "I can wait until after you move to officially move in. Plus don't be in such a hurry, you are scaring me" I added smiling.

"Oh no, it is not a question of courtesy or wanting to rush things" he said "in the Chinese culture, it is important that people start to see you as the new boss as soon as possible. You have to keep in mind; the managers would feel a sense of loyalty to me since I hired most of them. If we don't quickly move to show that you are now in charge, they will go into inaction while I am still here because they would want to wait to clear everything you say or ask them to do with me before they do it. To them, it would be disloyal to me if they followed you. The best way to cut through that quickly would be by showing both in our actions and symbolically, that you are it."

"I understand" I said

Rick looked at his watch and said "why don't we start to head to the conference room. I will start the meeting with a few words and then turn it over to you. I have to warn you that you should not be surprised if none of them says anything or asks any questions. It is a combination of things. Some will understand what you are saying while others won't but mostly it is cultural. They have been trained not to ask questions and simply follow orders."

"Let's do it" I said as I stood up and we started to head towards the conference room located on the same floor but on the opposite end of the building. Julie joined us as we started to walk to the conference room.

"By the way, I understand you have a manager by the Name of James Chang here in Tianjin. Can you introduce me to him when you have a chance?" I asked

"Yes, we do. James is one of our star hires. He is in Charge of our purchasing, logistics and distribution groups." Rick said "How do you know of him?" He asked.

"A friend of mine in Cincinnati asked me to say hello to him and be sure to sponsor him" I said "James apparently had worked for us a few years ago at the Dallas plant as part of an exchange program with China and he had left a very strong and positive impression on my friend, Terry, who sponsored him while in the US."

"I'll introduce you as soon as we wrap up the meeting. A small world, isn't it?" Rick commented as he opened the door to the conference room.

The conference room was long and narrow. It was laid out 'classroom style' with all chairs facing the front. All seats were taken with the exception of three seats that were set up facing the crowd and placed neatly at the front of the room.

Rick started the meeting by introducing me to everyone and giving them some information about my background, education and key positions I held with the Company to reassure them that they are in good hands.

Julie translated for Rick as he talked. Rick would say a thought and then stop giving Julie time to translate what he said into Mandarin for the group. Once she finished, he would pick up where he left off and continue. "It looks easy enough, I will use the same approach as Rick" I thought as I stood up to address the group when Rick turned the meeting over to me.

"I am very pleased to be here today" I started "as Rick had mentioned, I have been with the company 18 years and have had seven assignments with this being my eighth's and most important assignment."

"Why would I consider this to be my most important assignment?" I continued "the answer is simple. As Rick has just told you, I have had varied responsibilities including some very profitable businesses for the Company. I will tell you why it is very simple. Tianjin represents the future. Our soap business in China is non-existent at this point. But we are investing to build it and my job, along with all of you is to make this a very successful business for the company. What you may not know about me is that I am a very determined person. I have successfully turned around or significantly improved every business I have worked in to date, and I promise you, that together with you, we will make Tianjin the most successful soap plant the Company owns." I added.

As I was about to continue, Julie tapped me on the shoulder and asked "would it be ok for me to translate what you have said so far?"

"Yes, of course" I said "I guess I got carried away and forgot that you need to translate."

Julie translated the last comment first which got everyone laughing and then went back and translated what I had said so far. It wasn't as easy as it looked to be able to organize my thoughts in small sound bites as Rick made it look. I filed away that I needed to work on it. As I continued, I tried to stay on top of it, but got carried away again a couple of other times. After a few minutes, I was starting to get the hang of it, but it was not easy.

When I finished, everyone clapped.

I went on to say "I would be happy to answer any questions any of you have for me."

There was dead silence.

"The questions can be about me, my family, work, the US or anything else you want to talk about" I added to fill the silence.

Dead silence again. I waited awkwardly for a very long minute, but it looked like no one will be asking any questions. Rick stood up and said thank you to the group. I followed his lead, said thank you and dismissed everyone.

Several managers lined up to shake my hand and say welcome to me but there was no small talk. Shortly, I got to meet James, a tall handsome Chinese man in his thirties. He carried himself with confidence and my first impression was positive. After I conveyed Terry's regards to him, I asked him to set up some time with Julie so that we can chat. After everyone shook my hand, we headed back to the office.

"The sound of silence was deafening" I said to Rick as we walked back.

"I warned you before we went there" he replied "don't take it personally, it is cultural and, besides, you will get used to it."

That left me empty and wanting to better understand what may be going through those young managers minds. I have never been at an introduction meeting anywhere in the Company where I was not bombarded with questions. Typically, the questions are light and people are polite but there were always many questions that people had. Those Chinese managers can't possibly be any less curious about their new boss than other managers I thought to myself.

Back at the conference room, Rick asked Julie to start moving his things to the conference room and set me up in his office.

The phone rang and Maureen was on the phone. Rick reassured her that I did indeed show up to work. She asked him to let me know how pleased she was and that we will have to plan to get together again soon.

As soon as Rick hung up the phone, it rang again and Julie announced that Jack was calling from Guangzhou and wanted to speak to me.

"Hello Jack" I said "how is it going?"

"Fine" he said "I wanted to touch base and make sure all is ok with you on your first day at work."

"So far things are going well" I said "we met with all the managers and I had a chance to shake hands with all of them. A quiet bunch, but no surprises yet."

"Glad to hear it" he said "sounds like you are off to a good start. If anything comes up, be sure to call me."

"I will plan to call you towards the end of the week to give you an update" I said "by then, I should have a better feel for things and will probably have some questions for you. Rick and I are about to tour the plant."

"I'll let you go" he said. I thanked him and said goodbye.

We finally stepped out of the conference room and headed towards the stairs. We did not get far. As it turned out, two offices down the hall from my new office is Mr. Tian's office. Mr. Tian is the Deputy General Manager I met during my look-see visit who was assigned by BOLI (Bureau of Light Industry) and by extension, China's Communist Party as their appointee to the Joint Venture. Mr. Tian is an older gentleman who did not speak any English. He communicated with Rick and me through his assistant Kaitlin, a Chinese woman who spoke very good English. Mr. Tian wanted to let me know that he would like to spend some time with me to explain to me his responsibilities.

"I would be delighted to spend time with Mr. Tian" I told Kaitlin, "can you schedule an hour with Julie for us to meet later this week."

She translated what I said to him and I could see a disappointed look in Mr.

Tian's face.

"Since Mr. Tian and I will be having a lot of time together after Rick leaves, I want to take advantage of the time that I have with Rick before he leaves" I said "please explain to Mr. Tian that I am looking forward to working very closely with him."

Mr. Tian looked a little less disappointed, but at this point, I felt that it is important that I don't start my relationship with Mr. Tian by jumping when he says jump. I knew this needed to be a delicate relationship but, at the end of the day, regardless of the fact that he was assigned to the Joint Venture by the Communist Party (and we were in China after all), he was my deputy General Manager and he worked for me.

Mr. Tian spoke in Chinese for about five minutes. When he was finished, Kaitlin said he was explaining the importance of why he and I should meet, but the bottom line was that she would set up a time with Julie for us to meet. I thanked her and asked her to tell Mr. Tian that I look forward to spending time with him as Rick and I went down the stairs to start our tour.

"Tell me about Tian" I said to Rick.

"An interesting man" Rick said "he came to us with the Joint Venture. He appears to be very connected within BOLI. He is very suspicious of us and appears to think that we are here to take advantage of the Chinese. He is forever examining the financials and asking questions about every detail."

"How do you deal with him given his connections and the fact that we are in China?" I asked.

"After trying to work with him" Rick said "I finally decided that I will answer his questions, but mostly I try to ignore him. If you let him, he can become a full time job for you."

"I gathered that" I said "he was being a little too pushy for my taste; especially for a first conversation. I felt it was important to send him to Julie to set up his appointment. I wasn't sure how my interaction with him will be interpreted in the Chinese culture."

"My best guess" Rick said "is that he would feel a little disrespected since you asked him to arrange for the meeting through Julie. He is very hierarchy conscience. However; you softened it by asking Kaitlin to arrange the meeting and explaining your logic for not dropping everything to meet with him."

Rick stopped for a moment in contemplation and added "In China, a lot of times, it is difficult to know what the right answers are, but I thought you handled him with reasonable balance."

6

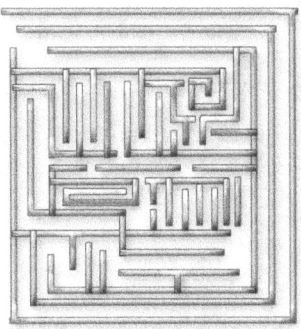

THE TRANSITION

Over the next few days we toured the plant several times as I tried to make sure I understood as much of the details and the thought processes behind them as best as I could.

The issues were numerous and I needed to make sure I had a handle on all of them.

By now, Rick had to spend some time in Beijing getting his belongings ready for shipment. Today, he had to stay home because he was expecting inspectors from one of the Bureaus responsible for making sure that antiques with significant historical value did not leave China unless they had a proper clearance and permission to export them. Those inspectors were going to inspect Rick and Maureen's belongings.

It wasn't until two years later, when Nancy and I visited Taiwan and toured the National Palace Museum in Taipei, that I developed an appreciation for why China felt a need to have a bureau dedicated to preserving their heritage and antiquities. The guide at that time explained that, after the Nationalist forces led by Chiang Kai-check were losing to the Communist forces led by Mao Tse-Tung, Chiang Kai-Check abandoned Central China in 1948 and Southern China in 1949 withdrawing to Taiwan. During that time, Chiang Kai-check had shiploads of valuable antiques moved to Taiwan where they can be seen today at the National Palace Museum.

The museum has impressive collections of paintings including famous calligraphy and watercolors, rare books and scrolls, tapestries, lacquer ware, enamel, jade, bronze and ceramics as well as artifacts used in the day to day life of the Chinese imperial families within the walls of the Forbidden City. The National Palace Museum has over 700,000 pieces, but is able to display only around 15,000, rotating them once every three months. It takes 12 years for the Museum to rotate all of the artwork that the museum owns. The rarest and most fragile objects are displayed each October.

"Call me if you need anything" Rick said.

"I will" I said "I am scheduled to spend about four hours with Dale, Todd and the engineers from Bechtel reviewing the modernization project. But if I need you, I know where to find you."

"Don't forget, tomorrow, we have Drew coming over for our lunch with Mr. Chen and others from BOLI" he said.

"I won't. Good luck with your inspections and I will see you in the morning" I said.

As I hung up the phone, I reflected on the fact that I have four different bosses. Not sure how I got to be so lucky I thought to myself. It usually is hard enough for most people to work for one boss. Trying to manage four is certainly going to be a challenge. By definition, they will have divergent needs and views on how to run the business.

Drew was the Company's most senior executive in China. He is the President of China and is responsible for all of the Company's businesses there with full Profit and Loss (P&L) responsibility. I report directly to the Vice President responsible for Personal Cleansing products in China. His name is Daniel. Daniel and I worked together very briefly several years earlier when I worked in the Company's Canadian Division. He will also be at the dinner tomorrow.

Mr. Chen is the Chairman of the Board of Directors of the Joint Venture. He is also the head of the Bureau of Light Industry (BOLI) in Tianjin which means he is a very important and influential member of the communist Party of China with very deep connections. As far as he and BOLI were concerned, he was my Boss since officially, I reported to the Chairman of the Board of Directors.

The Board of Directors consisted of Mr. Chen, Drew, and a representative of the Company's Hong Kong Partner.

I still have not met Drew or Mr. Chen in person. Tomorrow will be an interesting day, I thought.

My third boss is Jack who has functional responsibility for Greater China Product Supply. Jack reports functionally to Dick who is the Senior VP responsible for Asia Pacific Product Supply and is a Senior Executive Officer of the Company. Jack did not have P&L responsibility. His focus was on functional execution.

Finally, my fourth boss is Deepak. Deepak is responsible for the Personal Cleansing business in Asia. I would report to him for issues that relate to Personal Cleansing. His responsibility was functional. He worked with product introductions from a supply perspective. He did not have direct P&L responsibility. His focus was on execution. I still have not met Deepak yet, but I will get to meet him in two weeks at the Asian Product Supply Leadership Conference that was being held in Terrigal, Australia this year.

I went down to my meeting with the Engineering team which lasted three hours. They walked me through all the details and plans. I learned that in addition to the need to upgrade the technology, we had to reinforce all the buildings. I had not realized it, but Tianjin is in an earthquake zone and apparently had a serious earthquake that registered over 7.0 on the Richter scale in 1976 that resulted in a great deal of damage to buildings and took a serious toll on human life, although, the details of the damage were hushed up and mostly kept secret. At that time, China was in the depth of Mao Tse-Tung's rule and did not share much information with the outside world. The bottom line for me was that three buildings had to be reinforced with braces to make sure they can withstand another earthquake.

"So what does this mean for the timing to complete the project?" I asked Dale.

"I know this is not what you want to hear, but we are estimating nine months to reinforce the buildings and then we can start the modernization work which should take between two and three months for equipment installation."

Then we went on to look at the cost of doing all this work. The price tag was not inconsequential, so I turned to Dale.

"What would the cost be for us to start fresh on a vacant piece of land?" I asked.

"I suspected you may ask this question" he said and took me to another white board where he walked me through the numbers.

"It is going to be a little more expensive to do a 'green field' site" he said "but in my opinion, it would be worth every penny. We can't forget that we don't know what else we will uncover as we proceed with the upgrade work. A couple of surprises would bring the cost to break even."

"I assume that I am not the first to ask this question" I said inquisitively.

"We have talked it amongst ourselves within the engineering team, but not much beyond that" he said.

"The numbers you showed me don't include the money we already sunk into buying this plant" I said "am I correct?"

"You are correct. When you factor in our sunk cost so far, it would be a lot more expensive to walk away from this plant and build a new one" he said.

"Let's set this aside for a minute" I said "if we were to start from scratch, how long will it take to get us on line with full production capability?"

"Since I just arrived in China a little over two months ago, I don't have enough experience to project this with confidence; however, based on conversations I had with Bechtel engineers who have done projects in China already, I am told a very optimistic number would be eighteen months, but most likely, it would take two years assuming you have the land available now."

"That is way too long. We can't take two years or even the one year it would take to reinforce the buildings and upgrade this plant. We need to find a way to compress those timelines and get this business off the ground" I said.

"I understand" he said "but please don't forget that if we haven't learned anything else, we have learned that, in China, you need to get permission for everything you do. The permit process is very slow and laborious. People move at their own pace and in many instances, bureaucrats are afraid or unwilling to make decisions. As a result, most often, we face delays, get a 'no' answer or get referred to others who also are uncomfortable making decisions."

All of a sudden the lights went out and computer surge protectors started to beep in Dale's office where the only window was small and on the far end of the office where a partition blocked most of the daylight coming into the office area.

"Welcome to China" Dale said.

"Does this mean that production is down?" I asked hoping he would say no

"Unfortunately, yes" he said.

"How often does this happen?" I asked.

"At least once per week and often two or three times" he added.

"Is it reasonable to assume that we will get power back any moment now?" I asked.

"Not based on my experience in the past two months. It usually takes between one and four hours before power is restored" he said.

By now, I felt I had my fill of negative news for one day. I glanced at my watch and it was only noon. I asked Dale to closely examine what options we have available to us and try to speed the execution of the repairs as much as he can. I promised to give him all my support. I also asked him to continue to think about the green field option before heading back to my office.

When I arrived at the office, Julie asked me if I would like to have a hamburger and fries for lunch today.

I laughed "That is very cute Julie, but please don't tease me like that" I said.

"I am not teasing you' she said "we have a new McDonalds close to us. I can have your driver, Mr. Huang, go there and get you the hamburger and fries."

"Please do" I said laughing

I never thought that, of all people, I could get so excited about getting a McDonald's burger and fries for lunch. If someone told me six months ago that there would be a day when I would be grateful to be getting a McDonalds meal, I would have said, they must be delirious. But here I was very excited and it had only been three weeks since I moved to China.

Julie had accompanied me for lunch at the cafeteria for the past few days and I guess she must have picked up on the fact that I did not quite enjoy my lunches. The food that was served was filling, but as far as taste was concerned, it wouldn't be my choice. Plus, for the most part, I had no clue as to what was being served with one exception; the rice was easy to recognize.

A McDonald's hamburger and fries never tasted so good.

That afternoon, Julie had scheduled a meeting for me with James and another meeting with Mr. Tian.

James arrived a couple of minutes early and we spent some time talking about the time he had spent in the US. He explained to me that, at that time, he was working for the Tianjin Toilet Soap Factory and was chosen to spend six months in Dallas working at our Company as part of a US-China exchange program. That was how he met my friend Terry who was then the Operations manager at the Dallas plant. They became friends and Terry would often invite James over to his house for home cooked meals. James explained that he was very homesick, but Terry and his family made his time in Dallas much easier. They had stayed in touch ever since then and now communicate via e-mail once in a while.

The fact that James had gone through my experience in reverse plus the fact that both he and I had a common friend in Terry made James and I bond easily and quickly. As my assignment progressed, James became a close friend and a trusted adviser for me. He took it upon himself to help me better understand the Chinese culture.

My first lesson from him revolved around my puzzlement about the managers being so quiet when I addressed them on my first day at the plant. So I asked James to help me understand what was going on.

"How could it be that not even a single manager had a question for me?" I asked.

"Well" he said "in China, we have a saying that goes like this ... the grass that grows taller than the rest, gets cut"

"Oh" I said "that sounds harsh and final."

James simply answered "yes."

Julie knocked and peaked through the door to let me know that Mr. Tian had arrived for his meeting with me.

7

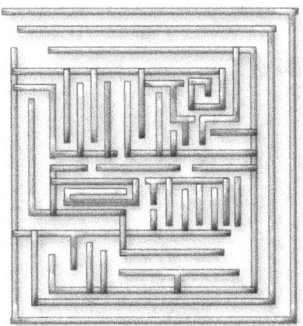

MY INTRODUCTION TO HOW THINGS ARE SUPPOSED TO WORK IN CHINA

"Mr. Tian, How are you?" I asked turning to Kaitlin and asking her also how she has been.

"Fine, thank you" she said as she turned to Mr. Tian to translate as he sat down and put a local newspaper on the conference table in my office. I thought it was strange that he would not have left his newspaper in his office, but decided to leave that thought alone. Maybe a question for another time I thought.

"Mr. Tian said that he is fine and wants to know how you and your family are finding life in Tianjin so far." Kaitlin translated.

"Tell him that everything is going very well so far, we are happy to be here. I appreciate him asking." I said "the kids are getting ready to start school. The Sheraton has been very good about looking after us. They are very helpful."

"Mr. Tian says he is glad to hear that everything is working out" Kaitlin translated "he also said to let him know if you need anything or if he can help in any way."

"Tell Mr. Tian, I appreciate his concern and offer of help. I will be sure to let him know if I need any help" I said.

"Mr. Tian wants to know what you thought about the plant. He also said that he knows you met with the Engineers this morning and wanted to know your thoughts about the project?" Kaitlin said.

"Tell Mr. Tian that it is too early for me to have many detailed observations about the plant and the project" I said "but my initial impression is that the plant has a great number of very good employees. They strike me as very hard workers."

"Mr. Tian is pleased to hear you say that. He personally selected the people that the Company would keep and the rest were transferred to TTSF. He made sure he selected the best" Kaitlin translated.

"Tell him that as best as I can tell, he has done a good job" I said adding "hen hao" as I gave Mr. Tian the universal thumbs up sign.

Kaitlin and Mr. Tian both laughed and commented that my Chinese was very good.

"You are both very kind" I said "but I just used most of the Chinese I have learned so far. The other words I know are 'bu hao', 'ni hao', 'ni hao ma', and 'zhe shi chen bi' which mean 'not good', 'hello', 'how are you' and 'this is a pencil'" I added laughing.

They both said they were impressed but I knew they were being polite. After all, Nancy, John and Elizabeth were able to learn about ten times the words I picked up when Mo was giving us private lessons before leaving Cincinnati. I had a sneaking suspicion that I wasn't going to be speaking like a native any time soon.

"The other day, Mr. Tian said he had something he wanted to talk to me about" I said trying to move the meeting along.

Mr. Tian talked for about ten minutes. He kept pointing at the newspaper. Then he flipped to another page and pointed some more.

"Mr. Tian said, yes, he wanted to talk to you about the need to increase our focus on safety and to double our efforts on improving it" Kaitlin translated.

"Tell Mr. Tian that I completely agree that we must have a strong focus on safety. It is a very fundamental belief of our company and we insist on it" I said "does Mr. Tian have specific areas that he feels we need to focus on?" I asked.

Mr. Tian talked for a few minutes before Kaitlin translated.

"Mr. Tian wanted to let you know that he also has several responsibilities as part of his Deputy General Manager of the Joint Venture. Aside from being appointed by BOLI, he is also responsible for the well being of the Chinese employees and that the head of the Union reports to him." Kaitlin said.

"Interesting" I said "I still have not met the head of the Union. I would like to meet with him shortly."

"Mr. Tian says that it is not necessary for you to meet with the head of the Union" she said "you can do all the dealings you need through Mr. Tian."

"Thank Mr. Tian for his kind offer" I said "but I can't possibly do that. I am a hands-on manager and I like to be close to our people. Of course, the Union head is an important person for me to know and build a relationship with."

"Mr. Tian says that the Head of the Union has to get Mr. Tian's approval before doing anything since he is appointed by BOLI and the Communist Party. So it would be more efficient if you worked through him directly." Kaitlin translated.

"Oh, I didn't know that" I said "tell Mr. Tian that I will keep that in mind whenever I need to work union related issues. I still think that it is important for me to meet with Mr. Li, the head of the union. I will be sure to let Mr. Tian know if I need his help."

"It is not a problem" Kaitlin translated.

"I want to go back to Mr. Tian's request that we double our efforts on Safety" I said "I may have missed it, but I am not sure what specifically he thinks we need to be doing or if he had any suggestions on what needs to be done in the area of safety?"

Mr. Tian was starting to look irritated as Kaitlin was translating my question to him.

Again, pointing at different parts of the newspaper he brought with him, he talked for several minutes before Kaitlin translated saying "he said we have to be diligent about safety and that we cannot forget how important it is. We must focus on improving Safety and redouble our effort to improve safety at the plant."

"He said a lot more" I said to Kaitlin "it seems like a short translation for how long Mr. Tian spoke. Also, what's in the newspaper? Mr. Tian keeps pointing at different parts of it. Why?"

"Yes" Kaitlin replied "he said a lot, but mostly, he repeated what he was saying several times for emphasis.

"Ok then, tell Mr. Tian I agree" we need to have high focus on safety "once I get past my initial transition into my role, I will make sure we keep that as a primary focus area. What about him referring to something in the newspaper?" I persisted.

Instead of translating my question, Kaitlin went on to tell me that Mr. Tian was simply conveying the message about the importance and need to focus on worker safety that was discussed in the local newspaper. Later I came to learn that since all newspapers were tightly controlled by the government, it was the norm to give direction to the masses via newspaper articles. The local Communist Party Leadership, would consider those communications as direction and work on executing them, hence the vagueness of the information.

As I eventually learned, China's equivalent to OSHA was concerned about a rise in the statistics of workers injured on the job and, as a result, had sent a directive that factories needed to put more focus on worker safety. That was the reason why Mr. Tian felt the need to convey the message to me but was getting frustrated when I asked for specifics. He could not be specific, because the direction from the government that he was trying to pass on to me was vague and unspecific, yet, during our conversation, I kept pushing him for specifics.

Later, I came to understand that culturally, Mr. Tian felt that by conveying the message to me, he would have done his duty as a local Communist Party Official; however, he did not feel that he had any responsibility beyond that. In effect, if there was a serious problem later on, he had covered his tracks and can say he told me, but I failed to follow-up. Sad but true, this is consistent with how most local bureaucrats would carry on their duties … do what you have to make sure that if there was blame to be had, you can pass it on to someone else.

With that, I decided to wrap up the meeting and said goodbye to Kaitlin and Mr. Tian.

Julie came in after Mr. Tian and Kaitlin left and asked me how my first meeting with Mr. Tian went.

"It went ok" I said not sure if I can trust Julie not to pass on anything I said to her about Tian.

"I was wondering if you shouldn't be at my meetings with him also." Kaitlin sometimes only translates part of what he says to me.

"I can do that, no problem" she said "he is long winded and tends to repeat himself several times when he says something."

"That is what Kaitlin told me also" I said "let's plan to have you with me and if we later find out it is redundant, we can change things."

"No problem" she said adding "since Rick is not coming in today, before you leave, I need you to sign some payment authorization forms and purchase orders so that purchasing and accounting can process some orders for the plant."

"Not a problem" I said looking at my computer screen "come see me when you are ready. For now, I want to catch up on my e-mails. It looks like I have over 150 unopened e-mails."

I started reading and answering e-mails. Many of which I was being copied on but were addressed to other people. A few e-mails, required my input.

When Julie knocked on the door, it was already 7:30 PM. I had lost track of time.

"Nancy called wanting to know when you expect to be back at the Sheraton" she told me.

"I lost track of time" I said "let me call her and let her know it will only be a few minutes before I leave."

Julie stepped out of the office while I dialed the hotel number and asked the operator to put me through to our room. As Nancy picked up, Julie walked back into the office with a stack of green papers that was about ten inches thick.

"Hi hon." Nancy said "I was wondering what is happening with you. It is already 7:30 PM. The kids are hungry."

"Go ahead and feed them" I said "I lost track of what time it is and Julie just walked in with a stack of papers that I need to sign because Rick did not come into work today. He had to stay at home to meet the people from the Bureau of Antiquities."

"Ok, we will be down at the lobby restaurant" she said "join us when you are finished."

I said "Will do" as I hung up.

What followed was interesting. Julie put the first piece of paper in front of me. It was all in Chinese. The only thing I recognized on the page was the numbers and the RMB sign.

"What am I looking at?" I asked.

Julie said "this is a payment to our supplier for the last shipment of coconut oil we received."

"That's a lot of money" I said "I feel uncomfortable signing it since I cannot read it."

Julie's face showed a great deal of concern at my comment. I realized that she may feel that I have leveled an insult at her and was questioning her trustworthiness. I need to find a way to salvage this I thought.

"Besides" I quickly added "since I have not officially taken over from Rick, I feel a little uncomfortable signing in his place especially for the big items. Out of respect, I don't want him to feel that I have already taken over while he is still here. Please don't think that I am questioning you."

I could see some relief in her expression, but I sensed that some damage has been done between us.

"Why don't we do this" I said "anything that you feel can wait until tomorrow when Rick is here, please set it aside and I will sign the rest before I go home."

Julie said ok and started to set some aside and hand me the ones that were urgent explaining to me what they were as she handed them to me.

Around 8:30 PM, we were finished; Julie called my driver, Mr. Huang, to let him know that I am on my way down.

When I arrived at the Sheraton twenty minutes later, Nancy and the kids had finished their dinner and were at the door heading out of the restaurant.

"Hi" I said "sorry to be so late. Just when I thought I was done, Julie walked in with a big stack of bills and payment authorizations for me to sign."

Nancy said she will sit with me while I grabbed a bite to eat at the restaurant and asked the kids if they wanted to stay or go up to their rooms. Both wanted to go up to their rooms.

"Sounds like you had quite a day" Nancy said.

"That is an understatement" I said.

"To start with, Rick had to stay at home. Apparently, before they can ship their belongings out of the country, the Bureau of Antiquities has to inspect their belongings to make sure that they are not smuggling valuable antiques out of the country" I said "so I lost a day from what is already a tight transition."

"Then, I met with the engineers and the news was disappointing all around. It sounds like the project is going to cost more and take close to one year to complete. A good project is completed on time and on budget. So overall, not good news." I added.

"To make things worse, we lost electricity while I was meeting with the engineers. When I asked them if this happens often, they said yes, sometimes they have several power failures in the span of a week and some last for several hours at a time."

"How can you run a business like that?" I asked rhetorically.

Nancy looked at me sympathetically and said "it sounds bad. What are you going to do?"

"That is not all" I went on "I met with Mr. Tian this afternoon. We spent almost two hours talking through his secretary and at the end of that, I was scratching my head wondering what the meeting was all about. He kept pointing at some newspaper article and mumbling about the need to focus on Safety, but every time I asked him to be specific, he rambled on for ten to fifteen minutes more without answering the question. Towards the end, he was starting to get upset when I asked him to be specific. I don't get it. Just because someone writes an article in a newspaper, Tian thinks that I am supposed to drop everything and focus on it? This is absurd" I added.

Nancy tried again to be sympathetic, but I wasn't done yet.

"Then, when I thought I was done for the day, Julie walks in with a big stack of papers for me to sign. It is all in Chinese and the only thing I recognized were the numbers. Some of them were very large numbers. I felt uncomfortable signing things I could not read and understand. She appeared insulted when I told her I was uncomfortable signing them."

"Why would feel insulted?" Nancy asked.

"I think she interpreted my concern as me not trusting her to make sure I only sign items I am supposed to sign" I said "I can see how she could feel that I was questioning her integrity" I said "I tried to tell her that I was trying to avoid making Rick feel that I am moving in too quickly, but I don't think she completely bought it."

"Sounds like you had quite a day. I am sure things will be better tomorrow" she said.

"I hope so" I said as I finished eating my salad and ordered a coffee as we adjourned to the lobby bar to try to relax.

8

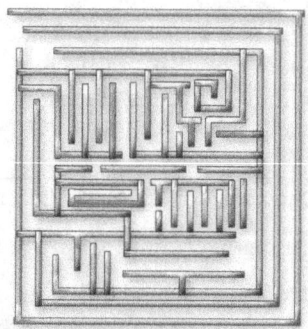

RICK'S GOODBYE LUNCH

Mr. Huang was waiting for me by the hotel entrance. I settled in the back seat

"Ni hao" I said to Mr. Huang as I fastened my seat belt. By now I was starting to get used to the chaos with all the bicycles and cars going in all directions.

"Ni hao" Mr. Huang replied and went on talking to me in Chinese with a high level of urgency in his voice.

Mr. Huang did not speak any English and I had no idea what he was saying, but he seemed determined to tell me something. All I could do was to keep repeating to him in English that I had no idea what he is saying. "Julie, Julie" I said. That appeared to finally make him stop and he said "ok" in English.

"Ok, Good, hen hao" I said.

A few minutes later, we pulled into the plant driveway. Mr. Huang dropped me at the entrance to the building and drove off to park the car. I went upstairs. Rick had not arrived yet, but Julie, had my desk all cleared up and ready for me to start the day.

"Good morning" I said "How are you this morning?"

"Very good" she said "thank you."

"Mr. Huang was talking to me in Chinese on the way from the hotel" I said "he appeared to have something urgent on his mind. Can you find out what he is trying to tell me please?"

"No problem" she said.

Rick arrived at that point and I was relieved to see him. I had a lot of questions to cover with him.

Julie went to get Rick's tea and my coffee.

Once Rick settled in, he told me about his frustrating experience with the Bureau of Antiquities representatives. They did not show up until three in the afternoon. He said that the inspectors wanted to go through everything they owned. After about two hours, they decided that there was nothing of historical value and gave them the stamp that indicated that they needed to show that their belongings were cleared for shipment.

"A most frustrating experience" he said "but, at least it is over. How was your day, yesterday?"

"It was a long and trying day" I said "I met with Dale, James and Mr. Tian. Then I was introduced by Julie to the procedures for signing purchase orders and payment authorization."

Rick laughed and said "yes, that is a lot of territory to cover in one day."

"I was concerned about how long Dale is telling me it will take to complete the project" I said "he is telling me that it will take at least a year and if you listen closely, you realize that there is also a high likelihood that it can take even longer before we have production from the new modernized plant. He also said that a Greenfield site would take even longer and cost more. What are your thoughts on this?"

"I agree with your assessment" he said "based on my experience so far, it will take longer than the engineers think. They want to please us so they give us their best and most optimistic estimates hoping they can meet it. More often than not, there are significant delays from the Bureaus responsible for issuing permits. In most cases, it takes several months before a permit to build or demolish a building is issued which means we have to wait before we can do anything."

"Why does it take so long?" I asked.

"No one really knows, or if they do, they are not telling us" Rick said.

I reflected back on my conversation with James and said "yesterday, I asked James to help me understand why I did not get any questions from the Managers when I first talked to them as a group. He told me that in China, they have a saying that goes something like this "the grass that grows higher than the rest gets cut.""

Rick gave me a puzzled look.

"Maybe I am reaching here" I said "but, can it be that people at the Bureaus are not comfortable making decisions because the system is not forgiving? In other words, if they don't make a decision, then they can't make a mistake. If that is culturally true, then, what we see as impossible bureaucracy is simply people trying to survive by playing it extra safe."

"You may be on to something" Rick said "I mean, in many ways, it is human nature to play it safe. It is not that unusual to see people in the West try to avoid making decisions in the corporate world. In a Bureau, I imagine it is the same, except the penalties can be more severe for making a bad decision."

Julie came in with my coffee and Rick's tea. I was happy to be drinking the instant coffee. At least it was coffee and I did not think to bring some with me from home. I am now treating coffee as a precious commodity because I still haven't found a local place where I can buy it. To get my caffeine fix, I have been mostly ordering coffee from room service at the Sheraton and I do not like the price they charge for it.

"Mr. Huang wants to talk to you" she said "so I set up a time for him to meet with you at 11:00 AM. At 11:15 AM we need to start heading out to get to Rick's goodbye lunch with BOLI. In the Meantime, I have asked Mr. Li, referring to Rick's driver, to head to the airport to pick up Drew and Daniel. They are on the flight from Guangzhou that gets in at 11:00. Mr. Li will take them directly to the restaurant."

"Great, thank you" both Rick and I said simultaneously.

"I will be back with Mr. Huang" she said as she went out of the office.

Rick said "let me go next door to the conference room and follow-up on some of my e-mails. I'll see you at 11:15."

"Very good" I said "I'll do the same until Mr. Huang comes in. I wonder what he wants."

After going through a few e-mails, Julie and Mr. Huang came in. After exchanging greetings, I asked Mr. Huang to sit down at the small conference table and I turned to Julie asking "What does Mr. Huang have on his mind?"

"Mr. Huang said he noticed that you put your seat belt on this morning and that you have been putting it on since Monday when he started to work for you" she translated.

"Yes, I have" I said smiling "the seat belts in the back are more awkward to use than the ones in the front, but I am starting to get used to them."

Julie was working very hard to conceal a smile and look serious as I was talking as she translated what I said to Mr. Huang.

"Mr. Huang says that he doesn't understand why you don't trust him" she said.

"Wait a minute; I don't understand what we are talking about. Is it possible that we are losing something in translation?" I asked "I don't remember saying anything that in anyway refers to me not trusting Mr. Huang. It is true that I don't know him very well yet, but I have no reason to believe that he is not trustworthy. Can you please explain that to Mr. Huang" I added.

After translating to Mr. Huang, Julie said "Mr. Huang believes that by using the seat belt, you are showing that you do not have any trust in his skills and abilities as a driver. He said that he has been a driver for 15 years and has never had a single accident which proves that he is an excellent driver and his safety record is exemplary."

"Ok, I think I understand the issue now" I said "the way Mr. Huang sees it is that if I had faith in him and his skills, I would not use a seat belt."

"Exactly" Julie said "he said, he would not want to work for you if you do not trust in his abilities and skills as a driver"

"Tell Mr. Huang that I am sorry to hear that" I said "however, please explain to Mr. Huang that in the US, it is the law to wear a seat belt any time someone is driving or riding in a car. That includes both the driver as well as the passengers. No exceptions."

Julie translated. Before Mr. Huang could say anything back, I continued "tell Mr. Huang also that in our culture, it is not a question of trust. When I drive myself, I always put my own seatbelt on and insist that everyone in the car also put their seatbelts on also. If it was a question of trust, then that would mean that I don't trust my own skills as a driver which would not be true since I have been driving for over 25 years without any accidents. I wear the seatbelt as a precaution and also out of habit."

Julie translated what I said. I could see that Mr. Huang's expression was easing somewhat.

I went on "also tell him that I think he is one of the most skilled drivers I have seen. I admire the way he maneuvers so skillfully in the heavy traffic and gets me to the office very quickly and efficiently. I hope he will reconsider and continue to work for me, but I feel that it is important for me to wear the seatbelt while I am traveling in the car. It is not a reflection on him, but more of an area of comfort for me. Ask him to think about it and if he still feels strongly about it tomorrow, we can discuss it some more."

Julie translated and Mr. Huang nodded and said "hao" which means ok or good in Mandarin.

I extended my hand to Mr. Huang and shook his hand saying "hao, hao."

Julie spoke to Mr. Huang as she escorted him out of the office. She turned to me and said "we need to get Rick and go down to the car." Mr. Huang will meet us at the entrance.

"Ok" I said as we went to the conference room next door. Rick was ready and we went towards the stairs.

"I would like to talk to you about Mr. Huang's concern" I said to Julie "maybe we can talk for a few minutes after lunch."

"Sure" she said.

The car was waiting in front of the entrance. Rick and I sat in the back and Julie sat in the front passenger seat. With hesitation, I proceeded to put my seat belt on and Rick did the same. I noticed that Julie did not.

Julie turned to Rick and me and explained the arrangements for the luncheon.

"I booked a private room with three round tables that seat twelve people each. The food has been pre-selected. Since there are only four foreigners and twenty nine people from BOLI, with Mr. Tian's help, I have Drew and Mr. Chen, the head of BOLI sitting at the same table as Rick since this is his party. I will have Daniel sit at one table and you can sit at the third table. That way, each table will have at least one of the foreign VIP's which will make the guests happy and help us avoid having anyone feel slighted."

"Sounds good" I said "I was hoping to spend some time with Drew and Daniel. I was also hoping to get to know Mr. Chen."

"I know" said Julie "I was trying to find a way to do that, but I wasn't able to find a practical way to do it. Maybe you can ride with Drew and Daniel to the airport. They are scheduled to catch a flight to Hong Kong at 5:00 PM. Drew wants to spend about half an hour with Mr. Chen also after lunch. He asked that you and Daniel also join them for the meeting. I arranged for a smaller room at the restaurant for all of you to meet."

"Excellent" I said "thank you. You are very efficient and I want you to know that I am very impressed."

Julie smiled and thanked me.

The car pulled to the front of the restaurant and we all got out. All the guests were already there and we were only missing Drew and Daniel. Julie took Rick and me towards a gentleman in the middle of the crowd. It was Mr. Chen. She introduced me and he welcomed me to China and Tianjin and said he was looking forward to working closely with me. Then he turned to Rick and it was apparent that some level of friendship existed between the two.

They talked like old friends albeit through Julie.

A few moments later, Drew and Daniel arrived. After the introductions were made, we all sat at our assigned seats. Julie sat between Mr. Chen and Drew to translate, Kaitlin sat next to me and Mr. Tian to translate for my table and Betty, Lou's secretary, was the third translator. She sat next to Daniel.

The servers started to bring out different food courses along with beer, wine and a local rice wine called Bai jiu which was being served in shot size glasses. While many people like Bai jiu, when I tasted it once before in Cincinnati, I did not like the way it smelled or tasted.

I was taking my time looking at the various dishes and since I wasn't sure what was what, I was trying to figure out what may be 'safe' to eat. I noticed that no one at my table was eating. Finally, Kaitlin whispered to me that they are all waiting for me to start eating before they would start themselves..

"In China, people don't start to eat until their guest of honor, or highest ranking official starts to eat" she said "so please start."

"Thank you for letting me know" I said as I reached for some food to put on my plate. I fumbled with my chop sticks since I had little practice using them so far, but, to my relief, I managed to get a piece of cooked vegetable on my plate without dropping it. That gave everyone on the table the go ahead and people started to reach for the food and lunch started at my table.

The server had served me a beer and a shot of Bai jiu. I ordered a Coke but noticed that everyone was drinking Bai jiu served in shot size glasses. As a few minutes passed, there was a lot of conversation with a lot of interest in my background and some questions about the USA. Mostly polite conversation and some curiosity, I thought.

As I was telling one of the guests about my children, I saw everyone stand up at Rick's table, raise their shot glasses and say 'gan bei', which means 'to your health' in Mandarin. Then everyone downed their drink. The waitresses came by and efficiently refilled everyone's drinks.

After a few minutes the same thing happened, except that a different person was doing the toasting. The same scene was repeated several times, but each time, a different person would do the toasting. People where now starting to go from different tables to Rick and do the toasting. Over the course of the next hour or so, I estimate that Rick had about twenty toasts and, of course, that translates to twenty shots on top of the drinks he had before the toasting began.

I was very concerned. In fact, I was downright panicked. I know myself and knew that if I was in Rick's shoes, there is no way I could handle this much alcohol. Aside from the trivial concern about the possibility of making a fool of myself, I would definitely pass out. The most I drank in an entire evening was during my fraternity days at University when I had a six pack of beer over the entire evening and I was quite wasted. Even worse, since college, I have been an occasional drinker with no more that two drinks in an evening and often going for days and sometimes weeks without drinking.

In simple terms, I knew I was a light weight when it came to drinking and what I was observing was very concerning.

I was brought back from my deep thought by Kaitlin saying "one of the gentlemen at my table, Mr. Lee, wants to have a toast in my honor and to welcome me to Tianjin."

I decided it was now or never.

"Please tell Mr. Lee, that I don't drink alcohol. It makes me ill" I added pointing to my beer which was still full and the shot of bai jiu that was still untouched.

"If he would be so kind to allow me to toast him back with water or Coke" I said "I would appreciate it very much."

As Kaitlin translated, I could see some disappointment in the faces of our guests, but with that toast, me with water and my tablemates with bai jiu, my cover story that I do not drink alcohol was born. While I would have an occasional drink when I visited with my ex-pat friends, ever since that day, I was very careful to stick to soft drinks in all business meetings.

Rick, on the other hand, was fine. He had a high tolerance for alcohol and seemed to stay cohesive regardless of how many toasts he had. Better than I expected.

Soon the party came to an end and Drew, Daniel, Rick, Mr. Chen and I adjourned to the smaller room after saying good bye to all my new friends. A lady was accompanying Mr. Chen whom he introduced as Madam Shen. He told us that she was an important member of BOLI and that she will be working closely with our Joint Venture as well.

The conversation that followed was very interesting.

In 1995 China, foreign companies had to have a local partner in order to own a business. As such, our Joint Venture was jointly owned by BOLI, or the Chinese Government, which owned ten percent. The remaining ninety percent was also jointly owned by us (seventy percent) while a Hong Kong partner owned thirty percent. Up to that point in time, all Joint Ventures in China were partly owned by the Chinese government through one of their bureaus or agencies.

The company had just made an offer on a piece of land in the industrial zone in Tianjin and the plan was to build a new plant to make shampoos for the Chinese market with a lot of space to expand and add other products and categories.

"As I said in our last conversation" Drew said looking at Mr. Chen "on the new plant, we have to have one hundred percent ownership."

Julie translated.

"I understand your desire, but in China, it is not possible to own one hundred percent. We can do ninety percent like we have with the soap plant" he responded.

"Mr. Chen, my friend" Drew said "I cannot do the deal unless we have one hundred percent ownership. After our last conversation, I went back to the company. I talked to my boss and he took it all the way to the Chairman of the Board of Directors. I can tell you that this deal was discussed in detail at a special meeting of the Board of Directors and the direction I am getting is that there will be no more investment or expansion in Tianjin if we can't have one hundred percent ownership."

"But we are only talking about ten percent" Mr. Chen replied.

"They were adamant about one hundred percent and, unfortunately, there is very little I can do" Drew insisted.

"How about five percent" Mr. Chen asked.

"Unfortunately, I don't have the authority to agree to anything less than one hundred percent" replied Drew adding "you know how much I would like to do business with you and expand in Tianjin, but the Board is very clear. If we can't have one hundred percent ownership, the company wants me to talk to other cities like Guangzhou, Shanghai, Souzho or Hangzhou ."

"Can you go back to the company with my latest offer of five percent and I will go back to my superiors to see if it is possible to do anything more. We want you in Tianjin, so let's take this step before we do anything else" Mr. Chen said.

"I can tell you that my boss will be very upset with me if I go back to him again on this, but I will do that for you my friend" Drew said and the meeting wrapped up.

I suggested to Rick that he should probably head home and skip going back to the office. He agreed. Julie called Mr. Li and we agreed that I would spend a little time touring Drew and Daniel through the plant and then have Mr. Huang drive them back to the airport.

As we settled in the car, I asked Drew to enlighten me about what was going on.

"I can't emphasize how confidential this is. Does your driver speak English?" he asked.

"Not to my knowledge" I answered "he hasn't shown any signs of understanding what I say to him."

"Let's wait until we get to the plant." he said "in the meantime, let me again welcome you to our organization. You come highly recommended. Peter is a friend of mine and he thinks very highly of you."

"Thank you. Peter is one of my favorite people. He is the best" I said.

"How is your family adjusting to China?" Daniel asked.

"It is quite an adjustment" I said "some good and some bad"

Both of them looked at me waiting for more.

"On the positive side, everyone has been very welcoming to us. People go out of their way to be helpful. We have met a lot of ex-pats already. The hotel has a gathering for all their guests every Tuesday evening. That facilitated us meeting many of the ex-pats that live in the hotel. Nancy joined the International Women's Club and she is starting to do things with some of the women she met. The kids met others their age and seem to be adjusting ok so far."

"On the negative side" I continued "last Saturday, we went to a local Department Store. When we were inside, Nancy and Elizabeth went to the clothing department while John and I went to the electronics and stereos department. A few minutes later, John and I noticed that there was a crowd gathered around Nancy and Elizabeth. We rushed over there to see what was going on. When we got there, both Nancy and Elizabeth looked absolutely panicked."

"What was going on?" Drew asked

"As we later found out, people are not used to seeing blond haired women. They were innocently curious and wanted to find out what blond hair felt like, so they were touching Nancy's hair. Of course Nancy had no idea what was going on and she was quite shaken."

"She told me later that it started with one or two people coming close to her and Elizabeth and within a few minutes, the number swelled into a crowd. To avoid them, she grabbed Elizabeth's hand and walked over to a different part of the store trying to find John and me, but the crowd moved with them, so she kept moving and they simply kept moving with them. Finally, one of the women reached over and touched her hair and then a second one did the same."

"When John and I arrived, the crowd backed off some but did not dissipate. We had to leave the store."

"At the time, it was very unsettling. When we got back to the hotel, we talked to Julia, our contact there, and she explained to us that this sometimes happens. She felt bad but kept reassuring us that it was a simple case of people being curious because they have not seen too many unescorted foreigners especially blond ones."

"I am sorry to hear that Nancy and Elizabeth had this experience" Drew said "since I live in Hong Kong and commute to Guangzhou weekly, I haven't had this experience. Both Hong Kong and Guangzhou have a lot of foreigners and people are used to seeing us there. I never heard of this type of problem there. I hope she is ok now."

"She is fine" I said "especially now that she understands what was going on."

Mr. Huang pulled to the entrance of the plant and soon we were out of the car. We went up to my office, dropped Drew's and Daniel' belongings and went back down so that I can take them on a tour of the plant which was customary for visiting executives. When we finally were by ourselves and outside the building, Drew started to explain to me what he was thinking and doing with Mr. Chen.

"In a nutshell" he said "we have had a partnership with the Chinese since we first arrived in China on a very small scale. The idea was that, as part of their ownership, the local Bureau of Light Industry (BOLI) would smooth things for us and be a helpful and enabling partner to us as we try to build the business. The fact is that they have been providing very little help and, at least in some cases, creating delays and slowdowns for us. In reality, they are part of the fabric of the Chinese government and the way they see it is that after you and I are long gone to our next assignments, they will still be here and have to live with the other bureaus and government agencies. So, given a choice, they would much rather have us be unhappy with things than upset the locals at the bureaus who they need to maintain their long term relationships with. In short, we come and go, their local friends don't."

"Interesting perspective" I said "I thought that 100% foreign ownership is not allowed in China and that is precisely what you were pushing for."

"True enough" he said "but my argument is that we already have four joint ventures with the Chinese government if you consider the operations we have in Guangzhou, Chengdu, Beijing and here in Tianjin. So my point with them is that they already have part ownership in our business. I am simply looking at our total business in China as a whole instead of looking at our JV's as four separate units, which is the way they tend to view it. Even if we were to look at it from the perspective of the Tianjin BOLI, they still own 10% of the business and the second plant even with 100% ownership, will bring in a lot of taxes and employment for the locals, many of whom are now working for defunct businesses that BOLI has to prop up to keep people employed. It is definitely a good deal for them."

Daniel jumped in and said "think of it as a parallel to the way we view our business, when the company talks about the business in China, they talk about it as a whole and not as four different businesses. We are asking the Chinese to view all of our business with them as a whole as well."

"Exactly" Drew added "we believe that they already own too much of a stake in our business. We bring in the capital, the technology, the brands, marketing and all the expertise. We already know through our other partnerships that, aside from minimal and, at times, questionable access, BOLI is not providing us with any benefits that would warrant the 5% stake they are asking for in Tianjin."

"I understand" I said "we have to ask ourselves, what value added benefits do they bring to our business? And the answer appears to be, not enough to warrant part ownership in it."

"You got it" Drew said "today's business is about forty million dollars, so you can easily say; their ten percent is worth about four million before taxes and expenses, etc. But fast forward ten years from now, how much do you think our business and brand equity will be worth?"

"I don't know" I said "a few hundred million?"

"You aim too low my friend" Drew said looking at Daniel.

Daniel said "try a few billion."

"Two billion would be a conservative number" Drew said looking at me and adding "you are an engineer so I assume you are good with math. What is 10% of two billion?"

"That is easy" I said "a cool two hundred million."

Drew then looked at me and said "as a shareholder of our company, would you think that the Board of Directors and the executives of this company are doing a good job if we gave away two hundred million dollars of the company's future revenue and weighed down our growth prospects by taking on yet another partnership?"

"Don't forget" added Daniel "that, based on our experience to date in our four JV's, the best we can hope for is that they are not a hindrance to our progress since they tend to view their role as one of oversight and compliance versus that of a partner who is eager to help grow and build the business. In short, the value of what they do to help the business is not quite there."

"That is why I am adamant that the new plant will have to be one hundred percent owned by us" Drew said. I am talking to Mr. Chen's counterparts in other parts of China and I believe that one of them will come through for us. We have to keep reminding them that the capital investment, the jobs created and taxes that will come from a new facility is not inconsequential. The plant we are talking about will start small with one business but will have a lot of expansion potential to accommodate many businesses. We will build it with the right infrastructure to support fast expansion when we finally get there."

"I completely understand" I said "this makes perfect sense. How can I help?"

"To start with" he said "do your job as the new General Manager of the Tianjin JV and the bar soap business. I need you to find a way to make things happen a lot faster than what I am hearing."

"I am clear on that part" I said "I just finished reviewing the project in detail and I drew the same conclusions. I am not happy with the proposed timing and I asked the engineering team to reassess and provide me with compressed time-lines. They promised me an update the middle of next week."

"Good" Daniel said "we have to find a way to get soap made and distributed across all of China" he added "it can't happen fast enough for us. The Beijing test market results are showing that we can have a thirty eight percent market share if we can only have the product to sell."

"I completely understand" I said looking at Daniel "give me a chance to finish transitioning with Rick and work on the timeline with engineering. I will touch base with you next week to let you know what I learn."

"Good" Drew said "the other thing I need you to do is lead the development of an infrastructure for the soap business beyond Tianjin. Your other area of responsibility as product supply manager covers all of Mainland China, Taiwan and Hong Kong. So far, we have had three infrastructures for the three countries that functioned independent of each other. We need to integrate all three and look for efficiencies between them."

"Besides" Daniel added "we need to be running test markets in China on other personal cleaning products besides bar soap. If you look at Hong Kong and Taiwan, we have a very strong franchise in shower gels, we believe that shower gels will be a big hit in China also but we have not run any test markets yet. We need to think about where we will produce the gels, ingredient sourcing, etc."

"As you can see we badly need you here" Drew said with a smile adding "so much opportunity and, naturally, we want everything yesterday."

Only now did Drew start to walk towards the production buildings for their quick tour. Fortunately, both of them had been through the plant and understood the challenges ahead. So I did not get any embarrassing questions I could not answer.

On the way back to the office, Drew said "in the next few days, I suspect that Mr. Chen will be trying to spend some time with you to try and get any information he can about the company's willingness to bend on the percentages."

"Yes" I replied "I suspected this much. How do you want me to handle him?"

"Meet with him" Drew said "listen to what he has to say, but don't say anything that can lead him to believe, even remotely, that there is any hope for changing the decision around one hundred percent ownership. Just keep re-emphasizing that the company was determined. And remind him that they already own a piece of your joint venture in Tianjin plus three other JV's across China. Tell him that you think it is a fair way to look at it from a Western perspective."

"Will do" I said "I will tell him that I am very surprised that the company has conceded to the ten percent ownership that they have with the existing JV's."

Drew looked at me with an approving smile and said "you are going to do fine in China. Be sure to call me anytime you hear from Mr. Chen. We will have to talk in code and may have to have you fly to Hong Kong for us to talk details."

Drew continued "I don't have to tell you that everything I told you is absolutely confidential and cannot be repeated to anyone."

"Absolutely. I understand" I said.

Drew felt a need to emphasize his point, so he continued "you can't repeat it even to our own people including the expats. Not even your wife. Remember what you were told at your security briefing. The walls have ears in China. That is why we are talking in the yard and not in your office."

"Thanks for the reminder, but I got it boss. Trust me" I said as I looked at my watch and said, "We should collect your things and get you to the airport."

9

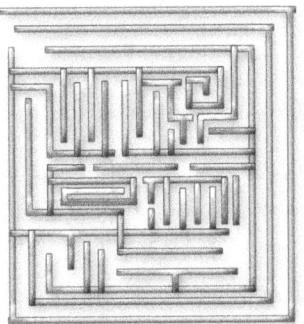

RICK LEAVES .... NOW WHAT

Over the next few days, people were coming out of the woodwork to have lunches and dinners with Rick and I would be invited as a courtesy. It gave me a chance to meet a lot of people and start to establish relationships. It felt like all we did was go from one meal to the next.

The pattern of drinking a lot of alcohol and the gan bei toasting was repeated endlessly. The good news is that my cover of being "allergic" to alcohol was taking hold and after a polite question about a drink, people were leaving me alone as far as alcohol was concerned. I was happy about that. The pressure was off.

The thing that I noticed was that Rick, and by default, the company was always picking up the bill even though the farewell events were being organized in Rick's honor.

I asked Rick about this custom. He laughed and said "yes, in China, you invite people, you pay, they invite you, you also pay" adding "in reality, the people cannot afford to pay the bill on their meager incomes and the bureaucracy around expense reports is daunting. It used to bother me, but I rationalized my way into accepting it as part of the overall China experience."

Needless to say, it was becoming increasingly more difficult to spend one on one time with Rick. The time Rick and I had left together was literally used up dealing with urgent questions in-between meals.

I heard from Mr. Chen on Rick's last day at the plant. Mr. Chen called to wish Rick the best in his future endeavors and took the opportunity to set up a dinner meeting with me the following Tuesday.

By early afternoon, I told Rick to feel free to head back to Beijing and finish getting ready. Maureen and he were scheduled to catch a flight to Hong Kong the next morning. We said our goodbyes and reconfirmed that I felt I was ready to take over and that he was only as far as the telephone.

On Monday, I met with the engineering team to get an update and things did not sound any more promising for advancing the timing, but the team was thinking more aggressively and being creative. While that fell way short of what I wanted to hear, I was encouraged to see that they were searching for 'out of the box' solutions and that they clearly understood the sense of urgency and magnitude of the opportunities that lay ahead.

The one thing that kept coming up as a concern, more so than any other, was the length of time it takes to get permits for construction and blue print approvals. When I asked Dale if there was anything I can do to help, he was quick to tell me that if I was able to somehow figure out the local bureaucracy and find a way to lean on senior officials to help speed things up, that would be the biggest help I can give to the engineering team. "That would allow us to shave time from the project schedule" he concluded.

"I will make it a top priority for me" I said "in the meantime, I am looking for you to keep driving the team to find ways to speed up project execution and get us ready to produce" I told Dale as we wrapped up our meeting.

"Not a problem, we are aligned on that" he said.

When I got back to my office, I asked Julie to set up a meeting with all the managers that afternoon. I felt that I needed to start working on developing the management team. I knew that what I needed to accomplish was simply too big for anyone to do by himself. I had to find a way to unleash the talent that is all around me.

While she was working on organizing the meeting, I called Daniel and told him that my meeting with the engineers was not coming up with any significant new information.

"I am convinced that their hearts are in the right place and they are absolutely focused on doing everything they can to speed things up" I said.

"I hear you, but there has got to be something we can do to get this business off the ground" Daniel said with some frustration in his voice. It was clear from the tone of his voice that he wasn't convinced that everyone was doing everything they can to deliver.

"I'll be honest with you" I said "based on my experience with big projects that are run under much more controlled and favorable circumstances than this team faces, I believe that if I push them any further, they will start to give me dates that they think I want to hear and hope for the best. That is not a position I want us to be in. We can easily find ourselves in such a predicament if we simply turn up the pressure any more than I already have. I think that we both need them to be upfront with us so that we can do our business planning based on commitments that can actually be delivered as promised or, at the very least, have a chance of being delivered within a narrow window."

"The problem" I continued "that keeps coming up as a common theme in every conversation I've had with them is that it almost doesn't matter how fast they work, once they apply for permits or look for approvals from a local bureau, the process comes to a dead stop. Approvals take a long time and frequently require a series of reiterations and re-submittals."

"Is this something that we are having trouble with because we are losing something in translation?" Daniel asked.

"There may be something to that" I answered "but, my understanding is that it is not that simple. From what I understand, the team works permitting through Bechtel, and they use local engineers and design institutes to manage the process with the bureaus. They often get Mr. Tian, who carries the weight of BOLI behind him, to provide his input before they submit paperwork and it still comes back. I think the issue is more along the lines that the rules and guidelines are written in such a way that they can be very broadly open for interpretation and, as such, present too many variables and moving targets. If you combine that with what I would call an ingrained fear by bureaucrats of making a decision for fear of making a mistake, you will have a stifling combination whereby getting anyone to make a decision is like pulling teeth."

"Believe me Daniel, I understand your frustration" I said "I am at least as frustrated as you are if not more by the pace of progress. I told Dale this morning that I am making working the permitting process a top priority for me. But I want you to hear me out on another approach for how we can have a breakthrough."

"I can't wait" he said with lack of excitement in his voice "what is your idea?"

"I think we need to have two parallel paths. One is building our capacity just like we are talking and the other involves identifying other sources of supply and quickly tapping them to make soap for us while we build our own capacity" I said.

"We already looked into that" Daniel said "the company does not have enough spare capacity in the rest of our global system to supply what we project the demand to be. On top of that, you have the cost of shipping to China, paying importation duty, etc. The tab becomes simply way too big for us to absorb" he said.

"That much I know" I said "I am not talking about tapping the company's capacity. I feel uncomfortable going through the details right now. I am scheduled to fly to Guangzhou for a product supply leadership team meeting with Jack on Thursday. Do you know if you are scheduled to be in town on Thursday?

"Yes, I will be here until Thursday afternoon. I need to catch the 4:00 PM train to Hong Kong" he said.

"Will you be available to meet over dinner on Wednesday evening?" I asked.

"That sounds great. Let's plan on dinner then."

"Good. Where are you staying?" I asked.

"White Swan Hotel, how about you?" he asked.

"I am booked at the China Hotel. I will have Julie switch my reservation to the White Swan. My flight gets in around 5:00 PM so I can probably meet you any time after 6:30 PM" I said

"Ok, let's plan to meet at 7:00 PM in the lobby of the White Swan. They have a good restaurant there that serves Western food" Daniel said as we wrapped up our conversation.

Next, I called Drew and gave him a quick update about my meeting with the engineers, the plans that Daniel and I had to meet on Wednesday evening and let him know that Mr. Chen called to say goodbye to Rick and that he and I are planning to have dinner on Tuesday night.

Drew asked me to keep him in the loop on what Daniel and I decide to do and to be sure to say hi to Mr. Chen for him and let him know that he is still following up on their conversation but was not optimistic. The Board is not happy that the question was brought back to them again.

I said I would and we hung up.

10

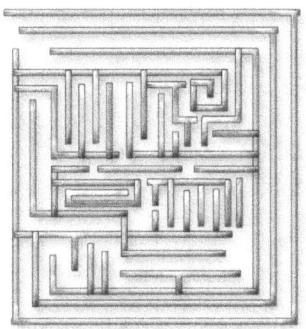

MY MEETING WITH THE MANAGEMENT TEAM.
THE JOURNEY BEGINS

Julie scheduled the meeting for 3:00 PM. Five minutes before the meeting, she came in and we both went to the big conference room. The room was still set up class room style. I was debating if I should have Julie translate or not. I was told that all the managers with the exception of Mr. Tian had studied English and generally had a reasonable understanding of the language.

I asked Julie what her impression was. She said "in general, they should be able to understand you, but the truth is that most of them have very poor English language skills."

"If I address them in English only, how much would you estimate they can understand? Would you say eighty or ninety percent?" I asked

"No, they may understand twenty or thirty percent. Some of them, like James will understand ninety five percent, but the majority will be lost" she said.

"That helps" I said "I will try harder to remember to stop and give you time to translate. If I get carried away like I did at our last meeting, don't hesitate to remind me to stop."

The conference room was full already and I automatically went to the front of the room and stood in what was starting to become a familiar spot for me.

"Good afternoon" I started "ni hao ma?" asking how everyone was doing.

Some of the managers chuckled at my Chinese.

"Today's meeting is going to be the first of a series of management meetings. The 'all management meetings' will be held weekly and you are all invited. Attendance is mandatory unless you are on vacation or away on business" I said, and waited for Julie to translate. I could see some unease but more curiosity in their faces.

"The objective of those meetings will be for us to learn about our company and our business. I will plan to communicate any information that I feel you need to know in order to do your job well. I will also update you on the plant modernization project and, just as important, we can discuss any problems we face and brainstorm solutions together" I said.

"As a start, I want to ask you to tell me what you would like me to talk about today. I am completely open to discussing anything that you may have on your minds. Ideas, suggestions or anything else?" I asked.

It was Déjà vu. I had an instant repeat of my first management meeting when Rick introduced me to the team. Once again, it was dead silence. I stood there for a long and very awkward minute not expecting anyone to say anything.

Finally, I said "I am going to pick the topic today, but for the next meeting, I want to hear suggestions from you. If you are not comfortable asking questions in the meeting, give your suggestions to Julie and she will pass them on to me."

"Today, I am going to tell you about the company that we all work for and talk about our corporate values"

I spent the next half hour talking about the company's values and why they were important. I talked about how their peers, in other countries, have the same common values and went on to explain how the company believes in treating its employee's right.

In closing, I quoted an old manager of mine who gave me advice when I was first promoted. He had said to me "managing the business in our company is very easy. All you have to do is take care of your people and they will take care of the business for you. It took a little time for me to fully understand that advice" I continued "but today, I am fully committed to leading this JV with this advice in mind."

"I need you to help me by letting me know if things are not right so that I can fix them or help you understand why things are being done a certain way" I said.

"I want to see some thumbs up if you agree to bring problems forward so that we can fix them together before I open the meeting up for question" I said.

Julie translated and I saw a lot of thumbs up. I was pleased to see that it was unanimous.

Interestingly, thumbs up appeared to be much easier to get from this group than the word "yes". Unfortunately, after the thumbs up, came the dead silence again. Again, I let the silence go on for another awkward minute then said "ok, I am going to let you get away with not asking questions this time only. Next week, no one can leave the meeting until I have three questions."

I dismissed everyone and said that I am looking forward to our meeting next week.

Julie asked me as we were heading back to the office why I decided to have weekly meetings?

"I think it is very important to have a means to communicate and have an open dialogue with the management team." I said.

"Rick only had meetings for special occasions" she told me "that seemed to work ok."

"I am sure it worked fine" I said "but I feel that if I want to develop the management team to be successful within the company, I have to teach them about the company, its culture and the way business is done in the West. If I don't do it, how will they learn? Also, they will be at a disadvantage versus their peers from other parts of the company. We will have a lose/lose situation on our hands."

Julie gave me a puzzled look "lose/lose?" she asked

"Lose/lose means that the managers from Tianjin lose because they will not be considered for promotions outside of Tianjin. The reason that they would miss out is that they will not know much about the Company beyond what they know about the Tianjin Plant. The Company has over one hundred thousand employees across the globe. That makes for tough competition and managers have to stand out to be recognized and promoted beyond a certain level. Does this make sense?" I asked.

Julie nodded and said "yes".

"The second lose refers to the Company losing because a source of management talent will go unnoticed because they were not developed and given the opportunity to reach their potential to perform beyond the Tianjin Plant. Because of that, all those smart and talented managers will not be tapped for assignments in other parts of the Company unless" I stopped for emphasis and saw that I had Julie's undivided attention, so I went on "unless they learn about the broader business and are able to show the Company what they can do to contribute to its success. Does this make sense?" I asked again.

"Yes" she said "that makes sense" she was silent for a moment and then said "very interesting perspective, but it's not going to be easy."

"No, it is not going to be easy" I agreed as I settled at my desk and Julie went to her office.

Today turned out to be an unusual day for me. The afternoon went by fast with no interruptions and I found myself finished with my work earlier than usual. Since there were no pressing issues that I needed to deal with, I decided to take advantage of the opportunity to leave early and surprise Nancy and the kids.

When I arrived at the hotel, I discovered that Nancy was out at an International Women's Club event and Liz was sleeping over at her friend's place. Only John was home.

"Why don't you and I go out for a walk; when we get hungry we can find a local restaurant and have an adventure" I suggested with a smile.

"Sounds good" John said "I know a place where they specialize in dumplings. I went there last week with my friends from school. It is called 99 dumplings because they have 99 variations of dumplings on their menu."

"Let's do it" I said as we headed out.

"So Johnny" I said "I know you were upset with me when I accepted this assignment, but now, you seem to be enjoying yourself. I have to admit that I was worried about you. I mean being 16 years old is usually tough enough without being transplanted half way across the world. How are things going for you now?" I asked.

John was finishing 10th Grade when we moved and started 11th Grade after his summer break. With us moving as often as every three to four years, it was hard on the kids since they had to start over with every move. John was born in Canada while I was on assignment in Hamilton, Ontario. It took a while for him to be accepted by the other kids when we relocated to Cincinnati. As a result, much of his social life revolved around his involvement in Tae Kwon Do.

"I have to say this" John said "I love China!! I don't care if it is Communist. Maybe that is because I wasn't even born yet when we had the "red scare", so I didn't really grow up with any prejudices against "the Communists". Or, who knows, maybe it was the three times a week I spent studying Tae Kwon

Do in Cincinnati for over 3 years where it was my life just before we moved to Tianjin."

He stopped for a moment to reflect before going on.

"I have to admit that, even though I was upset when I heard the news, I suppose I wasn't as upset as you may have thought. A part of me was full of wonder. I don't have to tell you that I saw the movie "Enter the Dragon" with Bruce Lee at least fifty times. You can say that I loved all that stuff. I guess after the initial shock of hearing that we might move to china, I started wondering what it would be like to live here. I wondered what the school in China will be like" he hesitated and went on "and I wondered if I will be getting a Chinese girlfriend and what that would be like."

"And ? ....." I said with a look that urged him to continue.

"I guess it is safe to say that I am happy to be here now. I mean I miss some of my friends, but overall I am doing just fine dad" he said "and I am enjoying myself."

"I am so glad to hear you say that" I said "I was torn because I was wondering if you and your sister will ever adjust. Seeing you do well is very comforting for your mom and me."

"You guys can stop worrying" he said "by the way, the 99 Dumplings restaurant is just ahead on the left."

"Good" I said.

We went in and seated ourselves at an open table. The waitress came over and started talking to us in Mandarin.

John would eventually excel in learning Mandarin. Not only did he work hard to learn Mandarin while we lived in Tianjin, but he also continued to study it at University as part of his International Business curriculum to the point where he learned to read, write and speak it fluently.

Unfortunately at this particular moment in time, with the two of us sitting at the 99 Dumplings restaurant, with the waitress talking to us in Mandarin, we were lost. Even though John's Mandarin was much better than mine, his Mandarin skills were still in their infancy and mine were almost non-existent. In less than a minute, it became abundantly clear that neither his nor my Mandarin were going to help us tonight.

As it turned out, when John came to this restaurant last week; his friends who spoke good Mandarin ordered the food.

Being the type of people who are not dissuaded easily, we both pressed on and tried to communicate, but eventually realized that we were not making much headway. Unfortunately, the old standby trick of walking around the restaurant from table to table and pointing at people's plates to place our order was not working this time. The reason it did not work is that from the outside, all dumplings have an uncanny resemblance to each other. One can't tell the difference in the fillings between one dumpling and another by simply looking at them. A dumpling filled with Chicken looks exactly the same as one filled with broccoli. This simple fact made it impossible to order by walking around tables and pointing at plates.

The second standby was also failing us this evening. In many cases, when foreigners find themselves in this type of situation, a local who might speak some English that happens to also be dining at the restaurant will come to their aid and save the day. Unfortunately, no one else at the restaurant spoke English and, as a result, no one was stepping in to help us tonight. We were truly on our own which meant that we had to find a creative way to get our order placed.

After a few minutes of frustration, I decided to call Julie and ask her to translate. Julie was a little surprised to get my call. As I explained to her what we were doing, she couldn't stop laughing. Eventually, she settled down and asked me to give the cell phone to the waitress. A few seconds later, the waitress handed the phone back to me. Julie explained to me that there were so many choices.

"Why don't we start with you telling me what you would like" she said.

"I would" I said "but I don't know what they have to choose from."

"Start with a category" she persisted "as an example, pork, beef, eggs, vegetables or chicken."

"I see" I said "let me ask John what he would like. Hang on."

After some discussion, we had Julie order a variety of dumplings and two Cokes."

I thanked Julie and hung up.

The dumplings were excellent. I can see why this particular restaurant was famous in Tianjin.

After dinner, we paid. That part was easy since we both were proficient with the language of money.

As we started to walk back towards the hotel, John asked me if I wanted to walk back using a different route than the one we took to get there. I said "yes" and we went in a different direction. As we walked, we came to an intersection where five different streets converged. We needed to cross to the other side of the intersection but the bicycle; car and pedestrian traffic was very heavy. I assumed my defensive position and was starting to stop and go, duck and weave as I crossed the street. We finally made it to the other side in one piece, but not without what sounded like a lot of grumbling from the cyclists and horns beeping at us, I turned to John and proudly said "we made it."

"Ok dad" John said "you almost got both of us killed."

"What are you talking about?" I asked with astonishment.

"Here is the deal" John said "when you cross the street, you simply have to look straight and keep a steady pace as you walk across. That way, people coming towards you can judge where you are and how fast you are walking. That allows them to predict where you are going to be as they approach you. When you are predictable, they can either go to your left or right to avoid hitting you."

"Interesting" I said "I guess I was so busy trying to avoid all the traffic that I missed that point and made myself more likely to have an accident."

"Exactly" he continued "when you stop and start and duck and weave like you did, you make yourself unpredictable which is what causes accidents. The other thing my friends told me was this. Don't make eye contact with incoming drivers or cyclists. If you make eye contact, they will assume that you are going to yield the right of way to them."

"Very interesting" I repeated "thank you for the Chinese traffic culture survival lesson."

"You are welcome" he said. We were almost at the hotel and could see a cab pulling to the main entrance.

A minute later, Nancy was getting out. She was surprised to see John and me walking towards her.

"What are you doing here" she asked looking at me "I wasn't expecting to see you for at least another hour. You know, your usual time" she added for emphasis.

"I had an unusual day today. I was finished early and decided to come home and surprise you" I said.

"Of all days" she said "this had to happen on the day of the International Women's Club meeting. Did you guys have dinner?" she continued.

"Yes, John took me to this restaurant that specializes in dumplings. It was very good. We'll have to go back" I said as John and I proceeded to tell her about our experience and how we ended up placing our orders.

11

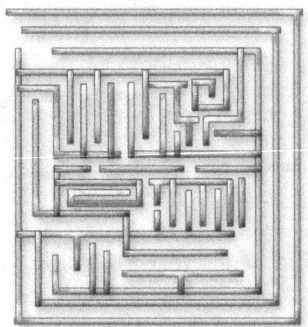

THE PLAN STARTS TO TAKE SHAPE

Tuesday went by very quickly. A lot of meetings were scheduled in the morning. In the early afternoon, I went for a walk through the plant.

On the way back, I stopped to see Dan. Dan and his family also moved to Tianjin from the US. They arrived one week after us.

"How is your transition going?" I asked.

"It has been very rough" he said "I don't know if you heard, but last night, we were in a miandi coming back from dinner at a local restaurant and we were rear ended by another taxi. Miandi is the Chinese name of the small vans that are abundant in China, typically used as taxis. To me, a miandi looks like a French bread delivery van. I came to find out that the word miandi literally translates to bread truck because they believe that those vehicles look like loaves of sliced bread.

"I am sorry to hear that" I said "No, I did not hear about the accident. Is everyone alright? Anybody hurt?" I asked.

"Fortunately, we were all ok. The boys and Salima were all shook up, but no one was hurt." Dan said adding "the miandi literally fell apart. Side panels and doors fell off."

"That sounds terrible but I am glad to hear that everyone is fine" I said "I have to admit that I still get knots in my stomach every time I am traveling in a car around here. I can't figure out the traffic. I am amazed that there isn't a lot more accidents the way the traffic moves. Please let me know if there is anything I can do to help" I said.

"I will" he said.

"I wanted to give you a heads up about something I am contemplating doing that can shift some of your assignment responsibilities" I said adding "I know you just got here and have barely started to do your job. What I am thinking about is expanding your role from what you and Rick talked about when you signed up for this assignment."

Dan looked at me and asked "what do you have in mind?"

"Why don't we take a walk while I fill you in on the details" I said.

While we headed out of the building, I started thinking to myself that I may be taking this whole thing about the 'walls having ears' a little too seriously. But then again, what if they are right? I asked myself.

Once outside, I told Dan about how long the project is expected to take before we start rolling out cases of soap to the marketplace. The frustration we were all feeling about having a very successful test market that showed we can have a thirty five plus market share if we could only get product to market.

I went on to explain what I learned from my discussions with the engineers and concluded by saying "we may be able to squeeze a month or two on the completion schedule; but realistically, there are enough unknowns that we are dealing with that it is more likely to have delays than acceleration of our plans."

By now, I could see that puzzled look in Dan's eyes. He was wondering where I was going with all this and how it related to him and his assignment. After all, his assignment as the new Technical Service Organization Manager was to train people on the company's technology and quality standards. A big part of his responsibility is to put a robust infrastructure in place that ensures that all products, made at the Tianjin JV, are manufactured to the same exacting specifications and standards as any of the company's products that are made anywhere else in the world.

"I know you are wondering where this is going" I said "before I go too far, I have to tell you that at this point, what I am about to share with you is an idea that I have. I still have to discuss it with Daniel and Drew and see if I can get their agreement to proceed. If they agree, I expect that we will be moving really fast which is why I am talking to you today."

"In a nutshell" I continued "I am going to ask Daniel and Drew to give me the go ahead to contract manufacture soap at as many local soap plants as I can find in China."

A concerned look appeared on Dan's face. He said "I don't think you can get agreement to go ahead with sub-contracting soap production. The big concern would be quality. There is a strong belief within the quality organization that the Chinese will take shortcuts wherever possible and I don't have to tell you about how fanatical we are about quality and protecting our brand image and good name."

"I know" I said "that is precisely why I am talking to you. In order for me to sell this idea, I have to be able to assure the company and the business that we are not going to do something rash or irresponsible. That means we need to develop a plan that will consistently deliver a quality product that meets the company's standards and specifications. The plan has to be practical and absolutely doable."

"Let's assume for a minute that we can convince the company to allow us to sub-contract out the manufacturing process for a minute. Do you realize how big a job it would be to deliver on this idea?" Dan asked.

"I know. It is a huge deal" I said "I think the trick is going to be to try and limit the number of suppliers we develop and qualify. The way I am thinking about it is that if we can get enough soap made by staffing up here plus find another say two to four other suppliers somewhere in China, I think we can manage it. It won't be easy, but I am convinced it is doable."

Dan was thinking deeply for a minute and then he said "I have to agree with the 'it won't be easy' part but I would have to think about how we may be able to do it."

"Can we bring in more ex-pats?" Dan asked.

I thought for a minute about Dan's question and then said "Yes, I am quite certain that I can get approval to bring more ex-pats if I push for it. Let's face it, we both know how eager the company is to build the business and expand quickly in China."

As I contemplated that thought some more I added "but, having said that, when I reflect on how long it took to go through the process to get us over here, if it takes the same amount of time to get new ex-pats here as it took us to get here, then, I must say that this idea is a non-starter. They would not be here in time to be of much help to us. We have to move a lot faster than that, I am afraid. While I like the idea, I don't think it would be practical for what we need."

We both stood in silence for a minute and then I said "I have it, here is what I can do that I think can help us move fast. I can lean on some of my friends and get us some people for a month or two on short term special assignments to help with the training and setting up the infrastructure to support what we need to get done. I can call my good friend Joe in Cincinnati; he heads the Quality organization and find out what he can do to help us. I can also call Deepak in Japan to see what he can do for us within the Asian organization. Getting people on loan would be a lot faster and easier. We would be talking weeks instead of months" I concluded with a lot of excitement in my voice.

Dan smiled and said "boy, you really want to make this happen and you want it now!"

"I do, I really do" I said "the last thing I want to do is to take a hardship assignment only to baby sit a project for a year or eighteen months. I came here to build a business, and that is exactly what we are going to do Dan. Are you with me?" I asked.

Dan said "Absolutely, you can count on me. I still have to caution you that this is not going to be a cake walk, but I will give it my best shot."

"That is all I can ask" I said "I would like you to put together a plan that explains how we will manage quality at sub-contractors to ensure that the company's specifications and standards are met consistently. From that, I need you to tell me what infrastructure support you will need, how many resources and what skills and expertise they need to have. If you know specific people, suggest them by name."

I added "your job is to make sure that you define a bullet proof plan and my job will be to get you the resources you need to execute the plan. If in doubt, err on the side of building too many safeguards."

"Sounds good, but not so fast" Dan said "for me to build a plan, I need to know how many plants you expect to sub-contract and their locations, volumes, etc."

"I agree" I said "the problem is that I don't really know at this point. Why don't you put together plans that assume we will sub-contract plants that are about the size and capability of this plant. Then we can use that information to guide us as we sign on additional plants. I realize that the use of a simple multiplier is not the best way to do this, but it will give us a good idea of what we need to do."

"I can do that" Dan said "when do you need this information?"

"As soon as you can get it to me" I said "I am flying to Guangzhou tomorrow afternoon. I realize you need more time than that, but let's plan to talk tomorrow over lunch. Give me whatever you have at that time."

"You don't ask for much, do you?" Dan said smiling "I'll see you at noon tomorrow.

I said "Great, I'll see you tomorrow and thank you. We are going to be a great team." adding "don't forget to say hello to Salima and the boys. Tell them that I am sorry about the accident and very glad that everyone is fine."

"I'll tell them" Dan said and we headed back to our respective offices.

12

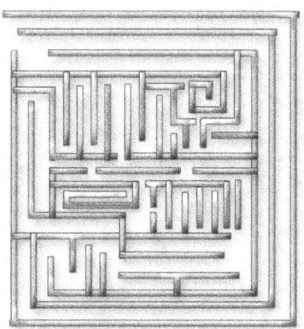

DINNER WITH MR. CHEN

Julie came in with the now familiar stack of papers I needed to sign reminding me that we had to hurry so that we can meet Mr. Chen at 7:00 PM for dinner.

I went through all the invoices and payment authorizations and signed all of them. Regrettably, I was starting to be a little comfortable with signing Chinese language documents that I did not quite know for sure what they were. I made a mental note to ask Jack what his thoughts were. I also need to understand what my personal liability was on this. I knew that it would not be very difficult to have me sign a piece of paper that authorizes payments to individuals that are not owed any money by the company. This was bothering me and I had to find a way to make it secure and more comfortable for me.

After I finished, we had about ten minutes before Mr. Huang will be picking us up. I dialed Jack's number. He picked up on the first ring.

"Expecting my Call?" I asked.

"No" he said "your call will be more pleasant. My wife is supposed to call me back but she is making me wait."

"What did you do this time?" I asked with a chuckle.

"She is not happy because I am not going back to Hong Kong tonight as originally planned. She had to cancel a get together that she had planned over two weeks ago with some friends of ours. I had to break the news to her that our partners in Guangzhou called a last minute meeting and Drew wants me to attend."

"I only know too well how this scenario works" I said laughing "better you than me boss."

"Thanks. I guess this too shall pass" he said "what's up?"

"I have a question for you" I said "every evening, Julie walks in with a stack of papers that she asks me to sign authorizing purchases and payments, some involve a lot of money" adding "I never had to do that when I ran businesses in the US."

"The rules are different here" Jack said "there are very strict guidelines imposed by the Chinese Government for JV's requiring the General Manager to sign off on those types of authorizations. The other GM's have to do this also at our other JV's."

"It bothers me that I don't know what I am signing for" I said.

"What do you mean you don't know what you are signing for?" Jack asked.

"I can't read Chinese Jack" I said "the way this works is Julie comes in with a stack of papers, I ask her what am I signing for and she tells me. If I have questions, I ask, otherwise, I sign and we move to the next paper in the stack to keep the business running."

"So what's the problem?" Jack asked.

"The problem is that Julie can tell me whatever she wants and I would not know any better" I said, quickly adding "it is not that I don't trust Julie, but the process makes me feel uncomfortable."

"I understand your discomfort" Jack said "but as an officer of the Company, when you sign a piece of paper, you are signing on behalf of the Company and the Company has to honor your signature" Jack said.

"I understand that part" I said "but at the end of the day, I feel that we have some vulnerability here. What would be my personal liability in the event of a mishap on this end?"

"There isn't a pretty way to say it" Jack said in his typical get to the point way "but it is your responsibility to make sure you only sign for things that are appropriate for you to sign. This is the official Company position" he added.

Before I could say anything Jack went on "the Company wants us to do everything possible to make sure we keep everything under control; however, there are a lot of safeguards."

"Like what?" I asked pointedly.

"Like that army of accountants that Marie has in the Finance group one floor below your office" Jack said "they go through each piece of paper you sign in detail to make sure that it is legitimate before making payments. Also, Mr. Tian and BOLI keep a very sharp eye on all the numbers and would certainly pick up any irregularities. Granted, if someone was determined, they can slip something through; however, it would require collusion by a number of people for it to go unnoticed. Yes, it can be done but it would not be easy" he concluded.

"That makes me feel a little better" I said.

"Do your best" Jack said "the bottom line is that while you are accountable and responsible to make sure that you know what you are signing, there are safeguards in place and the Company will only hold it against you if it was determined that you were directly involved somehow."

"Ok, I understand and I feel a little better about it" I said.

In the background I could hear Jack's cell phone ringing "I hear your cell ringing, so I better let you go" saying as we hung up "say hello to Sally for me".

Just as I hung up, Julie peaked through the door and announced that the car was already at the door waiting for us.

Mr. Huang dropped us off at the restaurant and, to my surprise, Mr. Tian was there waiting. I did not know that he would be there. Shortly after we said hello to Mr. Tian, Mr. Chen arrived with Madam Shen.

I was quickly learning about seating arrangements in China. The key principle is this. The most senior people sit next to each other with their backs to a wall, if a wall is close by the table, and face the entrance to the room. The Chinese typically use various sizes of round tables that can typically accommodate only a few or up to twelve to sixteen people. This fact takes care of the awkwardness that comes with dealing with the question of who sits at the head of the table. After that, since I needed a translator, Julie has to sit on my left while Mr. Chen sat on my right. To the right of Mr. Chen sat Madam Shen and then Mr. Tian who ended up next to Julie. From this seating arrangement, it is clear that Madam Shen was higher in the pecking order than Mr. Tian since Mr. Tian was sitting farther from Mr. Chen than Madam Shen. By the same token, since I am the highest ranking representative from the Company, I sat next to Mr. Chen; however, if Drew was at this meeting, then he would be the one to sit next to Mr. Chen and I would then sit next to Drew.

The food was ordered and drinks served. I ordered a Coke. After a few minutes of conversation, Julie was able to convince everyone that I was not being disrespectful or unsociable by not ordering an alcoholic drink, but that I was simply allergic to alcohol. "Good, my cover is working" I thought.

"How is your family adjusting to living in Tianjin?" Mr. Chen asked.

"We are very happy to be in Tianjin" I said "everyone we have met so far has been wonderful and eager to help us in any way they can."

"I am glad to hear that" he said "if at any time you face difficulties, be sure to let me or Mr. Tian know and we will take care of it for you."

"Thank you" I said "I will be sure to do that, but people have been great. The Chinese people are very gracious hosts."

"Thank you" he said.

"The kids started their School and, so far, are adjusting well to the change" I added "although it will take them a little more time to fully adjust, I don't see any problem."

"I am happy to hear that. How about your wife?" he asked.

"She is doing very well" I said "she met several women through the Tianjin International Women's Club. Also, she is getting to know several ex-pats that live at the Sheraton, so she is busy. On the week-end, we went to a local market that is across the foot bridge from the Sheraton and bought a lot of fruits and vegetables. They were excellent quality and very fresh. We were very happy to find this market."

"This is the same market I shop at" jumped in Madam Shen "I live in the tall white building on the other side of the canal, so I walk over there to do my shopping."

"Maybe the next time we go there, we will run into each other" I said and we all laughed.

"On the Joint Venture" Mr. Chen said "I am having a hard time convincing anyone to consider anything less than the five percent ownership I offered Drew."

"I appreciate your working on this" I said "I know Drew is also trying"

"I believe Drew is being unreasonable." he said "your company already has the lowest level we have allowed in Tianjin. With us owning only 10% of the Soap Factory Joint Venture, your company already has a higher percent ownership than any other Joint Venture. To show our good intentions, I was willing to go down to 5%."

"I completely understand" I said "this must be very frustrating for you."

"It is very frustrating" he said "I consider Drew a close personal friend, which is why I pushed very hard to get agreement to offer him the 5%. I don't understand why he is not accepting the 5% offer I made to him."

"I talked to Drew about this" I said "he is just as frustrated as you are about this. He told me that he took it as high up in the Company as he could but was told that he will not be getting approval for anything less than 100% company ownership."

"But that is unreasonable" he said "the company wants to do business in China, but doesn't want to share in the benefits it will be getting. That does not seem reasonable to me. Does it seem reasonable to you?" he asked me with a piercing look.

"I can see how you can think that Mr. Chen" I said "all I can do is try to explain to you how the Company views this. Especially, how people at the company's headquarters in Cincinnati would be thinking about this."

"Please, go ahead" he said.

"Very well" I said "to start with, the company does not have many Joint Ventures. It typically owns 100% of its facilities."

"I understand" he said "but it does have JV's in Guangzhou and from what I understand in Vietnam and some East European countries."

"True" I said "what you will find is that they only have JV's in countries that require it by law or where it would be very difficult to do business unless there was a local partner. Basically, it has JV's only when it must, but not by choice."

"Why does the company view the JV's so negatively?" he asked.

"I would not characterize it that way" I said "In general, the company makes and sells products that are constantly being upgraded. We spend over two billion dollars on Research and Development to find better products or improve our existing products and get even better performance from them. The constant innovation and product improvements are key to the company's ability to stay ahead of competition. Most innovations and upgrades are copied by competitors very quickly and whatever advantage those innovations bring is usually short lived."

"I believe that innovations and product upgrades are a good thing. Why would that be a problem?" he asked.

"You see Mr. Chen" I said "many of those upgrades require investing more money either on equipment purchases or the introduction of new formulas that sometimes cost more money. What the company has found is that partners don't want to spend money and then decisions are held up and often there are delays that cause the company to lose its advantage in the markets where it has JV's."

"What do you mean?" he asked.

"Well, let me see if I can help explain how this problem manifests itself and ends up hurting our business. As you know, we are a Global company and our competitors also have a Global presence. Let's say that the company is ready to introduce a product improvement that requires a capital investment. As I am sure you know, a very important factor in the success of any business in a competitive field is speed to market. The company that gets its innovations to market first benefits the most and gets the best results. Are you with me so far?" I asked.

"Yes" he said "please continue."

"Ok" I went on "now, let's say that the company decides to launch a global rollout of a significant improvement to one of its products with the expectation that a quick launch will allow the company to capture a bigger market share which will eventually result in more profit and better business results."

"I don't see any problem so far" Mr. Chen said "we all benefit from that."

"I agree" I said "but this is where I think the problem develops. Since those types of product upgrades take place often. Sometimes as much as two or three times per year for many of our products and, in most cases, money has to be invested. A decision to launch has the potential to turn an advantage into a disadvantage."

Mr. Chen was now giving me the Chinese equivalent to an 'are you kidding me?' look.

"Let me explain" I quickly added "since such product introductions often require us to make a capital investment. The decision to launch this product would be an easy one for the parts of the company that are 100% owned, but not for the JV's. For the JV's, a dialogue has to take place. Very often, there is a long lag time between the start of dialogue with our JV partners and the time a decision to proceed is made. In some cases, JV partners don't want to invest additional money or they don't feel an improvement is necessary. All of these things lead to delays and a lot of extra work to secure agreement to proceed."

"I don't see why the company cannot simply launch the product in the countries that they own 100% and then follow it up with a launch after they get the JV partner's approval" Mr. Chen said.

"It is not that simple" I said "I wish it was, but what really happens is that as soon as we introduce a product in one country, our competitors find out about it and immediately work to introduce improvements of their own or launch marketing campaigns or offer discounts on similar products in order to stunt our progress. So let's say that the company makes a decision to launch a product improvement. In this case, a single decision would be needed for the US, Europe and Latin America to immediately launch the improvements. The money would be appropriated and the company's focus will be on execution."

"For the other countries where we have JV's" I continued "since, it would be very easy for our competitors to work on copying our innovations and upgrades and likely introduce them into those markets. By the time the dialogue takes place with JV partners to get agreement to spend the capital or upgrade the formula or whatever other changes need to be made, we lose our advantage. Basically, we lose one of the most important weapons a business has … its ability to beat its competitors and be the first to introduce new products or improvements into the marketplace."

"We can make a commitment to work very fast through our channels to make sure that changes happen fast" Mr. Chen said "we have a very good relationship with Drew and your company and we will do everything possible to move fast."

"I have no doubt about that" I said "please do not take this the wrong way, but please understand that all of our JV partners have said the same thing, but in reality, they had to get agreement from people above them, especially when it comes to investing more capital. The process normally takes a long time to work through. In those types of situations, being ahead of competition by weeks, and sometimes even days, can make a big difference in our business."

"I can make most of the decisions in Tianjin" he said "so things can move fast"

At this point, I decided that I have taken this argument as far as I can and it was time to move on other points.

"I have no doubt that you are in a better position than other JV's" I said "based on our conversation so far, I already know that you will work very hard to help us. Unfortunately, I don't get to make those decisions. The important thing to keep in mind is that the people who can make such decisions are sitting at our corporate headquarters and they are determined to invest in a new site only if they can have 100% ownership."

"That is hard to accept for me" he said.

"Trust me on this" I added "Drew's hands are tied on this. He has already taken it all the way to the top and it was discussed in detail in a Board meeting. To be honest with you, I think that it is bad for Drew's career to ask again, but he told me that he will be trying again because he promised you that he would."

"I suppose that is all I can ask from Drew" he said.

"There is one other thing I should point out to you" I said "the Company thinks about each Country as a whole and not as parts or regions."

"Can you explain what you mean please" Mr. Chen said.

"Based on our discussion so far, I can see that you are looking at this deal as a separate deal that stands alone. Ten percent for the soap factory, five percent for the new facility. I think this is where a possible disconnect may exist between your position and that of the Company. The company sees all the investments it is making in China as one big investment. If you ask people on the Board of Directors, they would tell you that the Chinese Government is already a major partner with a large stake in the Company's business. They will list the JV's in Beijing, Chengdu, the two JV's in Guangzhou and of course our JV in Tianjin. To them, it is the total investment in China that they look at and not individual JV's."

"I think I understand a little better, how the Company thinks about these investments" Mr. Chen said looking very disappointed "unfortunately, in China, we look at things differently. Each area has a local Bureau of Light Industry (BOLI) and our leadership gives us individual goals to meet. It would be very difficult for me to explain why I was not able to get agreement to a JV even at a measly 5% while my counterparts in other cities, were able to get it."

"I understand the dilemma this presents to you" I said "I know I can't do anything to change the new plant arrangements, but what I can promise you is that I will move very aggressively to build the JV business that we have."

"What do you have in mind?"

"As you know, we are both losing money on the JV. It costs us over $22 to make a case of Soap and we are selling it for just under $18" I said "I intend to move quickly and aggressively to find ways to reduce our costs to get us to break even, at least until we are able to finish the expansion project. After the expansion project, we should be able to make some decent profit. In the short term, we need to stop the bleeding."

"One other thing that I may be able to do" I added "since the Tianjin Soap Factory is owned by BOLI, I may be in a position to contract them to make some soap for us. This can bring in additional revenue for BOLI and may possibly give you something to bring back to your leadership."

I could see that Mr. Chen was finally starting to see a ray of hope. Not quite what he wanted, but at least he will not go back empty handed to his bosses.

"That would be helpful" he said "how much are you thinking?" he asked.

"I don't have the specifics yet" I said "but before I can do anything, I have to get agreement from our corporate headquarters to contract production. I don't want to be misleading because it is usually very difficult to get permission to have other companies make our product for us. The main concern is usually Quality Control. The company works very hard to maintain high quality standards for all of its products."

"I understand" he said "you will find that the people at TTSF are very conscientious and very concerned about quality."

"I am glad to hear that" I replied "I am working to define how much we would need and, if I am able to get permission to proceed; I would be looking at creative ways to staff Quality Control. I am hoping to have my plans defined very quickly, maybe within a few weeks."

"Ok, good" Mr. Chen said "let me know as soon as you have information about this."

Mr. Chen then turned to Mr. Tian and Madam Shen and spoke to them at some length in Chinese. This portion was not translated to me, but then Mr. Chen turned back to me and told me that he instructed Mr. Tian and Madam Shen to introduce me to Mr. Li, the plant manager at TTSF and for both of them to give me all possible help to complete my analysis."

I thanked Mr. Chen and with that, my first dinner with Mr. Chen was over and we got up to leave.

13

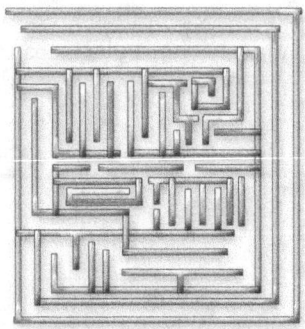

THE TRIP TO GUANGZHOU

The next day, before lunch time, I went to see Dale to find out if there was any new information about the project. There wasn't. The engineers worked very hard and explored different options to speed things up by moving as much of the project as they could in parallel. Unfortunately, all creative thought was stumped and the key obstacle and concern always came back to the same issue …. lack of confidence in being able to get permits and approvals to do the work. I asked Dale to keep working on it and to let me know every time he hits an obstacle.

"I had dinner with Mr. Chen last night and we are starting to build a good relationship. I am hoping to be able to leverage our relationship to try and get some of the bureaus to help us move things faster" I told Dale, adding "I also plan to assign Mr. Tian the responsibility to work on getting us the permits quickly."

"It would be a good thing if he is able to move things faster" Dale said "but be careful, I heard second hand from one of the Bechtel engineers working on our projects that their local contact had said that Mr. Tian is not willing to lean on his friends in the bureaus to make things happen."

"Thanks for the warning" I said "this will help me when I talk to Mr. Tian about this."

"I will let you know what develops" I said to Dale as I got up and headed for the door "I am off to the airport, I'll see you in a couple of days."

On the way back to my office and my meeting with Dan, I ran into Andrew, the Human Resources Manager. Andrew was waiting for me to get back. He asked me if he could introduce me to Ms. Chan.

"Ms. Chan" he said "is a professor at the Foreign Languages Institute in Tianjin. Her specialty is the English Language and she wants to meet you."

"I have a meeting with Dan in a few minutes" I said "but I can spend a few minutes and meet Ms. Chan."

"Ok, I will get her and we will meet you in your office."

Two minutes later, Andrew and Ms. Chan came in and Andrew introduced me. Julie told me that Ms. Chan was one of her professors when she was studying English.

Later I came to find out that the Tianjin Foreign Languages Institute was the Chinese equivalent to the Foreign Languages Institute in Monterey, California. It was very highly regarded in its field and many important people including diplomats and members of the secret service trained there to speak foreign languages like natives.

Ms. Chan was a very attractive woman with a big smile and a charming personality. Her English was better than mine. I was thrilled to be able to speak to a local Chinese who understood exactly what I said without having to go through a translator.

"I had heard that you were thinking about learning Chinese" Ms. Chan said "and I would like to be your teacher" she added getting straight to the point.

"You have heard right" I said "I have been so busy that I have not taken the time to find a teacher yet."

"I can give you private lessons and I am very reasonable"

"That sounds very good. How much do you charge per hour?" I asked.

"I normally charge 50 RMB, but since I came to you and Andrew has already bargained my price down, I will only charge you 40 RMB which is about five US dollars an hour. What do you think?"

"I am OK with 40 RMB" I said.

"Great" she said, when do you want to start?"

"I am catching a flight to Guangzhou this afternoon. How about you call me next week and we can try to arrange a time" I said.

"Excellent, I will call you next week" she said. As she was going out the door, she turned back and said "by the way, you can call me 'Angel', my English name."

"Ok Ms. Chan, I will call you Angel."

Dan was at the door.

"Come in" I said smiling "I can't wait to hear what you have to tell me. It took all of the discipline I can muster to not peek in and ask you for an update every five minutes this morning. I figured it would be wiser to let you work on the plans."

"I want to tell you again that this will not be easy or bullet proof, but the good news is that it is doable and I believe it will protect the brand and maintain our quality standards" he said.

Dan went on to describe the plan.

"To start with, I will have to do a crash training course for Jenny Chen, the QA Manager for this plant. She is sharp and has already had a lot of exposure to the company's Quality requirements and policies. We have to hire and train a local manager to work for her. She can free me up to focus on other locations."

"So far things sound good" I said "go on."

"The key to success will be for me to spend time training others like Jenny at the other sites to manage quality. This means that, as soon as you decide what locations you want to contract with, we would need to start training people as soon as possible" Dan said, quickly adding "I would want to personally interview anyone we plan to hire for those positions."

"I wouldn't have it any other way" I said "Can Jenny oversee a second site if need be? Is she ready to take on more responsibility yet?"

"She is bright and very capable technically" Dan said "her managerial skills however, still need more development. I was thinking of using her to help with the technical training, but for now, I am thinking of having myself oversee the other sites' Quality programs. If we end up contracting more than two, I will have to ask for more ex-pats."

"Fair enough" I said "how about ex-pats? Have you figured out if we need to borrow some experienced people from the rest of the region or other regions to help us get set up and execute a vertical start up?"

"Yes, I have" he said "it is difficult to give you details at this point, but the short answer is 'yes, absolutely yes', we should plan to bring in one ex-pat for every two sites."

"Do you have any specific individuals in mind that would fit the bill?" I asked

"I have sent some e-mails and will have to get back to you. I should have some names for you next week" he said.

"Excellent work" I said "thank you."

Julie walked in and reminded me that it was time for me to head for the Beijing airport. She told me that Angel called to set up a time to start my Chinese lessons next week and asked me what my preference was for time and day.

"I have so much going on right now, let's set something up after I get back" I said as I picked up my laptop and walked towards the door.

"Ok, I'll tell her" she said.

Mr. Huang was standing by the car and opened the door for me. I got into the back seat and buckled up my seat belt. Mr. Huang has given up on trying to convince me that I should not wear a seat belt because he is such a good driver. I am guessing that he has classified me as a fainthearted foreigner.

The flight to Guangzhou was on time and uneventful. The flight attendants gave all travelers a gift and shortly after that, a meal was served. It looked like sliced chicken and rice with some overcooked vegetables on the side." I ate some before getting my computer and starting to work on the basic math for how much production capacity we will need to supply all of China.

As I crunched the numbers using average consumption rates and factoring in the population of China and what our market research was showing we can expect as market share, I was coming up with numbers that were way too big. I came up with 799 million Bars of Soap per year. That meant that if we bought the highest speed soap packing lines in the world and ran them 24/7 at 85% efficiency, I would need just under four packaging lines.

Right off the bat, that told me that we may have trouble fitting all of this capacity into the plant. I also expected that we would have issues with storage tank capacity for raw materials like Tallow and Coconut Oil. While this was a concern, I knew that we can find a way to work those issues; however, guaranteeing about 800 million bars of soap a year was a scary proposition. "This is big, very big" I kept thinking to myself.

The flight landed and I found my way to the taxi stand. I got into the back of a taxi and told the driver to take me to the White Swan Hotel. That drew a blank look. The driver had no clue what I was saying. In the meantime, he had already started driving away from the airport. I kept repeating White Swan Hotel, but to no avail. Fortunately, I finally remembered Julie telling me as I was getting into the car that she had written down all the names and addresses in Chinese for me to show to the taxi drivers.

I opened my briefcase and there it was at the very front of my travel folder. I pulled out the paper and pointed to the Chinese writing next to the White Swan Hotel. The driver nodded and said something in Cantonese that sounded like he understood and knew where to take me now.

Guangzhou, formerly known as Canton to the Western world, is a bustling city located in Guangdong Province in the southern part of China. It is the provincial capital and is situated right at the top of the Pearl River Delta at the confluence of the North River, East River and West River. Rivers from the fertile Pearl River Delta discharge into the South China Sea at the half way point of the Province's 3,368 kilometers (2,100 miles) of winding coastline, which is the longest in the country.

Guangzhou is an ancient city with a history dating back 2800 years. It is named 'the spring city' because of its long summer. The city has abundant green plants and blooms with fresh flowers year round. Legend has it that Guangzhou was founded by Five Immortals riding five rams, each ram planted a stalk of rice grain which symbolizes abundance of harvest or prosperity. This is also how the city got its nickname, 'Yang Cheng' which literally means 'Goat City'.

Guangzhou is also the main communications center of Guangdong with railways, highways, bridges, airports and waterways. Ferries are still very much in use as a mode of transport, which also provides river excursion.

About half an hour later, the taxi pulled to the entrance of the White Swan hotel. A white high-rise building located at the riverbank with colorful neon lights illuminating large portions of the building and a huge sign displaying the name in English and Chinese.

The hotel lobby was very nice and luxurious with a lot of marble and granite tiles everywhere. It had a tropical look to it with palm trees, hanging plants, a two story tiered rock display complete with a waterfall, a pagoda with a golden roof at the top, a pond stocked with exotic fish at the bottom of the waterfall with a pedestrian bridge for people to cross the pond. I was greeted by a neatly dressed attendant and efficiently checked in. I had about twenty minutes before I was due to meet Daniel in the lobby, so I hurried up to my room and placed a quick call to let Nancy know I arrived safely.

Nancy was excited and in a talkative mood. She proceeded to tell me about her day.

"A friend of mine found this fantastic Chinese Art Teacher, Zhao Yingbin" she said "he is a famous and highly respected local artist and poet who authored several books. He agreed to give us all painting lessons."

"Fantastic" I said "that sounds very special."

"I know" she continued "it really is. There was a class this afternoon and I was able to join in. He does not speak English, but we have Sandy in the class and she speaks good Mandarin. So she is doubling up as our interpreter. He liked my work so far.....but it is still only the first class. We have to do homework which consists of each of us taking home a painting and copying it --- I chose a very tropical scene. You know I love Palm Trees. You'll see my first attempt when you get back."

"I can't wait" I said as we said goodbye.

I hung up the phone and quickly freshened up before heading down to meet Daniel. When the elevator stopped at the main floor, I walked out and almost bumped into Daniel who was just getting off an adjacent elevator.

"Hi Daniel" I said "I guess we are both right on time."

"Hey, good to see you. How was your flight?" he asked.

"Uneventful" I said "until I got in the cab at the airport."

"What happened?"

"The driver took off and, as it turned out, he did not know what I was saying when I kept repeating 'White Swan Hotel'. Thankfully, I remembered that Julie had given me all the information I needed on a piece of paper. Once I pointed at the paper, all was well again. For a couple of minutes, I was uncomfortable being in cab that was on the move without knowing where he was taking me."

Daniel laughed and said "welcome to China. This is China 101 training. Before you know it, it will become second nature. You will not take a trip without those magical pieces of paper."

Daniel and I started to walk towards the restaurant area. We were seated at a window table with a nice view of the river. The menus were in English and Chinese and I was pleased to see that they had filet mignon on the menu. Daniel said that they did a good job with the filet and I decided that I did not need to look any further. We ordered some wine and placed our orders.

"So what is the latest?" Daniel asked me.

"I want to give you an update on two things. The project and where things stand on that front and then I want to take a few minutes and walk you through a rough proposal on how we might be able to move forward very quickly." I said

"Sounds good, go ahead" he said.

"As far as the project is concerned, I have spent several hours with Dale and the engineering team since we last talked. Things keep coming back to the same point. I wish I had something big to tell you, but I have concluded that the engineers are being as aggressive as they can be. They really want to deliver the project faster, but the reality of the situation is that, if anything, we are at risk of not completing the project by the dates they are planning on."

"It concerns me to hear you say that" Daniel said.

"I know. It concerns me also to be saying it" I said "but I feel I owe you my most accurate assessment of where things really stand."

"Are you telling me that Dale and the engineers are making up dates?" Daniel persisted

"Not at all, I am not saying anything of the sort" I said "what I am saying is that they have put forward their most aggressive plans because we have repeatedly asked them to. They have factored in some delays; but we all know that, in China, more often than not, delays in getting approvals from the various bureaus can easily cost days and even weeks simply waiting for those approvals. Before they can proceed with construction, demolition, or just about anything else you can think off." I paused for a second before continuing "correct me if I am wrong, but I don't think I have said anything so far that would be news to you. Am I right?"

"Yes, this is typical of what I have been hearing since I came to China" he said allowing his frustration to show on his face before adding "I am looking for us to find a way to break through this!"

"I know" I said "and so am I. Unfortunately, I have yet to come across someone who has been able to break through China's bureaucracy. The bottom line is this. When I add up the fact that Dale's schedule is aggressive and that we have to rely on a bureaucracy that is predisposed to take its sweet time, I am concluding that there likely is a risk that the project can be delayed beyond the dates we are working with."

"Before you say anything" I continued "I will be the first to say that I don't believe, not even for a second, that we should roll over and play dead. But I firmly believe that we need to have a plan B."

"A plan B" Daniel said "I would love to have a plan B. So far, none of the ideas we explored have panned out. We looked at importing soap despite the extra cost, but there is not enough capacity anywhere else to fill the need if the numbers from the Beijing test market are anywhere near accurate."

"Here is what I am thinking" I said "we move on two parallel paths to get product to market quickly. The first path is to push as hard as we can to move the project forward as fast as we can without doing anything stupid. I will keep Dale and the engineers focused and on track."

"I am with you so far" he said.

"The second path would be for me to spend the next few weeks identifying local soap plants that we will contract to make the soap for us" I said.

Daniel cringed but before he could say anything, the waitress arrived with our food. I have to admit, the filet looked excellent. I had not realized how much I was missing western food already until I caught myself starting to salivate. Strange I thought to myself. The waitress topped up our wine glasses, asked if we needed anything else and left.

I cut into the filet and realized that it may look like a filet at a Morton's restaurant, but it was not exactly the same quality and nowhere near as tender as a Morton's filet. However; I had no complaints, it did taste very much like a decent piece of steak and I was more than happy to have it.

"How is your filet" I heard Daniel ask while I was deep in thought about, of all things, a piece of steak.

"Very good" I said "I did not realize how much I missed western food until I got served. Now I know where to go for dinner when I come to Guangzhou."

"This is not exactly Morton's of Chicago, but it will do" he said.

"Going back to looking at local soap plants" Daniel continued, "we looked at every possible plant before deciding to buy the JV in Tianjin. I know the Tianjin plant looks like it belonged in a museum of industrial history."

I was amused that we both had the same thought about where the plant belonged in the context of modern day manufacturing technology.

"Hard as it may be to believe" he continued, "Tianjin was the best of the lot. I will add that all the plants we looked at were so far below our standards that it wasn't even funny, but when you lined them all side by side, Tianjin's capabilities were better than those of the other plants."

"I suspected that much" I said "what I am proposing is to fill the gap until we finish building our own capacity by contracting the better ones under our strict supervision to make our soap."

"You will not be able to get Corporate Quality to sign off on such a move" Daniel said "we tried to get agreement once before but they raised so many concerns that we gave up on the idea."

"Here is my plan" I said "I know Joe personally and I believe that I have enough credibility with him that if I make a commitment to him that we will not allow any soap to be made or shipped under our brand name unless it met or exceeded our specifications and standards for quality, I believe that he will at least listen. I already have Dan working on a proposal that I think I can get Joe to agree to support. As a matter of fact, part of the plan is to enlist Joe's help in working through the issues."

"If you think you can pull it off, I will back you 100%." Daniel said.

"I really appreciate that very much" I said "I am very excited. This will give us the ability to move the business ahead while we build capacity."

"Right now, I can sell every case you can possibly make. We have a lot of people wanting to buy the soap and our sales people are frustrated because they can only sell into the Beijing test market."

"You said that we had assessed all the soap plants in China and ruled them out, so we must have a list of all the potential players. Who has this information and how can I get it?" I asked.

"Have you met Hugo yet?" Daniel asked.

"No, who is he?"

"He is on special assignment from our European division and is responsible to identify JV partners in the business categories in which we want to expand" he said.

"What is his background?"

"Business and Marketing" he said.

"How did he assess technical capability?" I asked.

"Once he identified a potential JV partner, he invited a team to go and assess their factory. It included people from finance, engineering, distribution and manufacturing. Rick was the manufacturing contact. Based on the team's assessment, they would make recommendations to move forward or drop potential players from the list."

"This is good news' I said "having this information will help us shrink the time we need to pick the better players and move fast."

"I will ask Hugo to work with you to establish contacts with the right people" he said adding "but before we get too carried away, don't you need to get agreement from Corporate Quality to proceed before we approach anyone."

Daniel continued "we have to be very careful not to create bad feelings between us and the Chinese suppliers on the list. Keep in mind that their expectations were already raised once when we went in to look at their facilities. When we finally made our decision to go with Tianjin, they were not happy when we told them that we were going to pass on them. I am sure that all of them still clearly remember that."

"I completely understand. I will treat this with kid gloves and I clearly will be in close contact with you to make sure that we are in alignment every step of the way" I said.

"OK, let me know if you need any help and be sure to keep me in the loop" he said "I will give Drew an update in the morning to make sure he doesn't have any major concerns with this."

"Great, I also need to touch base with him tomorrow to give him an update on my dinner with Mr. Chen" I said.

"How did it go with Mr. Chen?" he asked.

"As you might expect, he is very distraught over Drew's insistence on 100% ownership. I think his major concern is less about the percentages and the money and more about how his hierarchy will view him for coming back empty handed" I paused for a moment before I continued reflectively "I think we have to give him something to take to his bosses, otherwise, he will not cooperate. I think the question we have to help him answer is this – what would make it OK for him to accept zero percent ownership when all the other BOLI's we are dealing with have some level of ownership. Simply put, why should he be willing to settle for less than his peers?"

"Yes, Drew and I are acutely aware of this problem. If he goes empty handed, he will lose face and we will likely find ourselves having to deal with someone who is less friendly" Daniel said.

"Here is what I am thinking" I said "as part of our filling the gap and contracting out production to other plants, I can contract Tianjin Toilet Soap Factory (TTSF), which is part of Mr. Chen's responsibility, to make soap for us. I can probably get them quickly qualified and give them all the production they can handle. I know from talking to Mr. Tian that TTSF is losing money and BOLI has to heavily subsidize it. If I can get Joe to support us moving forward, we can move on TTSF first. That will give Mr. Chen something to take back and say he extracted that from us in return for the wholly owned subsidiary. Besides, such an arrangement will give him more immediate financial relief versus a small ownership position in a JV that would likely take a few years before it starts to pay dividends."

"That is a good thought. It will give us something to offer Mr. Chen" he said "Drew will like that."

The waitress stopped by and asked us if we wanted more wine or dessert. In my short time in China, I learned that, in most cases, desserts look better than they taste, so I decided to pass and so did Daniel. It was getting late and we both had early morning meetings, so we decided to call it a night.

I went back to my room, called Nancy to check in and make sure all is well at home.

"I am glad you called back" she said.

"Yeah, me too" I said "what's up?"

"I got a call from Julia from the hotel sales office. She told me that she found a Kung Fu expert who agreed to give Johnny private lessons."

"That is great" I said.

I had been feeling bad about pulling John away from his Tae Kwon Do lessons ever since we moved. Both John and Liz were only three months away from getting their Black Belt in Cincinnati. While Elizabeth was happy to get out of Tae Kwon Do, John really wanted to continue his studies. He really liked going to his lessons and excelled at. The last thing he wanted to do was to stop taking his lessons.

"I know" she said "especially, after the recognition he got from Master Kim about breaking the wood in three pieces."

"I bet he is happy to hear the news" I said.

"Oh, he is" she said "especially that the teacher is willing to teach him things out of the normal sequence since those would be private lessons. He really wants to learn how to use sticks and swords and the instructor said he will start him off with those."

"Great" I said "I wish Elizabeth would also continue her martial arts lessons. She was so close to getting her Black Belt also."

"Yeah" she said "it would be nice, but her heart isn't in it and besides, she was very clear that she does not want to continue taking lessons. We agreed and a promise is a promise."

"I agree" I said "I did promise her that if we moved to China, she would not have to take Martial Arts classes ever again. I don't think she is about to change her mind, so I have let it go."

After saying goodnight, I realized that I was too restless to go to sleep, so I decided to go down and take a quick walk. I stepped out of the hotel and went towards the river. After a few minutes, I started to feel a little uncomfortable. I did not have reason to be, but given the unfamiliar surroundings and the time of night, I decided to head back and stay closer to the hotel.

The next morning, I ran into Daniel and we shared a cab to the office. Once there, I proceeded to my Product Supply Leadership meeting.

After the meeting, I stopped by Drew's office. He was on the phone but ushered me in.

"Have a seat" he said pointing to the conference table in his office "I'll be with you in a minute."

Two minutes later, Drew finished his call and walked over to join me at the conference table.

"Daniel gave me a quick update this morning about your ideas" Drew said "I am excited, but we have to proceed with great caution. Fill me in on your dinner with Mr. Chen."

"It was a relatively good meeting" I said "he dwelled persistently on the question of wholly owned subsidiary versus a JV. He is taking some of this personally and is having a hard time understanding why you are not cutting him into the deal. He appears to dwell on the thought that you, as his friend, should be giving him the 5% ownership."

"Yes, that is the same theme he has been on for the past three months" he said "what did you tell him?"

"Basically, I tried to tell him that your hands were tied because those types of decisions are made by the Company's Board of Directors" I said "then I went on to tell him that, in spite of that, you were still going to bring it back to the Board."

"I stressed to him that in my opinion, I did not think that it was wise for you to go back to the Board after they clearly told you no, but that you felt it was important for you to keep the promise you made to Mr. Chen."

"At first" I went on "he came across as feeling he was being personally let down by you, but after I explained to him that the decision was beyond your level and that it had to go to the Board, he seemed to soften up. I reiterated that the fact that you were still willing to go back to the Board after you were told no, was, in my opinion a clear commitment by you and a reflection of how much you valued your friendship with him."

Before Drew could say anything, I quickly added "I realize I may have said too much on your behalf, but I hedged it by saying that this was my opinion or conclusions in case you wanted to go back and take things in a different direction."

"No, what you said is fine" he said "and it sounds like he is getting it."

"I have no doubt that he gets it" I said "in my opinion, the issue for him would be fear. I am guessing he would be afraid to go back to his hierarchy empty handed. They probably would be wondering why Mr. Chen is coming back empty handed when all the other BOLI's had a percent ownership in the JV's that we have in their jurisdictions. If I am right, we need to help him save face by giving him something to take back to his bosses in lieu of ownership in the new plant."

"I agree" he said "we need to give him something to take back. If we don't give him something to help him save face, we will be stuck in a stalemate like we are right now. Despite the fact that he dropped his demand for ownership from ten to five percent, I have consistently told him that we are investing over fifty million dollars in the Soap JV. On top of that, by the time we buy the land and finish construction of the new plant, we will be spending another eighty to one hundred and twenty million in Tianjin, not to mention the jobs we will be creating and the taxes that we will be paying. This adds up to a huge sum of money for the local economy."

"I understand and completely agree with what you are saying" I said "but, if my understanding of the concept of 'face' in China is accurate, his bosses will view him as having failed to extract enough concessions out of you and, therefore, he will lose face because his bosses would see him as a failure. If this is a reasonable assessment of the situation, then it is clear that Mr. Chen does not feel that he has enough from us to take to his bosses without loosing face."

"For someone who has been in China a short time" he said "you have a good grasp of the significance of 'saving face' in Chinese culture."

"Did Daniel give you a heads up on what I am going to try to do with TTSF when you talked this morning?" I asked.

"Yes, he did" Drew said "I like the opportunity it offers us. How long do you need to work the supply and quality issues out?"

"Given that as of two days ago this idea was only a pie in the sky, I don't have an exact plan yet" I said "but, now that I know I can count on your and Daniel's support to move forward, making this happen will be my primary focus. I am hoping to be able to move very fast. I am talking weeks, not months. I may need you to lean on some people in Corporate to inject a high sense of urgency and help move things along."

"You can count on my support" he said "once you have agreement to proceed and the plans are defined, let me know and I will talk with Mr. Chen to try and leverage this as part of closing the deal on the new facility."

"You will be the first to know" I said "but, I suggest you give Mr. Chen a call soon. I am going to have to meet with Mr. Li, the Plant Manager at TTSF and the Quality group will have to be working on all the details with Mr. Li and his people. I positioned it with him as a remote possibility. I emphasized that I had to get permission from corporate and went on at length about how difficult it is to get permission."

"I agree, I will call him later today" he said "Ideally, the story that we want to help Mr. Chen take to his hierarchy would go like this. He pushed us very hard to form a JV; however, the Company's Board of Directors is insisting that they will not proceed with investing in a new factory in Tianjin unless the company had 100% ownership. To help him make his case, we can provide him with numbers on how much capital we expect to spend, how many new jobs we will create and how much taxes Tianjin stands to collect if all goes well."

"Sounds right" I said "and once we get agreement to proceed with local contractors, Mr. Chen can talk about how TTSF is picking up extra production which gives BOLI new revenue and taxes now instead of in the future. I am sure that the fact that the JV is now losing money, can help his argument."

Drew turned to me and said "alright then, we have a plan. Keep me informed. I will let you know if anything unexpected comes out of my call to Mr. Chen."

"Very good" I said as I got up and prepared to go to my next meeting.

Next, I went to meet Hugo. He was very helpful and gave me his impression of the various soap manufacturers. He recommended that we look at plants in Guangzhou, Hangzhou, Suzhou and Chongqing. With TTSF across the street from us in Tianjin, that gave us five plants to look at in total.

"I have to tell you that the only facility that we did not already visit is Chongqing. With them, we would have to take a more in-depth look." Hugo pointed out.

"How quickly can you arrange for us to visit those facilities?" I asked.

"I can get us in next week, if you want" he said "they are very eager to do business with us. When they thought we were looking at doing a JV, they were bending over backwards for us."

"Good to know" I said "I am very eager to move fast to asses their capabilities, but I need to do things in sequence" I said "first, I need to get agreement from corporate quality to move forward. As soon as I have that worked out, I will call you to set up those meetings."

"Before we meet with them, we need to meet and strategize to make sure we don't create problems for ourselves" he said.

"Fair enough" I said "If we can, I wouldn't mind seeing all of them in one week, starting on a Monday and then traveling from one plant to the next."

"That can be a challenge" he said smiling "but, we should be able to pull it off."

"Great, thank you" I said "As far as us meeting to strategize, how about we plan to talk strategy over dinner the evening before each meeting?"

"That would work" he said "I was concerned that we may not be able to squeeze meetings in, especially with the fast pace we are trying to move at."

"Sounds like a plan" I said as I picked my copies of the reports on each of the factories and headed out of Hugo's office.

It was time for me to head for the airport to catch my flight back to Beijing. I asked the receptionist to call a taxi to take me to the airport. Five minutes later, the cab arrived. I had to find the list that Julie gave me. Number six instructed the driver to take me to the Guangzhou airport. I was starting to get the hang of using a translation list. Not bad, I was thinking to myself; but then I had a somewhat scary thought, what would I do if I lost my travel list?

The driver pulled in front of the main airport entrance while I was still deep in thought. I paid him and went to the counter to check in.

By now, I was getting used to people pushing each other through a line. I had discovered that in China, there is no such thing as a line or waiting for your turn. It is simply expected that one would elbow his or her way through to get a turn. So I started to strategically use my elbows and pushed my way to the front of the counter in about five minutes. No one minded me elbowing them just as I was at peace with being elbowed. It's just one of those things about China that one gets use to, I guess.

The flight back was packed. Next to me sat a young Chinese woman who spoke good English. She told me her English name was Griffith. We chatted for a little while and she asked me for my business card. I gave it to her before attempting to take a quick nap. However, as it turned out, I was not meant to take a nap on that flight. Two Dutch businessmen sat on the other side of the aisle. They were in the agricultural irrigation business. With me being the only other non-Chinese on the flight and Griffith being an articulate English speaker, conversations continued until we arrived in Beijing a little over two hours later.

Mr. Huang was waiting for me just outside the luggage area. He picked my bag and soon we were on our ninety minute ride back to Tianjin.

When I arrived at the Sheraton, Nancy had a big smile on her face. I asked her what is going on.

"John met this cute Chinese girl. Her name is Shen Yi. She came to visit him this afternoon and she is still here. Technically, she is his first date."

"That is interesting" I said "is she a nice girl?"

"I think so. She doesn't speak a lot of English but she manages OK" she said "she looks to be about the same age as him" adding "why don't you go meet her."

I went to John's room and met Shen Yi. She was about five feet, four inches tall with long thick black hair that went about halfway down her back. She was very pretty and had a bubbly and very outgoing personality. Despite her thick accent, her English was good and understandable.

14

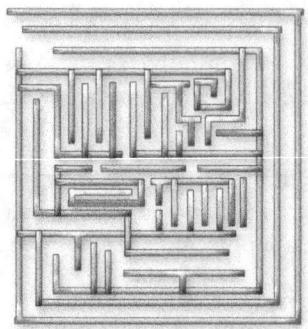

THE MEETING WITH THE MAYOR OF TIANJIN

The next morning, I went to the office. Julie brought out a large stack of paper with my instant coffee. The usual purchase orders, requisitions and payment authorizations were all there for me to sign. I went through them first.

"The Mayor has invited you to a lunch meeting that he is hosting today for the General Managers of the key JV's in the city" Julie informed me.

"I assume you cleared my schedule for this meeting" I said smiling "what is the reason for the meeting?" I asked.

"I don't know for sure" she said "but I asked Mr. Tian and he thinks that the Mayor is interested in feedback from the GM's on what needs to improve to support the JV's."

"I would like to get input from all the key managers on this" I said "can you contact all my direct reports as soon as we finish talking and put a list together of the difficulties they face in running the business. I would like to have the list at least an hour before we leave so that I can make sure I understand the issues and organize my thoughts."

"I'll have it ready" she said in her usual efficiency.

"I am going to see Dan" I said as I walked towards the door.

Dan was facing his computer terminal. He turned around when he heard me come in.

"Welcome back" he said "how was your trip?"

"It was a good trip" I said "I have Drew's and Daniel' support to move forward. They are both a little skeptical about us being able to get agreement to proceed, but are very supportive and interested in seeing it go through."

"That is good to hear" he said "I don't have any good news to report. All the people I contacted have responded. None of them is interested in coming to China, not even for a couple of months."

"This is not very encouraging" I said "it will complicate things considerably for us. Any ideas?"

"None, other than making them come by applying pressure from the top" Dan said.

"We can always do that" I said "but I am not sure how effective they will be if they come here kicking and screaming."

"For now, let's take one step at a time' I went on "I am going to call Joe tonight. I know he starts work early, so I should be able to catch him around 7:00 AM Cincinnati time. That would be 7:00 PM our time. If I can't get Joe on board, then everything else would be an academic exercise. Can you join me in my office at 7:00 PM for the call?"

"I will plan on it" he said.

"Good, bring all the data you can. You know Joe; he is going to want to know all the details."

"I know Joe" Dan said "he is going to be a tough sell."

"And so he should be" I said. Dan looked at me inquisitively.

"As responsible managers of the company, we would want him to be tough and demanding. The company has a lot riding on its ability to consistently deliver high quality products to consumers" I said.

"You are right" he said "I know all that. I guess I am dreading being grilled by Joe."

"I know" I said as I reflected back on my last meeting with Joe, a mere three months ago but felt like it was much longer than that …. so much has happened since.

"Trust me" I continued "I have experienced being grilled by Joe on more than one occasion. The good news is that at the end of the day, he was fair and supported me, which is all one can ask."

"That is good to hear" Dan said "My main concern is that we will not be able to answer many of Joe's detailed questions."

"I know" I said "but don't be overly concerned with that yet. The objective of this call is to find out what it would take to get his agreement for us to go forward. I am not looking for us to present him with a complete proposal and ask for his agreement. Instead, I want to engage him as a partner to help us work through all the issues."

"That would be a much easier conversation" Dan said.

"Good" I said "before I go, let me also give you an update on another detail. I met Hugo in Guangzhou; he is responsible to help the company identify companies that we may want to partner with in China. As it turned out, when they were looking at getting into the soap business, a group of people, including Rick, went around to all the potential companies, toured their facilities and analyzed their capabilities. They prepared reports on each of them." I have copies that I will give to you to look at. I do not want to make copies of them and you need to keep the information secure while it is in your possession."

"I understand" Dan said.

"My plan is to have you, Hugo and me visit each of those plants provided we get a preliminary agreement to proceed from Joe. There's a total of five factories. One is owned by our Guangzhou JV partner and is located in the same complex as our detergent JV, then we have TTSF across the street, a factory in Suzhou and another in Hangzhou, both of which are close to Shanghai and, finally, the fifth factory is one that is new to us. No one has been there yet. It is located in Sichuan Province, in the city of Chongqing in the middle of China."

"I told Hugo that I would want to go through all of them as soon as possible after I get Joe's ok" I added "he thought he can arrange visits for us on very short notice."

"Good" Dan said "the sooner we get started the better."

I said "I agree" as I got up and started to walk towards the door "stop by my office a few minutes before seven."

"I'll see you then."

As I opened the door, Julie was right there about to knock on the door.

"You have to get ready for the meeting with the Mayor. I have everyone's input except Dan's. I will get it now and add it to the list. In the meantime, you can go through what I collected so far. The list is on your desk."

"Great" I said "you are a life saver."

A few minutes later Julie came in and said "Dan's input is the same as the input from others, so the list you have is good. We need to leave in about ten minutes."

"I'll be ready" I said as I poured over the list. The issues were many, but the majority of them revolved around losing power several times a week, the length of time it takes to get permits and how many people within bureaus are not clear about what the requirements or rules are.

Ex-pats often learn about new rules after complying with what they were told were the requirements or rules, only to find out that there were other rules that they were not aware of or told about when they initially asked about the requirements. For foreigners, it felt like new rules were brought to their attention only when they had done all the things they were originally told were needed to get a permit or approval. This would send them back to do extra work to meet the 'new' requirements only to find out that there was even more rules and requirements that they were not told about that also had to be met. This was very frustrating and made it appear that bureaus develop rules as they go to suit the situation, which made it difficult for foreigners to know exactly what they need to do and inevitably led to long delays.

Those concerns are going to be tough to convey in a way that would not be offensive, I thought to myself. Julie came in to tell me it is time to go to the meeting. I put on my suit jacket and straightened my tie as we went down the stairs. Mr. Huang was waiting; he opened the back door for me while Julie got in the front passenger seat.

We arrived a few minutes early. I did not recognize any of the GM's. The room was set up with a series of conference tables forming a large rectangle. There were about 50 seats. Each seat had a microphone in-front of it and a name tag. Julie quickly found our assigned seats. To my left was a Japanese company GM and to my right was a Korean company GM. Neither one spoke English. Ironically, we had to communicate with each other by having what we said to each other translated first to Chinese and then back to our respective languages.

The Mayor arrived. The room turned quiet and everyone took their appointed seat. The Mayor welcomed everyone and asked us to introduce ourselves when it was our turn to talk. He said that he was very interested in learning how our businesses are doing, any difficulties we are facing and any suggestions for improvements that we may have for him. He wanted to make Tianjin very friendly to business and wanted to make our lives very easy. With that introduction, he turned to the first GM on his right and asked him if he would start by introducing himself and then providing his input.

The first GM turned on his microphone and started to talk. He was in charge of a Korean JV. He spoke at length about the problems with the infrastructure. He went on to describe the poor condition of the roads to his facility with a lot of pot holes. He complained bitterly about losing electricity quite often and how difficult and expensive it was for them to run their business. Finally, he went on to describe the difficulties and delays they had in getting permits to build, install or operate his equipment. It was very obvious that he was frustrated and his tone was a little condescending, I thought.

The Mayor was looking very uncomfortable and I was wondering if he already regretted having called this meeting. The Mayor politely thanked him for his input and turned the meeting over to the next GM. He was from Germany.

Aside from the language, the themes were identical although his examples differed a little, but there were no new complaints that came out. The tone of his voice was a little more condescending and unlike his Korean counterpart, he was much louder.

The Mayor looked even more uncomfortable. Again, he politely thanked the speaker and went on to the next GM who was running a Japanese JV. Once again, the complaints were the same. He was a little more soft-spoken, but his input was just as negative. He added a complaint about shipments being held up for too long before clearing customs at the Port of Tianjin.

The scene kept repeating itself with each GM giving his own examples but the tone was progressively getting louder and more negative as each speaker appeared to be feeding on the frustrations and negativity of the previous speaker.

By now, the Mayor was beyond uncomfortable and looking very angry. I had no doubt that; he was regretting having called this meeting. I thought to myself that if someone on the Mayor's staff had suggested to him that he should make this gesture and hold this meeting with the GM's of the foreign JV's in Tianjin, that person will be deeply regretting that he or she made that suggestion before this day is over.

I suddenly heard my name. It was my turn to speak now, so I turned on the microphone. I could tell that the Mayor was bracing himself for another GM repeating the same theme.

"Mr. Mayor" I said "I would like to start by thanking you and the people of Tianjin for the great hospitality that has been extended to me and my family."

The Mayor looked at me with some uncertainty. Wondering what I was up to but responded by saying "you are welcome."

"As you may know, my family and I moved to Tianjin about eight weeks ago. We received excellent treatment from everyone we met. Every person we met has offered to help us in any way they can. The generosity and kindness of the people of Tianjin is commendable."

Julie translated and the Mayor was looking a little relieved now and looked eager for me to say more.

"As far as our JV, we have received a lot of support from our friends at the Bureau of Light Industry (BOLI). They have given us advice and help in understanding how things work in China."

Again, Julie translated and the Mayor made a note as I was providing positive feedback about BOLI and wrote something down on his pad. Again, looking eager for me to say more.

"While we have been getting a great deal of support, we have also faced some delays. In some cases, the delays were the result of us not understanding and knowing how things work in China and particularly in Tianjin."

He nodded as Julie translated which I interpreted as him wanting to believe that the issues were there because the foreigners did not understand how things worked in China and, as a result, it took them longer to get things done. While I wanted to be kind, I still had problems that need to be dealt with and I did not want the Mayor to conclude that all is well, or that it is those foreigners' fault for not knowing how to do business in China.

"While it is reasonable to conclude that some of the issues are created by our lack of understanding of how to do business in China, there are some areas like those that some of the other speakers referred to earlier that can only be solved by government under your leadership."

Julie translated. The Mayor said "please go on."

"When we lose electricity, we are able to cope with the loss of electricity as long as service is restored within a few minutes; unfortunately, sometimes it takes longer than that. Mr. Mayor, my big concern is that I am looking at making a major investment to automate our factory and bring new technology. Unfortunately, the new technology is much less forgiving than the old technology. A single incident that lasts a few hours would put our factory out for several weeks. Every piece of equipment would have to be taken apart, cleaned of solidified soap and then reassembled."

"I understand your concern and the great inconvenience this creates to your business" he said "we are working to improve our electricity generation capacity to keep up with the growth in demand."

"Thank you Mr. Mayor" I said "I also understand the pressure you must be under in trying to accommodate the needs of all the foreign investors in your city. It takes time to build infrastructure. My dilemma is that even though I can deal with the inconvenience of the extra work and cost, what I cannot deal with is that a loss of even one week of production will force me to be short on supplying the demand of our product because we do not have sufficient capacity. After our investment in new technology, I will have enough capacity, but will not be able to lose a week or more of production in a year. If I do, I don't know what I would say to my superiors on why I am not able to meet the demand for our product after spending tens of millions of dollars to buy the new technology."

"I understand" he said motioning me with his hand to continue.

"The only other area of concern is the ability to get permits quickly. As I mentioned to you a second ago, I do not have enough capacity to meet the demand for our products. I am planning to make a large investment in new technology and need to modify and reinforce buildings. Anything that can be done to help us get approvals faster would be greatly appreciated."

"I will see what I can do" he said.

"Once again, Mr. Mayor" I said "my thanks to you and everyone who has worked hard to make me and my family feel welcome in your great city and thank you for your interest in learning about the issues and working hard to resolve them."

"Thank you and I am happy to have you here in Tianjin." With that, he moved to the next GM.

The GM who was two seats away from me was French. He had a unique problem that he brought forward. His factory was located in a village just outside the city but was still within the broader city limits. His issue was that the locals had set up some kind of a toll road and they were not letting trucks in or out without making them pay a fee to pass through. If they refused to pay, the locals blocked them in or out. He also had what sounded like more serious issues with loss of electricity. The Mayor asked for more particulars and once he was finished, the meeting was concluded with the Mayor promising to make wide ranging improvements and the meeting was adjourned. Interestingly there were no more forums like this one held in Tianjin, this turned out to be the first and last forum the Mayor held during the three years I was there.

I exchanged business cards with several of my counterparts from the other JV's and soon Julie and I were going back to the car. Julie turned to me and said, "You did a good job at the meeting."

"Thank you" I said.

"The way the other GM's were talking was very disrespectful. I doubt they will get much help from the Mayor. He looked very angry most of the time, but appeared to be more at ease with you and for the first time during the meeting he interacted. With the others he nodded and thanked them before moving to the next GM."

"I appreciate your assessment and feedback" I said "what is on the agenda for this afternoon?"

"I booked some time for you to go through your e-mails. At 3:00 Marie wants to see you. She has the preliminary financial results for the month and at 3:30 you have your weekly all management meeting."

"Good" I said as Mr. Huang pulled into the plant and stopped at the entrance to let Julie and me get out." He came out of the car, opened the door and walked with me towards Julie and started to talk.

Julie turned to me and said "Mr. Huang wants to know if it is ok with you if he uses the car on the weekends to take people back and forth to the Beijing airport?"

"Are you saying he wants to use my car, the car I am renting exclusively for my use as a taxi service?"

"No, Mr. Huang says, not a taxi" she said "he wants to take individuals to the airport and pick others from the airport and drive them back to Tianjin."

"Absolutely not" I said "I am paying an outrageous amount of money every month to have exclusive access to the car and Mr. Huang seven days a week."

"Mr. Huang says that you never use him on the weekends, so he is interested in earning some extra money by driving other ex-pats."

"Tell Mr. Huang that I am trying to be kind by allowing him to have some time to spend with his family on the weekends" I said "you can tell him that from now on, I will start to call him to take me places on the weekends instead of taking taxis."

Mr. Huang was getting angrier and angrier and started to raise his voice.

I decided I had enough of this nonsense. I turned to Julie and said "Tel Mr. Huang my decision is no and it is final. If he doesn't like it, he can resign" and I walked away.

Julie followed me to the office in a couple of minutes. "Mr. Huang resigned" she said.

"That is fine with me" I said and asked Julie "by local standards, was I being unreasonable?"

"Not at all" Julie said "he would never have dared ask such a question if he was driving for a Chinese official. I will call around and find another car and driver for you."

James was at my office door looking to see if I was available. I ushered him in and Julie left.

"I heard about Mr. Huang" he started.

"How did you hear so fast?" I asked curious because this was still an evolving situation in my mind.

"My driver was just in my office telling me" James said.

"News travels fast" I said "now that you mention it, your driver and Lou's driver were both standing close by the entrance to the building."

"Yes" James said "there are very few secrets in China. I felt bad when I heard about Mr. Huang's bad behavior. If you want, you can have my driver, Mr. Li, become your driver. He is very loyal and I promise you that you will not have any problems with him trying to use your car as a taxi service."

"Does Mr. Li speak any English?" I asked

"No" he said "but, like Mr. Huang, he will try to learn some English."

"What about the car?" I said "the company that Mr. Huang works for owns the car."

"Mr. Li said that if you are willing to sign a 1 year contract, you can tell him what kind of car you want and he will buy that model."

"That sounds good" I said "what will you do if I have Mr. Li driving for me?"

"Because I am a local, I will not have any trouble getting another driver. There are plenty of them in the village where I live." He said.

"Thank you my friend" I said to James "are you sure this works for you? As you know, I can just call HR and they will find a replacement for Mr. Huang very quickly."

"Not a problem at all" he said "it is my pleasure to help in any way I can.".

James left my office and with that Mr. Li became my new driver.

15

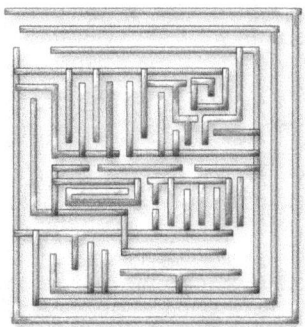

THE STRATEGY STARTS TO TAKE SHAPE

A few minutes before 3:00, Marie peaked through the glass in my office door. I waved her in and told her to pull a chair up to my desk. She did and sat across from me.

Marie is a brilliant young Chinese woman. She was slim, about five feet and three inches tall. She had a modern, short haircut and was extremely analytical. She thought through everything she said and, despite coming across as being shy, she was not afraid to tell me what she thought.

Like James, Marie and I became close friends over the next three years. She also took it upon herself to help me better understand the Chinese culture and made sure I understood the numbers well. Often, without telling me directly, she made sure I was aware of the numbers that were being shared with BOLI, through Mr. Tian.

This afternoon was my first official meeting with Marie in her new official role. She has just moved back to Tianjin from Guangzhou to replace Jimmy Chen, an expatriate from the company's Taiwan business. Jimmy accepted this temporary assignment but was eager to go back to Taipei and be with his family. He had accepted to fill the Finance Manager's role for the JV while a new manager was being trained.

Marie is originally from Tianjin, she had been hired by the company before I moved to China. She stood out amongst the new hires and was seen as a high potential manager and a quick study. She was sent to corporate headquarters in Guangzhou to train and work with ex-pat finance managers to learn how the company financial systems worked. The expectation was that she would return to Tianjin and be in charge of the JV's finance department – essentially, she was training to become the JV's CFO.

This essentially put her in a position of conflict since, as a Chinese, she was expected to be taking care of the interests of the Chinese government and BOLI. Anything short of that would be viewed negatively. On the flip side, she had been trained to be the top financial officer for the JV and, as such, the company had high expectations of here that she had to live up to. Both sides demanded and expected full loyalty. By virtue of her position, she would have access to information that one side did not necessarily want the other side to know. A very tough position for a young Chinese woman to be in.

Marie proceeded to walk me through the numbers for the past month. It was not a pretty picture. Bottom line was that we were losing seven dollars on every case of soap we were selling at this point. The fact that we were making an investment in the future of our business did not make this information any less painful none the less.

As I was thinking about how critical it is for us to move fast on the sourcing strategy, Julie knocked on the door to alert me that my meeting with the management team was in 3 minutes and we needed to head to the big conference room.

Marie, Julie and I headed to the conference room. Everyone was seated and the usual spot was reserved for me in the front of the room.

I greeted everyone with my Chinese greeting "ni hao" which brought smiles to everyone's face.

I started by reminding everyone of what I said at our last management meeting.

"Today is the day" I said "no one can leave the meeting until I have a minimum of 3 questions from the group."

Not too many managers looked me in the eye when I said that.

"Today I want to talk about the cost of making soap" I said asking "does anyone, other than Marie know what our cost is to make a case of soap and deliver it to the marketplace?"

Mr. Tian signaled that he wanted to answer. I motioned him to take the floor. In his usual fashion, he spoke for about five minutes. Julie translated the answer as a figure in RMB per ton. The Chinese measure, assign or allocated production to factories using tons.

"I am not sure if this is considered cheating" I said with a big smile "but Mr. Tian knows the numbers very well and, of course, he is correct."

"One thing to keep in mind is that the company uses a different measure than tons, for production cost, so please pay close attention." I said "whenever you are talking with ex-pats they will be confused by costs presented as RMB or even dollars per ton. You have to translate the information to dollars or RMB per case. The company finds it convenient to look at cost this way since we sell cases of soap and know how much we charge buyers for each case. It is simply a different way of looking at the same thing."

Julie translated.

"So, using this measure" I continued "a case of soap costs us about $24 to make."

I stopped for a second to let Julie translate and let the number sink in.

"Next" I went on "I want to ask if anyone other than Marie and Mr. Tian knows how much we sell a case of soap for?"

No one answered but many were shaking their head indicating they don't know.

"Would anyone like to take a guess at how much we sell a case of soap for?" I asked.

A young manager, Tammy, reluctantly raised her hand.

"This is great progress" I thought to myself.

"Tammy, how much do you think we sell it for?" I asked.

"$40 dollars" she said.

"That is a very logical number based on what we have been talking about so far" I said "but I am afraid it is not correct. Does anyone else want to take a guess?" I asked

Another hand went up in the air. This time it was Cindy, a bright young woman with a bubbly personality, sparkly eyes and curly hair, something you don't see often in China.

"Awesome, I had two people speaking up in one meeting. I feel as if I hit the jackpot" I thought to myself again feeling very good about how things were going so far.

"Cindy, tell us what you think we sell it for."

"At least $31 per case" Cindy offered "because in the market you can buy a bar of soap for 3.8 to 4.0 RMB, so I calculate that we must sell it for about

3.5 RMB which would be close to $31/case" she concluded with a very big smile.

"That is very clever and you used excellent deductive reasoning" I said to Cindy and turned to address the group "but I wish Cindy was right. The truth is that we would be very happy if we can sell a case for $31 or $40" I said "I am afraid, we are not that lucky. Would anyone else want to venture a guess?" I asked.

This time, there were no more volunteers. Still, I was very pleased.

"Before I tell you the numbers, I want to thank Cindy and Tammy for their participation. Let's all give them a hand" I said as I started to clap.

Everyone in the room clapped and the door was cracked open, ever so slightly, for participation in meetings.

"We actually sell a case of soap for about $17" I said and waited for a minute to let the numbers sink in.

I saw a lot of surprised looks on people's faces.

"That is right" I said "if you did the math right, we lose about $7 for each case of soap we sell."

Andrew, the Human Resources manager raised his hand and said "it doesn't make sense to sell for cheaper than what it costs us to make the soap. Why do we do it?" he asked.

"Excellent question" I said "would any one like to try to see if you can answer Andrew's question?"

I waited a moment and to my surprise, Cindy spoke up for the second time today.

"Because we are investing in the future of the business" she said.

Andrew jumped in again and said "yes, but how can we justify losing so much money. It will take a long time to recover our losses, even if we raise the price immediately."

This time Cindy remained quiet and so did everyone else in the room.

"This is a very good question and it gets at the heart of our business strategy" I said "I am glad we are having this conversation."

"Let me talk a little about how I see this strategy unraveling and about how business usually works in situations like this" I said.

"The first thing I will say is that Cindy is absolutely correct. We are making an investment in the future of our business."

"Our focus revolves around two areas" I continued.

"The first is to develop a solid understanding of the marketplace and the Chinese consumer preferences and buying habits. The way we are doing this is through the test market we are running in Beijing. What the test market is telling us is very encouraging. The results show that if our soap is widely available for people to buy today, there will be great demand for it. The test results show that 38 out of every 100 people will buy our soap instead of other brands that may be available to them if given the choice."

Frank, a soft spoken local manager who had a degree in Mechanical Engineering, raised his hand and asked "how can we know what our share of the market will be after we finish adding capacity and expand into the rest of China?"

"This is the purpose of us investing in test markets" I said "when we do a test market, we study the impact of many different variables on results. We study such things as the effectiveness of different advertising approaches and messages. Those would include the effectiveness of advertising on TV, in newspapers or the internet, giving samples to potential consumers and by hosting meetings with what we call 'focus groups'. Focus groups are made up of people who are typical of those who might buy our products. We meet with those groups, ask them for their input and opinions about our products, what they like about it, what they don't like, why they would buy it or, if they prefer a competitor's brand, we ask them to tell us what they like or dislike about each competitors' products. We also have them take different products home, use them and give us their feedback."

I stopped for a moment to let Julie translate and allow people a minute to absorb the information since most of the managers had engineering or other technical degrees. Then I went on to say "we don't stop there. Most of the time, we also test a number of variations of the formula and even experiment with different colors, shapes and fragrances. At the same time, we experiment with a variety of distribution channels and different ways to get our products to consumers."

"Sounds like a lot of work" I said "but it is the attention to detail in every step of a product's life cycle that sets our company apart and has been a key contributor to our success. We never take consumers for granted which is why we do all this work and take the time to analyze and understand what it all means as we incorporate the feedback into our plans. Those are critical steps that the company follows with all of our products before we would consider expanding a brand from test market to a national brand. This process can take several months."

"As a matter of fact, if consumer feedback is negative" I continued "the information goes back to R&D and they make modifications that may include changing things like the product formula, its shape or the fragrance. All changes and learning's are then fed back to the marketing team. Those are then incorporated into how the product is positioned in advertising. After they do all that, the focus groups get another chance to test the improved product and provide their input. This cycle can repeat itself several times before we get all aspects of the product exactly right. Only then would the company expand a brand on a national scale. Otherwise, a decision will be made to abandon a product instead of expanding it nationally. In either case, those decisions are made based on test market results."

I stopped to let Julie translate.

"In case you were wondering" I started after Julie finished translating "the reason that running a test market and completing those kinds of studies is critical is simple. It is very, very expensive to roll out a brand on a national scale."

"Let's take a few minutes and talk about the obvious and hidden costs involved" I continued "if you think about the cost associated with building capacity to supply the product nationally. Let's take our soap plant investment as an example. We expect to spend over $50 million dollars to build the capacity that our test market results tell us we need to have in order to meet the demand of the Chinese market. Let's assume for a minute that we don't do a thorough analysis and we end up either over or under estimating the demand for our soap in the Chinese market, what will that mean?" I asked and stopped to let Julie translate.

"Let's start by looking at the example where we are very optimistic and overestimate the need by 40%" I said adding "such an over estimate would mean that we only need 60% of the capacity we are planning to build at this moment. So the cost of being too optimistic can be as high as spending about $20 million more than what the business needs. The money would be spent on bigger buildings and more plant equipment that we will end up underutilizing. So we would have wasted capital that the company can effectively use to grow other brands and businesses. Not only that, but we would also be engaging more engineers on the expansion project whose skills and talents should have been used to expand other brands or businesses."

I noticed Julie was looking at me waiting for a break so that she can translate. But before she could start translating, Andrew piped in saying "we can't forget that such a mistake would also lead us to hire a lot of extra people that we would not need to support the business."

I let Julie translate before I continued "Andrew is right we can end up hiring a lot of extra people and then have to let some of them go. This does not make for good community relations and is unfair to the people who end up being hired and then later let go."

"Unfortunately, it doesn't end there" I continued "when we expand our product for sale nationally, our cost for advertising, shipping and holding inventory of extra product will also be a waste. Those numbers can easily run into the millions. Inventory is evil."

The group looked at me with what can only be described as a collective puzzled look. I continued "yes, holding too much inventory is bad. Not only do we have to be concerned with the amount of money that would be tied up in the actual product itself, which is not small when you consider the cost of the raw materials, the packaging, the labor and the other company costs we incur when we make our production. We also have to take into account the cost of shipping and storing this extra inventory in warehouses for which we pay rent. Sounds pretty bad, doesn't it?" I asked.

People were nodding in agreement as Julie translated.

"Unfortunately, that is not all" I continued "in my opinion, the worst thing about holding too much inventory is the fact that when you want to upgrade your product whether it is the formula, the fragrance or packaging, you basically have two options. The first option would be to discount the price on the product you have in inventory to move it out of your warehouses. This is usually a bad option since most often the company loses money when it does that. The second option would be to delay the launch of the upgraded product until the inventory is sold out. Does everyone follow what I am saying so far?" I asked.

After Julie finished translating, I went on "unfortunately, delaying the launch of improvements is a bad idea for the business even though it can make sense if one only looks at the cost. The reason it is a bad idea is that whenever we delay an improvement, we run the risk of our competition making the same improvements and beating us by being first to market with those innovations. Does everyone see how the best thing for our business is to have the absolute minimum amount of inventory that allows us to closely match our current business demand?" I asked.

A lot of heads nodded as Julie translated again.

I continued "having no or very little inventory allows us to be agile and also happens to be the lowest cost way to run the business"

"Does all of this make sense to you?" I asked again.

There was a collective nod.

"Does anyone have questions before we discuss the second area? Those are very important concepts and we should take whatever time we need to make sure everyone understands them."

I waited a moment but there were no questions.

I hope they are not just being polite, I thought to myself before I decided to continue.

"Before I talk about the second point, let's take a moment and look at what it means to the business if we were to underestimate how much capacity we need to satisfy the demand. In other words, what if we should be spending $70 million instead of $50 million on our expansion project. Any ideas?" I asked.

Cindy said "in many ways, not having enough product to meet consumer demand is worse than having too much inventory. It gives our competition an opening to jump ahead of us and convert consumers to using their products instead of ours. In this case, when there is demand for the soap but the consumer cannot find it at the store, they will buy someone else's product."

James added "when that happens, by the time we are able to react and build additional capacity to supply the extra demand, the customers would be hard to win back and during that time they can be developing brand loyalty to our competitors' brands."

"Cindy and James are right" I said "one other fact that I would like to add is that once we lose a customer, it is very difficult and expensive to win them back or convince them to switch brands, especially if our competitors have good quality products that are priced right."

"Do you see why it is critical to do all the test market analysis and thoroughly analyze our situation and options?" I asked, paused for a moment and continued "drawing the wrong conclusions can easily lead to very expensive mistakes and it can take us a very long time to recover from such mistakes. We simply have to get things right the first time."

"Let me now address the second point that is very critical to our success" I said adding "would anyone care to guess what the second point is?"

James raised his hand and said "we still have the problem of losing $7 for every case of soap that we sell."

"Thank you James" I said "you are 100% correct. We cannot stay in business for very long, even if we look at what we are doing today as an investment, if we continue to lose money for every case we sell. We have to do something about it. Any ideas on what we should do?" I asked.

Michael, a normally very quiet and soft spoken local engineer, raised his hand and said "we should increase our prices immediately so that we can stop losing money on every case we sell."

"That is one option" I said "let's look at what that means mathematically. Maybe Marie can help me figure out the numbers" I added asking Marie to join me at the front of the room and work the numbers on the white board.

Marie went through the numbers and translated them into RMB. I watched the group. Everyone was intently following the math, including me despite the conversation being in Mandarin.

"At today's exchange rate, the price we sell a case of soap to a merchant is $17 which translates to 1.96 RMB for a bar of soap. To break even, we will have to sell it for 2.8 RMB. To make about $5 profit per case, we would have to sell a bar for about 3.35 RMB" she concluded.

Michael jumped in and said with a big smile on his face "so we charge 3.35 RMB for each bar of soap and we can make money and fix this problem." It was obvious that Michael was feeling very proud of his conclusion.

"Very good point" I said "but that presents a problem for us. The test market showed that, as the price of a bar of soap goes past 4 RMB, the demand starts to drop. In other words, less people can afford it or are willing to pay that much for our soap. We have to keep in mind that we have to be competitive with other brands to be able to sell our soap. If our price is much higher than the price others charge, people will not buy our product. Don't get me wrong, we can demand and get a higher price because of the higher quality of our products, but there are limits to how much more consumers are willing to pay for it. Does anyone here know how much TTSF or other local or imported soap sells for?" I asked.

Several people raised their hands saying that between 2 and 3 RMB would be a typical price for a good quality bar of soap. Local soaps of average quality typically sell for as little as 1 RMB.

"Interesting" I said "does anyone know how much our soap is selling for in the Beijing test market?"

Mr. Tian raised his hand and said "3.8 RMB."

"Exactly right" I said "by now some of you are wondering why we are losing money when a bar of our soap sells for 3.8 RMB. Am I right?" I asked.

I saw a lot of heads nod, so I went on.

"The difference between the 1.96 RMB we get for it and the 3.8 RMB it sells for are the cost of the sales organization, the cost to advertise and other marketing expenses, the cost of shipping and other distribution costs and finally the profit that the final merchant needs to make to sell our product."

"Does this make sense?" I asked.

I saw more heads nodding so I went on "if we took Michael's advice and sold the soap for 3.5 RMB instead of 2 RMB. What would the final selling price for a bar of soap be when you take into account all the other costs I just mentioned?" I asked looking at Marie.

Marie said "it is simple; we add 1.5 to 3.8 which gives us 5.3 RMB."

"How many of you would be willing to pay 5.3 RMB for a bar of soap?" I asked.

Cindy piped in saying "5.3 RMB would be too expensive for many people."

"Exactly" I said "and that is consistent with the results of the Beijing test market results. Our study and analysis of the price point we need to be at is 4 RMB or a little lower if we are going to be competitive. A price over 4 RMB would be too high."

"Does this make sense to everyone?" I asked again.

I got an almost unanimous "yes."

I looked at my watch and it has already been an hour and a half since we started our one hour meeting. I needed to wrap up, but there was a lot of energy in the room, so I decided that I will send everyone with a homework assignment for our next all management meeting next week.

"Let me make one final point before we wrap up today's meeting" I said "since we are limited to 4 RMB maximum on how much we can charge, then the only other alternative that is available to us in order to make a profit is to reduce our cost. Does everyone agree?" I asked.

Again, everyone nodded.

"Here is what I am going to leave you with. I am giving you a homework assignment. I want you to think about what can be done to reduce our costs. Think about what your department or group can do. What you personally can do. Also, don't be afraid to make suggestions for what others can do to help us reduce costs."

"I have to remind everyone that there are three key boundaries that cannot be crossed" I said "first, nothing that you propose can have a negative effect on the quality of our soap; second, it has to be in compliance with the laws of

China and, third, it has to be consistent with our company's principles and guidelines. Those are the areas that cannot be compromised in any way."

"Is everyone clear on the assignment and what you need to think about between now and next week's meeting?"

I saw people nodding. With that, the meeting was adjourned and the group dismissed.

Dan joined me on the way back to my office. It was a few minutes before 5:00 PM. We agreed that he will join me in my office a few minutes before 7:00 PM so that we can call Joe in Cincinnati.

A few minutes later, Julie brought in the usual stack of requisitions and payments for me to sign and before I knew it, Dan was knocking at my office door. It was already 6:55 PM. Within minutes, Julie had Joe on the phone.

Joe asked "how are things going so far?"

"So far so good" I answered "so much opportunity but the challenges are unbelievable. I am on a steep learning curve about how to effectively function in the Chinese culture, but there is so much that I still have to learn."

"This should not be a surprise to you, I hope" Joe said.

"A surprise, no, but in reality, things are even different than what I had envisioned or read about. It is one thing to understand things on an intellectual level and quite another to live it" I said adding "I hope you will plan a trip to China soon. I know it has barely been over a month since I left Cincinnati, but it feels like it has been such a long time. I always thought that things in the US moved at a lot faster pace than they did in other countries, but, I have to tell you, the way things are moving here, I think I am reassessing my definition of what fast paced means."

Joe laughed and said "you are still young, you can handle it."

"I agree, I can handle it and I am truly having a lot of fun. When you come to visit I will tell you all sorts of stories" I said "for now, I have Dan with me and we wanted to get your input and thoughts on a plan that is germinating in our heads."

"Hi Dan" Joe said "I hope your transition is going well."

"All is well" Dan said "thank you for asking."

I went on to explain to Joe the plan to contract between four and five plants to manufacture soap for us until we finish building our own capacity. As I was talking, it was clear to me that Joe was less than enthusiastic about our plan; however, I knew that Joe was also a businessman and would have a hard time making a decision that would not support the business. So I pressed on.

"As you might imagine, our other multinational competitors are assuming that it will take us about two years to build our capacity and they are working as if they have all the time in the world to secure their market share before we can come on stream" I said knowing that Joe felt as strongly as I did about this competitor who had successfully taken market share from us in the US market while we were stuck in corporate indecision. I knew that, like me, Joe would dearly like to see us catch them off guard.

Joe asked "How does their market share compare to ours?"

"They have 37% share on a national level and we have zero nationally." I said.

"Wow" Joe said "they already own the market. It is going to be tough to unseat them."

"True" I said "however, in Beijing where we have a lot of data and are now running a test market, our product is seen as superior and within a few weeks, we moved up to 38% market share while they dropped to 17% in spite of the fact that they have already been in this market for a few years."

"That is what I like to hear" Joe said.

"It gets better" I said "one of our mutual customers was telling us that our competitor's sales people are telling clients that their estimate is that we will not be able to have our test market product available for at least 18 to 24 months. This tells me that we can truly catch them off guard if we are able to pull this off and move swiftly."

"We have to find a way to do that" Joe said.

"I agree" I said "that is exactly why I felt strongly that we need to have a plan that allows us to keep our quality standards intact while we bring capacity on line within weeks."

"Ok" Joe said "why don't you and Dan walk me through how you propose to do this."

I went on to tell Joe about the plan to start with a plant tour of the 5 plants we identified to ascertain their capacity, their willingness to give us control of their process and quality control and their technical capability. After that, we will do the math and bring them on-line as quickly as we are able to train them and put our people and controls in place.

"How do you propose to manage their quality control?" he asked.

"The idea is to have Dan oversee the big picture. Since he can't be in six places at once, we plan to hire our own people, train them and put them in place on location at each of the plants. To get them trained, we may need to fly experienced people from other parts of the company to help train and oversee the start up."

I could tell that Joe was uneasy about this plan.

"How do you propose to ensure that things will not slide as soon as the ex-pats leave?" he asked.

"We have not finalized all the details and would be more than happy to implement any ideas that you might have for us" I said "but the plan is to have our people who are on the ground stay very close to Dan and augment that with having samples shipped from daily production to our lab in Tianjin to check the quality of what they are producing."

"As I think about it" I added "we can also send regular samples to Cincinnati for analysis until we determine that we have a predictable and reliable process."

There was a long pause. Then Joe said "I am not crazy about the plan."

There was another long pause, I motioned Dan to stay quiet and decided to wait for Joe to say some more about what he was thinking.

"On the other hand" Joe started again "I can see this plan working with a lot of detailed oversight and management."

Dan and I smiled and came very close to doing a high five.

"You can tentatively proceed with your plant visits. I will ask Jon to fly to Tianjin and work with Dan to finalize the plans."

"Thank you for your support" I said "how soon can you have Jon fly over" I asked "I am anxious to move full speed ahead."

"I will talk to him right after we hang up" Joe said "I will see about having him there next week."

"Again Joe, thank you" I said adding "you are the best."

"I am going to have to make the trip to China sooner than I had anticipated" he said as we said goodbye.

16

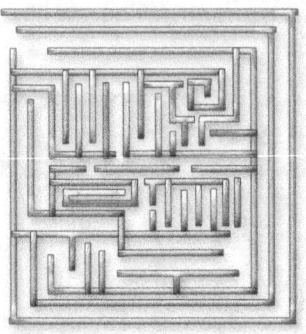

THE TRIP TO HONG KONG
AND THE START OF MY CHINESE LESSONS

Back at the office, Julie brought me the usual stack of bills and purchase orders. By now, I was so used to it that I ordered a signature stamp to speed up the process of signing all the paperwork. As we wrapped up, she told me that Hugo had arranged for us to visit four soap plants next week. We would start by visiting the plant in Guangzhou on Tuesday. On Tuesday afternoon, we will fly to Chongqing and tour the plant there on Wednesday. On Wednesday afternoon, we will fly to Shanghai where we will spend the night and then travel by car to Suzhou to tour the plant there. That afternoon, we will again travel by car to Hangzhou where we will spend the night and tour the plant there on Friday morning. On Friday afternoon, we will travel back to Shanghai and fly back to Beijing. She informed me that she was able to get the flights for myself and Dan arranged and that Rick and Hugo will also be joining us. She will travel with us to translate.

"That sounds excellent" I said "I think it will be a long and grueling trip" I added.

Before Julie could respond, the phone rang and she picked up. She turned to me and said "Angel, your Chinese teacher is on the phone. She was asking if it is possible to talk to you."

"Sure" I said as I reached to take the phone.

Angel started by asking me how I was doing and quickly went on to ask me about my plans for starting my Chinese lessons.

"I know" I said, feeling a little guilty "I have been so busy that I have not been able to find the time to schedule any lessons."

"Will things change soon?" she asked.

"Good question" I said as I reflected on the fast pace that everything was moving. In all honesty, I could not see myself having spare time for lessons any time soon, but I did not have the heart to break the news to her. Before I could say anything, it occurred to me that the only time that I have available is the time I spend in the car going back and forth to the Beijing airport. It was unproductive. The first few trips were interesting since everything was new, but now, the novelty was starting to wear off.

"I have an idea" I said "but I don't know if you would be open to it."

"I am very flexible" she eagerly said.

"The way my schedule looks, I expect to be traveling to Beijing airport once or twice every week" I said "it usually takes about two hours to get to the airport from here. If you are willing to do it, I can have my driver pick you up and you can give me a lesson in the car on the way to the airport. Then, when I come back, you can come to the airport with him and give me another lesson on the way back. What do you think?" I asked.

She was silent for a long moment so I added "of course, I will pay you for four hours each time since you will be spending two extra hours on the drive back to Tianjin. What do you think?" I asked again.

This time there was no hesitation in her voice and she said "that sounds great. When is your next trip?"

Julie jumped in and reminded me that I am traveling to Hong Kong on Friday for the week-end, but since I was going with my family, the car will be full. The next trip will be on Monday morning and that she will arrange for Mr. Li to pick her up.

With Angel off the phone, I asked Julie "is there anything else that I need to do before I go home?"

"You are all set" she replied "I just need to give you your trip folder for the Hong Kong trip."

She stepped out of the office and returned within 10 seconds with a nicely organized folder containing 4 airline tickets, the hotel confirmation and all the other details for the weekend trip.

I couldn't believe that it has only been a little over one month since we moved to Tianjin. So much has happened already, but for now it is time for our first R&R trip to Hong Kong … starting tomorrow..

Mr. Li was waiting downstairs. He opened the door for me and Julie got into the front seat as usual. Twenty minutes later they dropped me off at the Sheraton. I went up to our apartment where I found Nancy and both kids sitting around the kitchen table talking about their day.

Nancy has already figured out how to pace herself and coordinate with Julie around my schedule. She had prepared a nice meal for us this evening. She was already taking Chinese lessons regularly as were the kids. They were all becoming proficient and starting to function in Mandarin at a very basic level. I was the exception but felt good that on Monday, I will be officially starting my lessons.

When we finished dinner, the phone rang. It was Craig, an old friend of mine who moved here with his family in anticipation of working on the project to build the new plant that Drew and Mr. Chen were discussing. He asked if Nancy and I wanted to meet him and his wife Shelly at the lobby bar for a drink. I said we will be down in about 10 minutes.

We went down. They were already seated. The Filipino band was just getting back from their break and they started to play.

Craig and I enjoyed exchanging stories about our experiences. The stories ranged from the interesting to the bizarre. Around 11:00 pm, Nancy reminded me that we still needed to pack for our trip in the morning. We excused ourselves and went up.

The next morning, Mr. Li was waiting for us. I could see the car from my window parked at least 45 minutes before he was scheduled to pick us up.

The flight was uneventful. We quickly cleared customs and soon we were checking in at the New World Harbor View Hotel.

After dropping our bags at our rooms, we decided to take the subway to Pacific Place Mall. The Mall is accessible from the Admiralty Station interchange and is part of a huge complex that is touted as being Hong Kong's most elegant shopping destination featuring luxury brands, a stadium seating cinema and an array of gourmet dining. The complex also houses several luxury high rise hotels including the JW Marriott, Conrad Hong Kong, Island Shangri-La and the Pacific Place Apartments, where our friends Rick and Maureen now live.

As always, there was only so much shopping that I could stand to do. We decided to grab a late lunch at Dan Ryan's Chicago Grill. It was nice to have an English speaking waitress and a menu that was totally familiar.

Nancy and Elizabeth wanted to go to a few more stores. John and I decided we could not stand the sight of another clothing or shoe store, so we agreed that we would split from them and go to check camera and electronic stores. We agreed to meet back at the hotel no later than 5:00 PM since Nancy and I had plans to meet Rick and Maureen for dinner.

At 5:30 we arrived at Rick and Maureen's place. We had a drink together and caught up on each other's news. For dinner, we decided to take a leisurely walk towards an area that had several restaurants and see what catches our fancy when we get there.

As we walked towards the area, I could see a sign outside an Indian Restaurant that read "if you don't eat here, we both will go hungry". We all laughed and thought it was a clever sign. Rick told me that he had eaten there several times. The food was good and the owner was very attentive. So we decided to give it a try. True to Rick's words, the food was very good with a lot of main dish choices and excellent fresh na'an bread that was made to order.

After dinner, we walked to an Italian café and enjoyed a cappuccino and biscotti before saying goodbye to Rick and Maureen and going back to our hotel.

Both kids were still up when we arrived. They had an adjoining room with a door between them. We visited for a while and agreed to take the bus to Stanley Market tomorrow morning.

The next morning, we had a buffet breakfast in the dining room overlooking Victoria Harbor and the new convention center that was under construction at that time. I always found the busy harbor and boat traffic fascinating to watch. The sail boats and fishing boats had very unusual and ornate designs to them. While we were finishing our breakfast, the hydrofoil boat that travels between Hong Kong and Macau went by. It was very interesting to see the boat hovering over the water and traveling at high speed. It made the other boats appear stationary in comparison.

The bus that took us to Stanley Market was a Double Decker bus. We found that sitting on the right hand side on the second level of the bus gave us the best views. The trip took close to one hour. On our way there, we passed by Repulse Bay and a big condominium complex with a big hole in the middle which was part of the unique design of the building!

Stanley market is like a one stop market for souvenirs. It is a dry market frequented by tourists and located in the southern part of Hong Kong Island. It had an abundance of the usual oriental-looking gifts you can find across

Hong Kong and much more. There were a few shops that specialize in making Chinese stone seals that they would engrave with your Chinese name. If you don't have a Chinese name, no worries, they will give you one much faster than your parents gave you your original name.

In addition to the market, there is a strip by the water with a row of bars and restaurants. Many of them have outdoors dining on the weekends when the street is closed off to motorized vehicles.

Down the road is a small shopping center and a historical building that was moved there stone by stone. This rustic building, Murray House, is now home to a few fine restaurants. One has live music every night - a trio singing from table to table!

The adjacent Stanley Beach is the location of dragon boat races during the Dragon Boat Festival which draws local fishermen and corporate expatriates and ends up being quite a party.

We did break for lunch at an English Pub overlooking Stanley Bay. I had fish and chips (what else) and a pint of English beer. By late afternoon, we were loaded up with bags and feeling exhausted as we headed back to the bus stop and caught the next bus back to Hong Kong.

At the hotel we freshened up and decided that we would take a short walk to the Italian restaurant we liked near the hotel. Since it was a Saturday night, we decided to have the concierge make reservations for us in advance.

After dinner, we were all too tired to do much, so we decided to have an early night. The plan was to get packed up tonight so that we can get up early in the morning and go to Victoria Peak for an early lunch before catching our afternoon flight back to Tianjin.

As planned, the next morning, we took a taxi to the base of Victoria Peak at the central district. Victoria Peak is a mountain located in the western half of Hong Kong Island. It is also known as Mount Austin, and locally as The Peak. Its 1,810 ft altitude makes it the highest mountain on the island proper. The actual summit is occupied by a radio telecommunications facility and is closed to the public. However, the surrounding area of public parks and high-value residential land is the area that is normally meant by the name 'The Peak'. It is a major tourist attraction which offers spectacular views over central Hong Kong, Victoria Harbor, and the surrounding islands. It also has two malls. Peak Tower and Peak Galleria.

As early as the 19th century, the Peak attracted non-native, prominent residents because of its panoramic view over the colony and its temperate climate compared to the sub-tropical climate in the rest of Hong Kong. The sixth Governor of Hong Kong, Sir Richard MacDonnell had a summer residence built on the Peak in 1868. The original residents reached their homes by sedan chairs, which were carried up and down the steep slope of Victoria Peak.

The opening of the Peak Tram funicular in 1888 created demand for residences on the Peak. Between 1904 and 1930, the Peak Reservation Ordinance designated the Peak as an exclusive residential area reserved for Europeans and government officials. They also reserved the Peak Tram for the use of such passengers during peak periods. The Peak remains an up market residential area, although residency today is based on wealth.

After taking in the views and picking up a couple of souvenirs, we went to the Peak Lookout Restaurant which is housed in an older and more traditional building which was originally a spacious house for engineers working on the Peak Tramway. It was rebuilt in 1901 as a stop area for sedan chairs, but was re-opened as a restaurant in 1947. I enjoyed a bowl of Tom Yam Soup but we had to make it quick to be able to get to the airport and catch our flight this afternoon.

To avoid any delays, as soon as the tram arrived at the base of the Peak, we jumped into a taxi and ten minutes later we were at the hotel. I went to check us out while Nancy and the kids went to the rooms to get the bags ready. A few minutes later, the bell boy picked up our luggage and we were on our way to the airport. As it turned out, we were still not finished shopping, the Duty Free shops at the airport were too tempting and Nancy and Elizabeth picked up a couple more souvenirs.

The flight was uneventful as was the ride back to the hotel.

Monday morning came too fast. The alarm went off and half an hour later, I was on my way down. When I opened the door, Angel was waiting in the back seat while Julie was sitting in the front seat. Mr. Li started the car and we were on our way to the Beijing Airport.

Angel asked me "what areas I would like her to focus on for my Chinese lessons."

"I want to learn words that would be commonly used in business" I said.

"I suspected you might say that" she said "how about we start with words you will need to check into a hotel or use at a restaurant to place an order."

"That would be a good place to start" I said reflecting back on Johnny's and my experience having to call Julie on my cell phone to get some help ordering at the 99 Dumplings restaurant.

Angel started to teach me words and worked on my pronunciation. She explained to me that Mandarin had eight tones. Simply put, that means that a given word can have eight different meanings depending on the context and which tone is being used. I was having a tough time relating to the concept of eight tones when she went on to tell me that Cantonese was a little more complicated than Mandarin because it had 16 tones. That fact made me feel grateful that Mandarin was the official language of China and that all native Chinese were required to learn it.

I asked her to teach me how to ask for an official receipt when I was at the hotel. When I was doing my first expense report, I discovered that simple receipts showing charges to my American Express Card were not accepted for official accounting purposes by the Chinese government. There was something called a 'fa piao', which is the word that describes a receipt that bears an official government stamp. Anything else was not accepted for official government or tax deduction purposes.

Angel taught me how to ask for a fa piao, but I was having trouble getting the tones right. She asked me to keep practicing and working on my tones as Mr. Li pulled to the departures level at the airport. I promised her that I would as Julie and I got out of the car.

Julie handled checking us in. She efficiently took care of all the details and soon we were on our way to Guangzhou for our first plant tour.

17

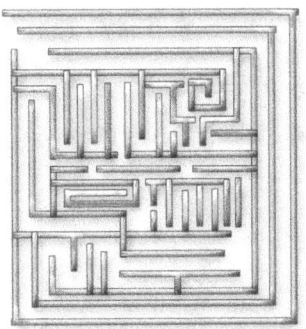

THE WHIRLWIND TOUR

That evening, dinner with the team was planned for 7:00 PM at a local restaurant. I was promised a memorable experience that I was certain to enjoy. I was a little concerned that we may not have enough time to prepare for our meetings. We needed to discuss the key issues and work through the areas we need to penetrate in depth, but I decided to have faith and not say anything.

In stark contrast to my last trip to Guangzhou, this time, I did not have to worry about any of the details. Julie was on the job. She efficiently checked us in at the China Hotel. Once she handed me the key to my room, we agreed to meet at the lobby at 6:30 PM to catch a cab and head to our meeting.

I went to my room and worked for about 2 hours refining the list of questions and concerns I wanted the team to assess during each of our plant visits. At 5:00 PM, I called Nancy to check in and make sure all is well with her and the kids.

On the second ring, Nancy picked up "I thought this might be you" she said.

"You were right" I said laughing "it is me. I wanted to check in before I went to my meetings. How are things going with you and the kids?" I asked.

By now, we all had a full month of getting used to the nuances of living in China. I knew that Nancy felt that we were so lucky to be able to live in the

Presidential suite of the Sheraton Hotel. She referred to it as "luxury in a most 'unluxurious' place".

"Yes" she said "everything is fine. Looks like the kids have settled into their school and adjusted to their teachers and new friends."

"Glad to hear it" I said "I was worried about being stuck with them feeling that I am the monster responsible for ruining their lives. Sounds like I just might live that one down" I added laughing.

"I know" she said "looks like we are getting past that. By the way" she continued laughing hard "you may want to tell the company they need to update the information they send to ex-pats about life in China."

"What are you talking about?" I asked.

"Well, this morning, I was reading some of that literature we received before leaving Cincinnati. There is a section that talks about buckets for human excrements being left outside each person's door. You know, for the purpose of fertilizing their crops?" she continued laughing "well I am glad to report that, to date, the hotel staff has not asked us to do that yet. I think that whoever wrote that must have meant back some 50 years ago and maybe outside farm house doors out in the countryside. In any case, I thought you might want to remind the company to update their ex-pat pamphlets. Something like this can scare prospective ex-pats from thinking about taking assignments in China."

"Yes ma'am, I will make this my top priority" I said laughing "I, for one, am glad I did not read all the literature HR passed on to us".

With that we said goodbye and she wished me luck with my meetings.

As soon as I hung up the phone, it rang again. This time, it was Rick on the phone. He told me he had already checked in and asked if I wanted to meet him at the bar for a beer. I said I will be down in ten minutes.

Rick looked good and greeted me with a big smile.

"You look younger than the last time I saw you" I said with a big smile.

"Not you my friend" Rick said joking "I think you look like you have aged about two years in the past few weeks."

We both laughed but I have to admit I was wondering if there was some truth to what he said. I have been jumping from one thing to another without stopping to take a deep breath. I made a mental note to have a talk with myself later about this.

Rick ordered two beers. I asked him about his and Maureen's transition.

"We love being in Hong Kong and enjoy the hustle and bustle of the city" he said.

"I know what you mean" I said "Hong Kong reminds me of being in Manhattan ... you can almost feel the pulse of the city. When I am there, I feel both excited and energized. Tell Maureen that I am jealous. I guess we will have to visit you guys regularly."

We went on to discuss the Guangzhou operation and what he knew about it. He had visited it several times since it is owned by our joint venture partner there. As such, he had easy access to it and took advantage of that access by visiting when he was in town. Overall, he had a positive impression of the plant.

"It needs some work to bring it up to our standards and get it on line, but it is not too bad compared to other plants I visited" he said "the advantage they offer is that they have already gone through their basic education when we did the detergents JV with them. In general, they know what to expect and we should be able to bring them on board fairly quickly."

"That sounds good but what I don't understand is why we did not bring them on board from the very beginning?" I asked.

"They wanted way too much money for what they had to offer. Their equipment is as antiquated as what you have in Tianjin and they don't even have a continuous process. On top of that, they have limited capacity. We calculated that we would need to add at least two mills plus two to three packing lines."

"I see" I said "do they have space to add the equipment and what about raw material storage?"

"They do" Rick said "we could have made it work, but they were negotiating very hard and, at that time, we needed to get their attention about issues related to the detergent business. They were acting like they held all the cards and were being very demanding. Drew got fed up with them. As a matter of fact, when he told them that he would do a JV somewhere else, they thought he was bluffing."

"Do you think they will be any easier to deal with now?" I asked.

"I do" he said "they regretted not working with us and tried very hard after we signed the deal with Tianjin's BOLI, to get us to reverse our decision. By then, it was too late."

"So they should be ready to deal at this point" I said

"I think so" Rick said "one thing that surprised me was that even when they were trying to win us back, their prices were still high."

"I would have thought they would have been very competitive at that point" I said "what were they thinking?"

"I think there is some justification for higher prices in Guangzhou compared with Tianjin. Everything from land to labor is cheaper in Tianjin" Rick said "however, not by the margin they were asking for."

"We will soon find out if time has softened their position" I said.

I heard someone say "Hi guys", I turned and it was Dan "I figured I would find you two at the bar" he said.

"Glad we were able to live up to your expectations" I said laughing and checked my watch. "It is time for us to meet everyone at the lobby. It is already 6:25PM" I said

Rick signed the bar tab to his room and we all headed for the lobby. Julie was waiting there with Hugo. She was so excited to see Rick and went over to give him a big hug. She was his assistant for the nine months that he was in Tianjin.

Hugo told us that Simon, from corporate finance will not be joining us in Guangzhou because we already have all the financial information we need about it. But he will join us for the flight tomorrow afternoon to Chongqing and then on to Suzhou and Hangzhou."

We all piled into two taxis for our ride to the restaurant. As it turned out, the restaurant was run by people from Hunan Province. Their food is different from the typical Cantonese cuisine. Drinks and food were ordered and we started to discuss our objectives and the approach we need to take. We eventually agreed that each of us should ask questions related to their area of specialty. However; when asking their questions, it was critical that no one give the impression that anything we are discussing is a done deal. All questions by our hosts should be referred to me and I will redirect them if and as needed.

After going through my list and a few other questions by others, I felt that we were as ready as we were going to be.

At about 9:00PM, loud music started to play and several dancers dressed in very colorful costumes came out to the center of the restaurant which happened to be right next to our table. The men wore green jackets and loose pants with elaborate and colorful designs while the women wore long red gowns with lots of colorful designs. Both the men and women were taller than the average Cantonese person you see in Guangzhou. They looked like they could be descendants of Chinese mixed with Northern Europeans.

After a few folk dances that I was told represented typical dances from Hunan Province, a group of twelve men also dressed in colorful costumes came out. They were in pairs with each pair carrying two bamboo sticks that were 3 to 4 inches thick and about 8 feet long. The men formed a square. Each side of the square was manned by three men. Along with the three men opposite them, they formed a pair. Each man held the end of two bamboo sticks creating a set of six bamboos in parallel. Those, along with the other set of six bamboos held by the other six men on the other two sides of the square, essentially formed what looked like a giant eight foot tic tac toe square.

Then, in unison, the men started to click the bamboos together and then separate them to the beat of the music forming an ever moving array of squares that alternately formed and closed on either side of the bamboos in rhythm with the beat of the music.

Essentially, the men were constantly shifting the squares from one side of each bamboo to the other as the men clicked their sticks together first having the two bamboo sticks they are holding touch each other which closed the squares in the middle while simultaneously opening adjacent squares. Keeping in mind that when all 12 men had their bamboos apart, the player was dealing with nine squares. When one pair of men clicked their bamboos together, the nine squares turned into six squares. The same would be true when the other pair of six men clicked their bamboos together. Finally when all the men brought their bamboos together at the same time, the number of squares dropped to four.

Next, some of the men in colorful costumes as well as some of the dancers started to hop through as some of squares opened while others closed around their ankles. The objective of the game was to try and make it to the side opposite from where you start without having your ankles clipped by the bamboos I have to admit that the men and women doing it made it look easy and appeared to be moving with the rhythm of the music as the bamboos clicked on. However; based on personal experience; I can verify that it looked a lot easier than it actually was. Being clipped by the bamboos can be a little uncomfortable but the experience was fun and worth it.

Soon, the women dancers started to go from table to table inviting guests to jump through the ever moving squares. Some did very well while others did not do as well. Eventually, it was my turn and I figured I should be able to do it. I just had to move with the beat. Unfortunately, it wasn't that simple. Eventually, I got to the other side after getting clipped by bamboo three or four times. It was a fun game and everyone participated. Rick tried to get a pass based on seniority, but eventually succumbed. He did at least as well as me.

It was getting late and we decided to call it a night. I paid the bill and we all went back agreeing to meet in the lobby at eight the next morning

Back at the hotel, I called Nancy again. Both John and Elizabeth were still up so I said hi and caught up on their latest news before they went to sleep.

After we finished talking, they put their mom back on the phone.

"I am glad you called" she said "I was hoping to talk to you before you went to bed."

"I just finished my dinner meeting" I said "they took me to a restaurant that served food from Yunnan Province. They had entertainment including some folk dancers and local music. I will have to take you to it when you visit Guangzhou."

"Sounds nice" she said "you'll never believe what happened after we last talked."

"What?" I asked.

"Oh, I am now the new President of the Tianjin International Women's Club" she said adding "by default, actually."

"Wow" I said "I had no idea you were interested in doing that."

"I wasn't" she said "but if you remember, when we first got here, I offered to help and reluctantly accepted when they voted me in as the secretary. Well, at today's meeting, both the current President and Vice President resigned and as the only other elected official in the room, they turned the job of president over to me. It seems that the club is divided into two factions, the Europeans and the Americans. I think I haven't been here long enough to make waves with either group, so I am it."

"Quite a turn of events" I said "you will make a great president" I added.

"Well, things are about to get a little bit more hectic for me" she said "it'll keep me busy I suppose."

"I am sure you will have fun" I said faking a French accent "Madame President."

"Thank you monsieur" she replied "I guess I will give it my best shot and see how it goes."

"I am sure you will do great" I said.

"Oh, I almost forgot" she said "I signed us up for Tai Chi lessons here at the hotel. I hope you will have time to make some of them at least. I know you work late, but they start at 7 PM every Wednesday night and at 10 AM on Saturdays. Also, there is talk of a ballroom dance class starting up in the evenings at the hotel --- I figure that one you may want to mull over, before committing to it" she added laughing.

"I can dance" I said "but ballroom dancing might be a stretch."

"Yes" she said "it would be. Think it over and we can decide when you get back. Aside from that, not much else to report except that the kids and I miss you and can't wait for you to get back home, I mean, back here to the hotel...see that? Guess it didn't take us long at all to start calling this place home" she said as we said goodnight.

The alarm went off at 7:00 and by the time I got out of bed; room service was knocking on my door. I had placed my coffee and breakfast order before I went to bed. I was glad I did, I needed that coffee. After taking a quick shower, I ate breakfast as I listened to CNN World. I was glad to be able to get CNN. It helped me feel somewhat still connected with the US, although the World News channel covered much broader world news than its US counterpart, something I always thought was missing in the US. We tended to know less about what is going on in the rest of the world than our European friends.

At five minutes to eight, I was at the lobby. Within a couple of minutes, everyone was there. We took two taxis to the plant where people were waiting for us. We went through the introductions and other formalities for about 15 minutes. I asked if I could tour the detergent plant after our meeting and our host said he would be delighted to tour me through.

The plant was about on par with the one in Tianjin with kettle soap making and a single packing line. Our host showed me where additional equipment can be added. We toured their lab facility and their tank farm where the raw materials will be stored. I was getting excited because I thought this could work, but we still faced the same challenge of having to wait for equipment. So I started to ask more questions.

As it turned out, there was local suppliers that manufacture milling equipment in China. They have a 3 week lead-time I was told. Mr. Chang went on to explain that the packing lines will take longer but they will do the packing by hand, similar to what we were doing in Tianjin.

My first reaction was to wonder how he would know about how we pack in Tianjin, then I reminded myself that we were in China and that all manufacturers belonged to the government. As such, they had full access to everyone else's plants, prices, etc.

I asked Mr. Chang to give me a quote that showed the price he will charge, the maximum volume they can produce and how quickly they can be up and running. I also emphasized with him that Dan and eventually someone from our Company will be responsible for quality. Mr. Chang indicated that he completely understood since they already have a JV with us. He went on to reassure me that he understands our requirements and emphasized that he did not foresee any issues in meeting our needs in every detail.

We wrapped up the meeting and I asked Mr. Chang if he could give me a quick tour of the detergents plant. Everyone wanted to take the tour with me, so we headed towards the plant on the other side of the property. He took me up a set of stairs to the Plant Manager's office located on the second floor where I had a major surprise. The Plant Manager was an old boss of mine. I had worked for Dick about twelve years earlier for two years before he moved to Corporate. Dick is a tall, heavyset man with a full head of thick blond hair. He is a chain smoker and has a booming voice. For a while, we stayed in touch, but after a few years, we lost contact with each other. I did not know he was now working for the company in China.

After the initial surprise passed, Dick took us through the plant on a quick tour. Again, the operation was much more manual than what I was used to seeing, but they were doing the job. Dick and I agreed to connect on my next trip to Guangzhou. He said he would be happy to help answer any questions I have about his JV. I told him I will be in touch shortly but before leaving, I made sure he met Dan.

It was time for us to head for the airport to catch our flight to Chongqing. The traffic was heavy and I was starting to worry about us missing our flight. But things kept moving albeit slowly. Once at the airport, we had little time to spare.

The flight was uneventful and we arrived in Chongqing around 5:30 PM. After Julie efficiently checked us in; we agreed to meet for dinner at 7:00.

Chongqing is a port city with the largest municipal area in China. It is situated in the upper reaches of the Yangtze River at the confluence of the Yangtze and Jialing Rivers in southwest China. With an area of 31,800 square miles, Chongqing shares borders with the provinces of Hubei, Hunan, Guizhou, Sichuan, and Shaanxi. Besides the Han who form the majority of its total population of 30.9 million (around 6 million live within the city proper), numerous ethnic groups reside in Chongqing, including Yi, Tibetan, Miao, Qiang, You and Tujia.

Since its founding 3,000 years ago, Chongqing has been called Jiangzhou, Yuzhou, and Gongzhou, before getting its present name nearly 800 years ago. Since the Qin Dynasty (221 BC-206 BC), many dynasties have set up administrative institutions that have endowed the city with brilliant cultures. Perched beside the Yangtze, the "Golden River," Chongqing symbolizes Yangtze River civilizations and is the cradle of Bayu culture.

Today, Chongqing is a modern city, China's fourth municipality after Beijing, Shanghai, and Tianjin. Within its borders Chongqing encompasses a wealth of water reserves, mineral resources, dense forests, and abundant flora and fauna. The focal point of the unique Yangtze Three Gorges Dam, Chongqing is a tourist attraction as well as a commercial city.

Chongqing has a rich cultural heritage and is the starting point for the Yangtze River Cruise, which explores the stunning scenery of the Three Gorges. Other attractions include the Dazu Rock Carvings, valuable works of art carved during the Ninth Century, Gold Buddhist Mountain, a rich repository of diverse animals and plants; and Fishing Town, one of three ancient battlefields in China.

Chongqing is famous for its hot Sichuan cuisine and world-famous hotpot dishes. Street vendors as well as restaurants feature exciting spicy delicacies for the adventurers. The particular restaurant we went to was fancy and the service was world class with several young waitresses anticipating our every need. The only problem for me was that the food was very hot; as in "cayenne pepper" hot. Based on my limited experience, it seems that hot peppers are used in all recipes. I had innocently taken a mouthful during dinner which I immediately regretted. The food was painfully hot. I felt as if my mouth was set on fire and that single mouthful brought tears to my eyes. It seemed that no amount of water could begin to wash the burning hot sensation away. With that, I lost my sense of taste for most of the evening.

The group and I went over the same list again despite the fact that my tongue felt like it was three times its normal size. We all expected tomorrow's visit to be much more demanding since this factory was one that was new to us. No one from the team has been there before.

After dinner we agreed to meet at 8:00AM and retired for the evening.

The next morning, we took two taxis to the factory. The city of Chongqing is in a mountainous part of Sichuan Province. Houses are built on the sides of hills and it felt like we were always either going uphill or downhill, but seldom on flat ground. It was very scenic; however, it struck me as being very smoggy or 'hazy' as Julie was quick to correct me. The air felt very thick especially early in the day.

About 20 minutes later, we arrived at the factory and were soon introduced to the key players. It quickly became apparent that the big boss was a woman whose name was Madam Kong. She was a very serious woman and was eyeing us with suspicion.

As the meeting progressed, it was becoming clear to me that doing business with Madam Kong will be a challenge. She had an attitude and it showed. I tried to avoid letting my personal view of Madam Kong affect my judgment, so I pressed on with our questions. Finally, we took a tour of the facility. As it turned out, the plant was built on several layers of the hill. Raw material tanks were down hill from the kettle making and the packing area was located a little higher up on the hill. The layout was a complete nightmare from a sound engineering design and efficient flow of materials perspective. If Madam Kong's attitude towards us did not kill it for me, the way the factory was laid out and our tour of their quality control facility did.

I thanked Madam Kong for her time and hospitality. I told her that we were visiting a few factories and that we will let her know what our plans are after we complete our visits.

After saying goodbye, we headed for the airport to catch a flight to Shanghai where we will spend the night. The trip to Suzhou will be made by car the following morning.

Shanghai was quite interesting. It is the largest city in China, and one of the largest metropolitan areas in the world, with over 20 million people. Located on China's central eastern coast just at the mouth of the Yangtze River, the city is administered as a municipality of the People's Republic of China with Province-level status.

Originally a fishing and textiles town, Shanghai grew in importance in the 19th century due to its favorable port location and, as one of the cities opened to foreign trade by the 1842 Treaty of Nanking, the city flourished as a center of commerce between east and west, and became a multinational hub of finance and business by the 1930s. After 1990, the economic reforms introduced by Deng Xiaoping, resulted in intense re-development and financing of the city.

The city is a tourist destination renowned for its historical landmarks such as the Bund and City God Temple, its modern and ever-expanding skyline including the Oriental Pearl Tower, and its new reputation as a cosmopolitan center of culture and design. Today, Shanghai is the largest center of commerce and finance in mainland China, and has been described as the "showpiece" of the world's fastest-growing major economy.

We stayed at the Westin hotel there and I discovered that the city offered a wide range of restaurants that served almost any food one might want. I suggested we go to an Italian restaurant that night. The food selection was good and I enjoyed my dinner and a glass of Chianti. By now, the team was familiar with the list and we did not need to spend much time strategizing.

The next morning, a van picked us for the drive to Suzhou. Our ride took about ninety minutes.

Suzhou, occasionally nicknamed the "Venice of the East" or "Venice of China", is located on the lower reaches of the Yangtze River and on the shores of Lake Taihu in the province of Jiangsu. The city is renowned for its beautiful stone bridges, pagodas, and meticulously designed gardens which have contributed to its status as a great tourist attraction. Since the Song Dynasty (960-1279), Suzhou has also been an important centre for China's silk industry and continues to hold that prominent position today. The city is part of the Yangtze River Delta region.

We met the key players. The top man was Mr. Chen. Hugo and Rick had met him before. Mr. Chen was very eager to do business with us. He already had a minor contract with a US based soap manufacturer. The brand and company were not serious competition for us; however, the issue of confidentiality concerned me. As we discussed it, Mr. Chen indicated that he would be ready to discontinue his relationship with their current customer if we were serious about a JV with them. While that was what I wanted to hear, it also concerned me since I wasn't sure how quickly Mr. Chen will drop us if he got a better offer while he was working with us.

On the other hand, the Suzhou factory was a little better organized than anything I had seen to date in Chinese Soap manufacturing. They had what appeared to be good quality control and a decent lab. This was a plant that I felt can be brought up to speed quickly. We went for lunch with Mr. Chen and his deputies. I asked him to provide me with information on his pricing, the capacity that he can dedicate to our production and how he will manage confidentiality. I explained to him that we were looking to place one of our people at his facility, if we decide to go forward, to manage quality control. He was agreeable to the idea and indicated that he would be willing to do whatever was needed to support the business; however, he was less than enthused about the fact that we were looking to contract his capacity instead of forming a Joint Venture with him.

After lunch, we took the van to Hangzhou. Hangzhou is the capital of Zhejiang province and its political, economic and cultural center. With its famous natural beauty and cultural heritages, Hangzhou is one of China's most important tourist venues.

The City, the southern terminus of the Grand Canal, is located on the lower reaches of the Qiantang River in southeast China, a superior position in the Yangtze Delta and only 180 kilometers (112 miles) from Shanghai. Hangzhou has a subtropical monsoon type climate with four quite distinct seasons. However, it is neither too hot in summer nor too cold in winter making it a year round destination.

West Lake is undoubtedly the most renowned feature of Hangzhou, noted for the scenic beauty that blends naturally with many famous historical and cultural sites. Visitors to Hangzhou can enjoy outstanding views of the lake, mountains and monuments. Hangzhou's natural surroundings have caught the attention of visitors for centuries including that of the famous 13th century explorer, Marco Polo.

Hangzhou has a number of national museums of Chinese culture. Fine examples are the National Silk Museum and National Tea Museum. Along with the other museums in Hangzhou, they provide a fascinating insight into the history of traditional Chinese products.

We stayed at the Shangri La Hotel located on the shore of West Lake in a very serene and beautiful setting. After checking in, I decided to go for a walk and quite liked the feel of the place. I quite enjoyed being surrounded by the beautiful scenery and was awestruck to think that I was probably walking along a path that Marco Polo may have walked so many years ago. As I walked past the teahouses and pubs overlooking West Lake, I was reminded of the many contrasts one sees in China. The old and the new, the local and the foreign all existing side by side as China moves forward towards modernization.

Dinner that evening was very good. Hangzhou dishes are noted for their elaborate preparation, sophisticated cooking and good taste. We enjoyed what we were told were their most famous local specialties including Beggar's Chicken (a chicken baked in clay), West Lake Fish in Sweet and Sour Sauce (vinegar coated fresh fish caught from the lake), Dongpo Pork (braised pork) and Fried Shrimps.

The next morning, we repeated the same drill during our meeting with the Soap Factory in Hangzhou. The top official was Mr. Wang. He was also eager to work with us. We took a plant tour and I decided that Hangzhou is also workable and that I can do business with them. We concluded our meeting with me asking Mr. Wang to provide me with the same information about pricing, capacity and how quickly they can come on line. Mr. Wang was also agreeable to us placing our people at his plant to oversee quality control; however, like Mr. Chen from Suzhou, he was less than thrilled about the fact that I was looking to contract his capacity instead of forming a Joint Venture with his factory.

The trip to the Shanghai Airport seemed to take forever after a long week on the road. I was happy to finally get on the airplane and head back to Beijing. I tried not to think about the fact that I still had at least a one and a half hour ride once we land in Beijing before I am back at the Sheraton in Tianjin.

I fell asleep on the flight back. This helped a bit and before I knew it, we landed in Beijing and Julie and I went to the baggage claim area. Mr. Li was there with Angel. I had forgotten about Angel and my Chinese lesson. The last thing I wanted to do at this point was to take a lesson. I was mentally and physically drained from all the things we did during the past week; however, Angel was enthusiastic about giving me my second lesson and soon her enthusiasm rubbed off on me.

As we were approaching the Sheraton hotel, I asked Julie to confirm with Mr. Li at TTSF that I was still planning to go over to tour the factory as we had agreed through Mr. Tian. I told her to arrange for Dan, herself and me to be there for 10:00 am on Monday.

"Mr. Tian is also planning to accompany you" Julie told me.

"That would be fine, let him know about the time" I said adding "I would also like to set up an all day meeting with my direct reports on Wednesday."

Julie said "will do" as the car pulled to the hotel entrance. I said goodbye to Angel and Julie, wished them a good weekend and told Mr. Li that I will not need him to drive me this weekend.

While on the way up, I was thinking to myself that I was feeling a little tired and hoped that Nancy did not have any big plans. Yes, I thought, I would like to rest this weekend before I do anything else. As I was deep in thought, the elevator stopped on the fifth floor and Shelly got on. We chatted while the elevator made its way to the sixth floor. I was about to say goodbye to Shelly but she was following me out of the elevator and kept walking with me until we arrived at my home.

She could see my curious look and said with a big smile "you don't know, do you?"

"No, what is going on at my place?" I asked.

"Nothing big, we are getting together with Andy and Eric and their wives. We are starting with drinks at your place and then going to a new restaurant that Craig and I discovered last week" she replied.

"That sounds like fun" I said as I opened the door and said hello to everyone. I excused myself and went to freshen up and get ready. "So much for a slow weekend" I thought.

A few minutes later, Craig came up and half an hour later we were on our way to another new China adventure.

The restaurant was very nice. It was in an old building with a lot of character that was located in what was the old Dutch section of Tianjin. We were quickly seated and soon discovered that they did not have an English menu and the waitress did not speak a single word of English. I turned to Craig and Shelly and asked "how did you guys order when you came here last week?"

"We came here with Ping. She ordered for all of us" Craig said laughing adding "it was very easy you know."

"Alright then" I said "let's see if we can figure this out."

We already knew how to say beer in Chinese, so we ordered beer, but had no clue how to say wine. So I turned to look around at other guests and fortunately, there was one couple that had a glass of wine. I pointed at the table but the waitress had a puzzled look.

I decided to walk with her to the table and point more specifically at the wine glass. The woman thought it was funny to have this foreigner walk the waitress to her table and point at her wine. The waitress was happy, because at least now she knew what else I was ordering. There was only one minor problem, the woman had a glass of white wine and I needed two glasses of white and another two glasses of red. At this point, no one cared what brand the wine was. Red or white was as deep as I thought we can go with choices.

"Lianga" I said showing the waitress two fingers while I was pointing at the woman's glass of wine. However, I was stuck now. I did not know how to tell her about the other two. I decided to show her 4 fingers; however, she clearly thought I wanted four glasses of white. So I said "no, no, no, lianga jaiga" as I pointed to the white wine again which meant "two, this" and then pointed at a red curtain and said "lianga, jaiga" as I pointed at the red curtain. The confused look on the waitress' face was priceless. I quickly figured that she is thinking that I am trying to also order two red curtains.

I decided that I needed to try and do this in stages. So I went back to asking her for two glasses of white wine and the four beers. She went off to get the drinks and I went back to the table. As I told everyone what happened, I almost fell to the floor I was laughing so hard. Then all of a sudden it dawned at me, I should go to where the waitress went and point at a bottle of red wine. I quickly walked in the direction she went and she was just about to leave with the drinks when I showed up. She looked at me again puzzled about what I was doing there and probably thinking she should have called in sick this evening.

I walked to the shelves and there was a bottle of red wine sitting there. I then pointed at the bottle and said "lianga" while showing her two fingers. She smiled and rambled on in Chinese, but it was obvious that she had figured out what I was doing pointing at the red curtains. She went back and poured two glasses of red and she and I went back to the table. We toasted each other and decided that we were going to have fun tonight, English menus or not.

A few minutes later, the waitress came back ready to take our orders. We decided, pointing worked for us so far and given that we did not have much of an alternative, we will have to continue to point as we place the rest of our orders. So we all got up and walked the waitress from one table to another pointing at plates that looked good. Fortunately for us, no one appeared to be upset, they seemed to be taking it in stride and mostly finding our exchange with the waitress entertaining.

By now, we were not sure what we ordered or how much. Nancy pointed out that we did not come across any vegetable servings or dishes. We were not planning to order salads. The risk of contaminated vegetables was too high, but cooked vegetables would be fine.

I decided to look at the list of the items we ordered to see if we had pointed at or ordered enough food. I counted 10 orders. There were eight of us. I quickly decided, this was bigger than me. I knew there was no way we will be able to sort through what is what, so I said "hao."

Nancy prodded me "what about some vegetables?"

"I have a plan" I said.

When the waitress headed for the kitchen, I told Craig "let's go" and we followed her. She was looking at us curiously, but I kept saying "hao, hao" and pointed to her to go on.

When we got to the kitchen, I was glad Nancy did not come with me. She would never have eaten anything they served. Simply put, the kitchen was not what one might call clean or sanitary. To allow myself to keep going, I reasoned to myself that they boil or fry everything.

Craig and I went around the supplies in the kitchen and pointed at various vegetables with me saying "iga" meaning "one" as I pointed to each vegetable.

About 20 minutes later, the food was served. The dishes both looked and tasted good. Andy observed that it only took 20 minutes to prepare and serve the food, but it took us 45 minutes to place the order. We all laughed and I said "imagine telling our friends back home about how it took longer to order our meal than it took to cook and serve it to us. Only in China!" I added as we all laughed.

We enjoyed a few more drinks and soon it was time to call it a night, so we paid the bill and two minutes later we were on the street flagging two taxis. On our ride back, I started to reflected on our evening and dinner. I wondered how frustrating this evening could have been for the eight of us if we had the wrong attitude. We could have as easily become frustrated and angry about the lack of English language menus, our inability to communicate and worse, we could have been stuck with those feelings. Attitude, I thought, has got to be the key. It is what makes the difference between simply surviving such an assignment or thriving and enjoying the experience. I was deep in thought when the taxi pulled to the front of the Sheraton.

Ironically, as Nancy, Craig, Shelly and I paid the driver and got out, we could hear shouting. It was two guests from Germany who were on assignment in Tianjin and they were all mad and screaming. As best as I could tell, it was some disagreement about the amount of the fare the driver wanted to charge. I recognized them and remembered that I had met the husband two weeks earlier at the Hotel weekly cocktail hour and all he did then was to tell me how terrible the Chinese were and how Tianjin was so backward. I remember thinking "get over it, this is not Berlin."

Attitude, I thought again, it makes all the difference in the world.

18

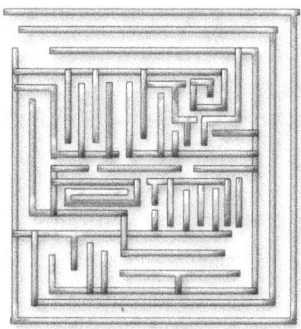

THE STRATEGY

On Monday morning, Mr. Tian, Dan and Julie came to my office a few minutes before ten. We all walked over to TTSF for our meeting with Mr. Li.

On the way over, Mr. Tian asked Julie to tell me that on the way back from our meeting with Mr. Li, he would like to show me the plans for the temporary bicycle parking.

"Temporary bicycle parking?" I asked inquisitively.

"Yes, temporary bicycle parking" he told her and asked her to explain to me that "just like companies in the U.S. provide parking space for cars, in China companies need to provide parking for bicycles."

"That makes sense" I said "tell Mr. Tian, I look forward to it."

Mr. Li was waiting for us by the entrance to the factory and escorted us to a conference room that looked more like a living room with three black leather couches, a middle table and three accent tables.

"Mr. Li, I like your conference room a lot better than mine" I said laughing.

"When your company bought your factory, the room where your conference room is now was furnished just like this one" Mr. Li said "but Rick insisted that they get rid of the couches and he had them replaced with the conference table and chairs you have now. I am sure you can go back to the old conference room if you wanted to."

Mr. Tian jumped in and said "I tried to convince Rick that he should leave the conference room the way it was, but he wouldn't listen."

"In the West, using a conference table and chairs, like we have now, is very typical. In our culture, especially in a manufacturing organization, having sofas would be viewed negatively by the workers and the shareholders. The shareholders would view it as extravagant and wasteful."

"But this factory is in China, it is not in the US" Mr. Tian responded in a critical and sarcastic tone that cut through the translation. He then added trying to soften his criticism "I am sure you will be given leeway by the company to accommodate the local culture. When we have local officials visiting us, we don't have the type of meeting room they are used to using and often comment negatively about our conference room."

"Tell Mr. Tian that his input is well taken" I said and then moved the conversation in a different direction by turning to Mr. Li and thanking him for hosting us on such short notice.

Mr. Li offered us some tea, but I asked if we can have tea after we toured the facility.

The factory was similar in many ways to the factory we bought from BOLI, but it had a glycerin refining facility which was also refining our glycerin. It looked a little better laid out than ours, had kettle soap making and manual soap packaging.

When we went back to the conference room, which by now, I knew better than to casually comment on, Mr. Li explained very openly that he was very eager to do business with us. He went on to explain that the brand of soap he is producing has been losing market share. He has a lot of spare capacity and people by the hundreds that had nothing to do, but he still had to pay them.

Mr. Li also presented information about how much capacity he can dedicate to us and his pricing. It was very clear that Mr. Li had spent a lot of time and energy preparing for our meeting. I told Mr. Li that I am very interested in doing business with him, especially since BOLI has ownership in both of our factories which makes us sister companies.

I went on to explain to him about the quality requirements and how I would be looking to have Dan oversee quality at TTSF as well as for our factory. He was fine with that and explained that he would do whatever it took to support us.

I decided that we will be doing business with TTSF, so it was time to attack the price he was asking for, so I asked him to review his pricing again. I explained to him that it was a little higher than I was expecting. I could see that Mr. Tian was about to object and Mr. Li appeared to want to say something, so I decided to be pre-emptive. I already knew that Mr. Li, through BOLI and Mr. Tian, who used to work for him, knew very well how high our costs were. After all, Mr. Li knew that my complete cost across the street was about $22/case and he was offering to charge me a manufacturing cost of $1.93/case to make and pack the soap . We would buy and supply him with all the raw and packaging materials.

"I know that you are offering me an attractive price compared to where my costs are today, but I can assure you that those costs will not be true for too long. I can tell you that I expect our costs to fall in line with our costs in other countries which are in the $1.0 - $1.20/case range."

I knew that Mr. Li knew in detail where I spent last week. It would not surprise me if I found out that he had already talked to the factory managers that I met last week. So I went on "I am not sure if you know this already, but last week I visited four soap factories."

"Yes, I know" Mr. Li said

"As you know" I went on "the projections for our volume are huge and we are going to need more than one or two factories to meet the demand for our soap. In any case, all four factories were very eager to do business with us and all of them are going to provide me with what I expect would be very competitive proposals" I concluded.

"I understand your concern" Mr. Li said "what is your price target?"

"The lower, the better" I said "unfortunately, the only numbers that I know today are the ones I mentioned for the cost of making soap at our own factories in other parts of the world. I can also tell you that all the factories are trying to find ways to reduce their costs, so those numbers are a moving target."

I went on "as of today, I still don't have any prices from the other factories that I met with last week. Although, I have to tell you that my company rules and guidelines prevent me from telling you what those prices are even if I knew what they were. The company believes that if our suppliers really want our business, then they would offer their best prices upfront. If we allow a vendor to reduce their price, then we are required to give all the other vendors the opportunity to bid again on the business. Otherwise, we would be penalizing the vendors that gave us their best price from the very beginning."

"Interesting" Mr. Li said "it is very different from how we do business in China. Over here, we like to bargain."

"Yes, it is very different, but I think you and I are going to work very well together" I said adding "please forgive me for repeating this, but I have to ask you to be sure that you are as aggressive as you can be on price. It is my intention to make decisions very quickly. Possibly as early as the latter part of this week."

"In that case, I will get back to you later this afternoon" Mr. Li said.

I decided it was time to add an incentive for Mr. Li to make sure he keeps his pencil sharp. I leaned over towards Julie and Mr. Li and said in a low conspiratorial tone "I will be honest with you, Mr. Li, my preference is for us to have your factory produce the maximum amount of soap that you can produce and to only farm out what you and I cannot produce at our factories."

"Now that we talked and you know the situation" I said to Mr. Li "it is my hope that you can offer me much more competitive pricing than the $1.93/case you already mentioned. I am hoping for a price that would be less than $1.00/case."

I paused for a minute to let the numbers sink in before I continued "after all Mr. Li, you were one of the first people I met when I moved here and we have since become personal friends."

"Of course, we are very good friends" he said.

"On a personal level" I went on "we have to find a way to agree on a price that works for both of us. After all, we both are part of BOLI and ultimately have to answer to Mr. Chen."

"Mr. Chen would be very disappointed if we cannot agree on a price" he said

I paused for a moment before adding "I agree, he would be disappointed. I also have people in the US that I have to answer to."

"I know, I know" he said "with you being so close, I am sure we can find a way to get to a price that is better than what other competitors can offer you. I will take a hard look at the prices and get back to you this afternoon" Mr. Li concluded.

"Again" I said "thank you my friend and I am looking forward to talking to you this afternoon."

With that I stood up and everyone else followed. Mr. Li escorted us to the main gate and said goodbye.

As soon as we crossed the street, we were on the curb outside the fence on the west side of our factory. Mr. Tian told Julie that he would like to show me where the temporary bicycle parking will be.

Mr. Tian pointed to an area that had street vendors congregated. He explained that the area where the vendors were was part of our property.

The plan was to set up temporary parking there.

"What will we do with those vendors?" I asked.

"We will move them to the open space across the street" he said.

"Remind me, why do we need to set up temporary parking?" I asked.

"Construction inside the factory will start soon" Mr. Tian said "and the engineers need the area where people park their bicycles now cleared before they can start construction of the new glycerin refinery building."

"Ok, I understand" I said "any security concerns about parking being outside the fenced area?"

"No, the bicycles will be safe here" Mr. Tian said.

"Where will the new permanent parking be if this is temporary parking?" I asked.

"It will go in where the engineering building is. Dale said the building is not seismically safe and would have to be torn down after the project is finished" Mr. Tian said.

"Good" I said "the plan makes sense to me and the new permanent parking will be conveniently located near the main entrance."

"Then you agree?" Mr. Tian asked.

"Yes, I agree" I said "good job Mr. Tian, thank you."

Mr. Tian smiled and was obviously please to get positive feedback from me.

"Interesting" I thought.

Back at the office, I asked Julie to put a call through to Daniel and then to Drew. A minute later, Julie came in and told me that Daniel was in a meeting with Drew.

"In that case, call Drew's assistant and see if she can call us back when they finish their meeting. Make sure that she knows that I need to talk to both of them please" I said.

Five minutes later, my phone rang and I had both Drew and Daniel on the phone. I gave them an update on where things stood.

"In a nutshell" I concluded "I think all signals are a go. We have Joe's support on the quality front. I believe that TTSF, Guangzhou, Hangzhou and Suzhou can all be viable players. It will be a challenge to bring them all on board together, so I will manage the process of bringing capacity on board in step with business demand."

Drew and Daniel were very excited about this news and Drew asked "when will you have the capacity numbers, costs and timing for how quickly you can ramp up?"

"Starting this afternoon" I said "and I expect to have all of it by the middle of this week."

"Why don't you schedule a conference call when you have all the information so that we can finalize our plans" Drew said.

"In the meantime" Daniel said "I need to mobilize the soap brand team and sales group to quickly ramp up our expansion plans. Until today, their focus has been to complete test markets and develop launch plans that we thought would be implemented 12 to 18 months out."

Daniel asked me "what is your best estimate of how soon you can start to deliver soap beyond the Beijing area?"

"If you plan to have the Sales and Marketing teams ready in a month; that would be perfect. My best estimate today which is very aggressive but I believe doable, is that we can start producing to build inventory within a month" I said, adding "this would allow us to start expanding beyond Beijing."

"That sounds very aggressive" Drew said.

"It is" I said "my reasoning is that, I can get some of those suppliers on line very quickly. Specifically, I am referring to Guangzhou and TTSF. We will focus on them first. I will bring Suzhou and Hangzhou on line in step with the demand. In the meantime, I have Lou and Gaston working on getting more production out of our factory. We can make more soap in the kettles, but do not have enough packers to handle that so we will start hiring and training packers in the next few days. We have space on the third floor of the packing building where we can locate about 60 to 80 people per shift with tables and boxes to manually pack the soap."

I continued reflectively "this is one of those times where we just have to push forward and ramp up as fast as we can. Clearly, we have to expect that we will hit a few bumps in the road, but if we can hold hands and say we will work together to deal with the bumps as they come up, I think we can successfully pull this off and build this brand a lot sooner than anyone expects."

"Good thoughts, but it still sounds very aggressive" Daniel said "it is definitely risky, but it may be the best we can hope for at this point."

"If we at least directionally agree" I said "then as soon as you can get the execution team working, I will need a roll out plan that tells me what geographical areas we will tackle first and most important, I need to know volume projections of what we need to successfully execute the sales and Marketing plans. Obviously, it is going to take some time to fill the pipeline for the first time as we expand nationally, so markets and volumes need to be listed in priority order."

"Very exciting" Drew said "we obviously have a lot of work ahead of us if we are to pull this off. Let us know when you get the numbers and let's make sure we keep each other informed as things develop."

"Will do" I said as I hung up the phone.

Julie walked in with a McDonald's Fish sandwich and fries for me as she informed me that she thought that fish was healthier for me than burgers. I agreed but pointed out that the fried and breaded fish probably had a lot of extra fat that may offset the health benefits of fish. But that did not prevent me from eating the sandwich anyways not to mention the fries.

I walked over to Dan's office and said "I just talked to Drew and Daniel. It's a go."

"I knew that the day Joe said he will support us" Dan said.

"Yea, me too" I said "no sales or marketing executive in their right mind would tell us to stop. I told them that we will focus on TTSF and Guangzhou first and then take our time bringing Suzhou and Hangzhou on line. My plan is to bring those plants one at a time as we ramp up, like I have been saying, we will bring capacity on line in step with demand."

"That is good" it gives us some breathing room" Dan said

"Also, I talked to Dick in Guangzhou and he offered to help us by getting Chris on the team. As you know she is experienced at managing quality at contract manufacturers and already knows the detergent plant."

"That is great news" Dan said "if Chris focuses on Guangzhou and I focus on TTSF and on bringing Jenny along, we can speed things up considerably."

"I agree" I said "Let's do it!"

"By the way" I said on my way out of Dan's office "since we are still haggling over price, do not repeat what we discussed to anyone, including Jenny or even the ex-pat managers."

With that, I went back to my office and asked Julie to have James come up and see me. Ten minutes later, James was seated across the desk from me.

I explained to him what I was thinking. I asked him to find out how quickly we can get tallow, coconut oil, perfumes and all the ingredients and packaging materials delivered. We needed to review lead times for suppliers and develop a ramp up plan for materials.

"The locally supplied materials will be easy for us to ramp up quickly" James said "what I would be worried about are the imported materials. The good news is that we have just received big shipments of tallow and coconut oil and the tanks at the port are full. We ordered some extra materials in anticipation of us improving efficiencies at our factory. That will give us a head start, but it is far short of what we would ultimately need. I would also need to know where we will be delivering those materials to."

"I know" I said "I will have that information for you by the end of this week. Would that work?"

"We'll make it work" James said. He is normally very even keeled and thoughtful in what he says and how he says it. Despite that, I could sense his excitement as he left my office saying "I will start working on this right away."

As James was walking out of my office, he almost bumped into Mr. Li who was about to knock on the door. I waved Mr. Li in and invited him to have a seat. I asked Julie to come in to translate for me.

Mr. Li said that, as promised, he has revised numbers for me. He went on to explain that he simply breaks even with his costs at this rate. If he was to cut his price any further, he would lose money which would create a major problem for him.

"I understand" I said "I appreciate all the effort you have put into this."

Mr. Li's new price was $1.40/case and we buy and provide all the ingredients. This is $0.53 cents lower than his first price and compared favorably with some of the best costs that the company had per case globally.

I asked "how quickly can you ramp up production?"

"This afternoon" Mr. Li said to emphasize his eagerness.

"Excellent" I said "tomorrow morning, I will have Dan and Jenny come over to your plant and start working with your quality control people to set up procedures. I will also have James come over to discuss the logistics of getting the raw and packaging materials to your plant. If all goes well, we should be able to ramp up quickly and start production within a week."

"I look forward to working with them" Mr. Li said getting ready to get up and leave.

"One other thing" I said "I will have Mr. Chao, our attorney from Guangzhou, contact you to set up a time to go over the legal contract language. Before we can go too far, we would need TTSF to sign an exclusivity agreement promising not to supply soap to other clients who may be competitors of ours unless you get our written agreement in advance."

"From our previous discussions" Mr. Li said "it sounds like you will use up all of my spare capacity, so this should not be a problem."

"That is correct" I said "and if things change, you will have the ability to ask us to reconsider this requirement."

With that, we stood up, shook hands and said good bye.

I walked over to Dan's office, asked him to walk with me to James's office and updated both on the TTSF agreement. Both said they will be there along with Jenny first thing the next morning to get things started.

Over the next two days, I received packages from all the factories we visited. I went through the same routine with each of them except for Chongqing. I asked Hugo to contact Madam Kong and let her know that we appreciated her time but are not planning to use her factory in the short term. Needless to say, Hugo was happy not to have to deal with Madam Kong, but was a little uneasy about breaking the news to her.

The cost quotes varied widely between the remaining three players and all were higher than TTSF's proposed pricing. As I pushed them to lower their prices, none of them went down to the same level as TTSF, but Guangzhou, our detergent business partner finally conceded a price of $1.85, $0.45 cents higher than TTSF's but between $0.20 and $0.30 lower than the other two. I decided after a lot of push and shove that we have gone as far as we are going to. They are not going to drop their price any lower than what they had given me.

To confirm my conclusions, I called Dick and he confirmed that I should not expect to see much movement if any. His perspective was that Guangzhou had two things that influence its willingness to reduce their pricing any more than they already have.

"The first" he explained "is simply that labor wages are higher in Guangzhou than they are in Tianjin. The second is that they are profitable and have viable brands. Because of that, they would not be willing to do what TTSF has done and sell to us at cost. They don't have the same pressure as TTSF does to do a deal. In short, they will only do a deal if they can make money."

With that, I decided to stop pushing for further concessions and move forward with qualifying them to start production quickly.

I reminded Dick about his offer to have Chris manage quality for us and he confirmed that his offer was still good. I thanked him and told him that I will have Dan contact Chris to start working the details before hanging up the phone.

With Suzhou and Hangzhou, I let them know that I still wanted to work with them, but did not expect to be in a position to use their services for at least a few months. I asked them to keep working on their pricing and asked if they would be willing to sign an agreement with us that requires them to notify us if things change and they decide to do business with one of our competitors. Both agreed to sign an agreement giving us the right of first refusal in return for some money. I agreed and let them know that our attorney, Mr. Chao will contact them and work out the details.

With that, the strategy shift was complete. From this point forward, the strategy was no longer based on how accurately we can project the demand and then use that projection to build capacity. Instead, the strategy now shifted to one that sought "to bring capacity on line in step with market demand".

I gave Drew and Daniel an update and both were very excited.

"You are going to be ready before us" Daniel said "I have marketing going full speed ahead. We should be ready within four to six weeks."

"I am pressing full speed ahead" I said "Anything I can get will be warehoused until you are ready."

In closing, Drew told me that he was glad I was on his team. I was very happy to hear that; but I knew we still have a lot of hard work ahead to pull this off.

19

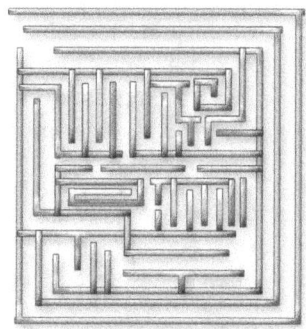

THE EXECUTION PLAN

By Wednesday of the following week, I finally had a few minutes in my office where things were quiet. I reflected on where things stood and concluded that overall, I was pleased with how far things have moved in the past couple of months. I have the agreements with TTSF and Guangzhou in place; both were ramping up to start production.

James worked quickly with suppliers and diverted supplies that were destined to our factory to TTSF and Guangzhou. He was also able to accelerate other orders and place new ones with the net effect that TTSF will be making its first production this afternoon while Guangzhou will be on line next week.

Dan and Jenny were comfortable with the Quality Control procedures and felt that between them being close to TTSF and Chris overseeing Guangzhou, we should be in good shape. Joe agreed when we updated him yesterday afternoon. Jon arrived yesterday from the US and so far has not raised any major concerns about the systems, procedures or the safeguards we are putting in place.

I was feeling good about the work going on at the other factories and was hopeful that nothing was missed. I had faith in Dan, Jon and Chris' skills and capabilities. Jenny was stepping up and I was feeling very good about how quickly she is coming along. Even Jon took some time to tell me he was impressed with her work.

Moments of reflection are nice, I thought to myself, but before I allowed myself to get too comfortable and declare victory, I had to remind myself that I still have a $50 million dollar expansion in progress and I need to build a world class organization that will be making soap for China for decades to come.

Ah, yes, I thought, details, details .... I guess I had to come back to reality and my reality is that I have a management team that consists of four experienced ex-pats who, like me, will only be around for the next one to three years. The primary focus needs to be on getting the 30 inexperienced local managers who currently have no clue how to run a business and make independent decisions ready to take over the reigns. From where I am sitting at this moment, the job ahead seems daunting.

This is a whole new experience for me. Ever since I joined the company 18 years ago, I have always managed people, who for the most part were experienced professionals, running their piece of the business.

After allowing myself to go from a high "high" to a low "low". I decided to allow myself to feel a little discouraged for about 30 seconds, but now it was time for me to snap out of it and start to map out how I planned to teach those kids how to run a world class business. It was time to detail our plans for building our capacity for the short and long term including bringing additional capacity on line in step with market demand.

As I was deep in thought, I could see Tom and Ian's faces back in Cincinnati. Two years ago I was leading a training session for my peers about strategy development and deployment, the systems and processes that can be used to bring strategies to life and how to successfully deploy and execute those strategies.

At that time, I had a feeling from the comments and questions being asked by Tom and Ian, the Sales and Marketing managers, that they did not quite buy the company's approach. I remembered inviting both for a drink after the session and as they loosened up, I asked what they thought about the new approach. Tom told me he thought that all this strategy "stuff" is fine, but he felt it was "too process". In short, while he did not say it in so many words … he basically thought it was for other people and not him and his people.

I remember thinking that, unfortunately for the business, unless Tom sees the value inherent in strategically running his part of the business, his people will not see it either. As his peer, I knew that I can only try to help Tom see the value of applying this methodology and the use of a disciplined approach, but could not make him believe in its value. What I wanted was for him to believe with a passion, but knew that I most likely will get an organization that will go through the motions. Sadly, the business will pay the price of lost opportunity as Tom and his team fall short of their potential as the company pushes towards more discipline in execution.

I went to my filing cabinet and pulled out my notes from that session and started to read what I had put down.

<u>CONTENTS OF A GOOD STRATEGY</u>:

A good strategy is a conscious set of choices that define how you and your team intend to beat competition, on a sustainable basis, in meeting customer or consumer needs.

Key components include:-

<u>A CLEAR VISION</u>: A statement of where you see your business 5 – 10 years from now. Examples include - market share, geographies, volumes, profitability.

<u>KEY ELEMENTS FOR SUCCESS</u>: A statement of what can <u>truly</u> drive winning in the marketplace. Examples of key elements include – superior consumer/customer service, quality, value, speed to market, and marketing considerations.

<u>CONSUMER/CUSTOMER NEEDS</u>: Recap basic consumer/customer needs your products aims to fulfill. Focus on identifying poorly met or overlooked needs.

<u>COMPETITIVE REALITIES</u>: A statement of what we and our major competitors bring to the marketplace.

<u>GENERAL STRATEGY</u>: A statement of the <u>broad</u> choices you are making. Generally, broad choices include areas such as the ability to leverage, build on or exploit any and all competitive advantages the company has to fulfill unmet customer/consumer needs. This includes such disciplines as manufacturing, supply chain, R&D, technology, branding, partnerships with vendors and customers, ability to leverage size or exploit innovations on a global scale.

<u>SPECIFIC STRATEGIC CHOICES</u>: This is where leadership must start to make specific choices about what to do, and, just as important, what <u>not</u> to do to gain sustainable advantage in meeting customer and consumer needs.

<u>ISSUES</u>: A statement of the basic risks built into the strategy and how those will be managed.

<u>COMPONENTS OF STRATEGY DEPLOYMENT</u>.

<u>LONG TERM DIRECTION</u>: Defines why the company or division exists and where the business is headed. Simply put -- you can't get there if you don't know where you are going.

<u>DEVELOP STRATEGY</u>: Develop the strategy making sure that the key components of a good strategy are addressed and then translate them into Objectives, Goals, Strategies and Measures (OGSM's).

Definitions:

Objectives and Goals describe "what" you want to achieve in words and numbers.

Objectives: Describe what you are trying to achieve (1 choice). Use simple words that people can easily understand.

Goals: Describe how you will measure progress toward achieving objectives. Use numbers.

Strategies and Measures describe "how" the Objectives and Goals will be achieved.

Strategies: Use words to describe how you will achieve your Objectives and Goals.

Measures: Use numbers to describe how you will measure progress toward achieving the Strategies.

DEPLOY STRATEGY: Define individuals and groups responsible for delivering the Strategies/Measures and develop the next level of detail defined as Action Plans/Action Targets/Accountability for execution.

Deployment links individuals and groups to the Company's strategy. It helps people understand their role in delivering the company's strategy and, ultimately, their personal contribution to the company's success.

CAPABILITY/REALITY CHECK: Confirm that the Action Plans, if executed as planned, are sufficient to deliver the Strategies and Measures. Also confirm that the organization is capable of delivering the plans.

DO THE PLANS: Execute Action Plans and track progress.

REVIEW & ADJUST: This is where the Strategy comes to life and becomes action, accountability is established and people learn.

MONTHLY REVIEWS: Action teams check their progress vs. targets. Where there are gaps (both positive and negative), they are analyzed and adjustments made to get back on track if target is missed. If targets are exceeded, the gaps are analyzed and used as a learning event to help accelerate progress in other areas or rebalance and reallocate resources.

QUARTERLY REVIEWS: Action Teams review progress with Management exposing them to what is working, what else is needed, what was learned and how the team plans to maintain improvements. This is the time to ask for additional help and resources as part of gap analysis and plan adjustments to stay on track.

Reviews are the "heart" of the system. Done right, reviews create focus, commitment and a learning environment. Done wrong, they create lack of focus, compliance and a fear environment. Managers need to be active partners in making sure the team gets the support it needs to stay on track and in nurturing a learning environment.

When I finished reviewing my notes, I decided to use what I had as is. I concluded that it was not necessary to modify the contents to adapt them to the Chinese culture. While I have only been in China for about two months now, I felt that I had enough of a feel for the culture to know that this methodology transcends cultures. Besides, I thought, since I am about to teach my new team about strategy development and deployment, it was appropriate to start from the beginning. All of a sudden it dawned on me that in this case, their inexperience should be a big positive. In all of my previous assignments, both my peers and subordinates alike felt that they already knew how to get things done and there was a constant need to sell them on using the tools.

As I reflected on the big difference between the two situations, I remembered what Mindy, an Organizational Development expert, had told me at one point. She had explained that the organization will go through four stages.

The "Compliance" stage (1-3 months) – My boss wants me to do this. I'll do it, it's just another program; if I wait and keep a low profile….this too shall pass.

The "You've got to be kidding" stage (3-12 months) – Too much discipline, what happened to creativity, too much paper….when can I get back to real work?

The "It Works….results are improving" stage (12-18 months) – Individuals and teams are empowered and clear about what to do. Leaders are in the system, supporting, learning, creating focus, alignment and execution….changing the way we do work, not trying harder.

The Approach becomes a System that is part of the corporate culture (5 years) - Focus, alignment and rapid execution… this is just the way we do things around here.

I hoped that, in this instance, I can move the organization a lot faster through the various stages. I did not have that much time to bring people along and build the culture. The fact that I can go straight into teaching people how to get things done using this system should be a great help. I do not have to deprogram people from using their methods since they were all new and eager to learn. I started to get excited about the prospect.

The phone rang. I picked up and it was Nancy. She wanted to confirm that I remembered about our dancing lessons tonight. She had gone ahead and signed us up to take ballroom dancing and she was looking forward to our first lesson. I told her I remembered, but I was still glad she called to remind me. I could have easily lost track of time and missed our first lesson.

After I hung up, I walked over to Julie's desk next door asking "is the next all management meeting scheduled as usual this week?"

"Yes" she said "the same time."

"Good" I said "can you extend the time to three hours?"

"No problem" she said "I will notify everyone."

"Good" I said handing her my notes "can you type these and have them ready to distribute at the meeting?"

She looked at the notes and said "I will take care of it. I am working on some reports that are due to BOLI this week. If it looks like I need some help, I will ask Betty, Lou's assistant, to help me."

"Excellent" I said "thank you."

The next day, at the all management meeting, I taught the team about the development and deployment of strategies and formed a team to help lead the development of the strategy for the Joint Venture.

In a nut shell, everyone was in agreement that we had to find ways to reduce our cost by a big margin. I recapped the basics from our previous meeting where we discussed the costs in detail versus what the marketplace would allow us to charge.

Cindy raised her hand and asked "what should our target cost be if we wanted to make sure that Tianjin is successful and will be an important player in the Company's future?"

I was impressed. I felt she had cut straight to the heart of the matter.

"Excellent question" I said "the best cost we have right now is about $13.85/case out of our Cincinnati plant. Keep in mind that the plant has the most modern equipment and the most efficient layout of any of our plants. It also produces a large volume."

"So if we can get our cost down to $13.85/case we will be doing well" Tammy jumped in.

"That would be a good start" I said "however; I think that Tianjin needs to be lower than that."

Many looked at me somewhat puzzled, so I continued "here is my logic. If you look at the cost I gave you. That includes the price of shipping from Cincinnati to California. The way I see it is this, if we are able to get our price down such that we can make a case of soap here and then ship it to California for less than the company can deliver it from Cincinnati; then I think we would be doing very well."

I turned to James and asked "do you know how much it costs to ship from here to California?"

"We recently looked at the cost of shipping soap from the US to help fill our short term needs" James replied "the quote we had was for $2/case. I think we can get a little lower price if we decide to ship in large quantities."

"If we do the math" I said "I come up with $11.85/case as our target to break even with Cincinnati."

I wrote the number on the board and waited a minute to let the number sink in.

"I now have to ask you" I continued "is breaking even with Cincinnati good enough?"

Everyone was looking intensely at me, and then Cindy jumped in and said "no, because if our cost is the same, why would they buy from us?"

"Although it is not our objective to establish ourselves as a supplier for the US market, the only way we can be sure that we are in the lead and have a place in the company's long term plans is to be better than everyone else" I said "Cindy is right, if we were to ship to the US, then they have to deal with shipping schedules from China, inability to make quick changes to plans, the need to clear product through customs, etc. In order to make ourselves competitive, we have to offer the same quality for a lower price.

For now, let's say if we are able to produce a case of soap for $10.85 and then add the $2/case shipping, we will offer a $1/case advantage. This should be ok for now, although we have to keep in mind that Cincinnati and all the other plants are not standing still. They also continuously work to find ways to reduce their cost and increase their efficiencies"

With that, the $10.85 price target was born and it became a key driver in developing focus and the plant's new Strategy.

Over the next few weeks, the leadership team completed the development of the Plant Strategy. The Objectives, Goals, Strategies and Measures were all developed. Next those were deployed to the various teams who, in turn, developed their Action Plans and Targets and within 6 weeks, we had started the monthly reviews. A very pleasant surprise was that I never needed to do much selling. As I had anticipated, I did not need to deprogram old habits and beliefs before we could move forward. People were ready and eager to move towards their goal over the next 2 years.

When I left Tianjin about three years later to return to the US for my next assignment, the cost was $12.55/case and everyone was working diligently to achieve the $10.85 target.

I returned to visit Tianjin 18 months later while on a business trip to Asia and Frank, the new Plant Manager walked me proudly to a board that displayed key measures and results and showed me the cost and the other key results that they had continued to track. Frank proudly announced that the plant has now achieved a cost of $11.35/case and they only had 50 cents to go. I remember being choked and full of pride. This made all the long hours and hardship that my family and I had to endure during our three year assignment in Tianjin worthwhile.

20

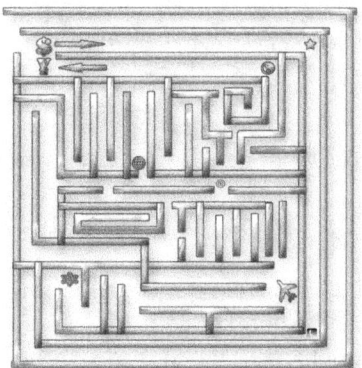

MR. CHEN'S DISAPPEARANCE AND OTHER LESSONS ABOUT RELATIONSHIPS IN CHINA

The phone rang. It was Drew on the line. He was meeting with Daniel and they were reviewing the launch results. They wanted to let me know that they were pleased with the progress we made in getting production up and running.

"Thank you" I said "I am very pleased too. I am afraid to claim victory for fear of jinxing things. I keep thinking that, with so many moving parts, I could be calling you with bad news at any time."

"Wrong attitude" Drew said "take your wins whenever you can. If something goes wrong, we will deal with it at that time."

"Good point and thank you for the reminder" I said "how is the roll out of the new TV advertisements going? Are we getting a good response?"

"Better than expected" he said "Daniel was just showing me the numbers and we are ahead of target. As a matter of fact, one of the reasons for this call is to ask you if you are able to give us more if this trend persists?"

"I can ramp up Suzhou and Hangzhou quickly" I said "the plan was to bring one plant on line at a time so that we can manage risk. Once we commit to one, we will have to give them enough volume before we can ramp up the next one."

"I understand" Daniel said "Don't do anything yet. We will let you know as things develop"

"Just in case we need to move fast" Drew asked "how quickly can you react?"

"I can squeeze a little more out of TTSF and Guangzhou" I said "but as far as the other two; I can have some production within a month to six weeks once I get the go ahead from you or Daniel."

"Fair enough" Drew said "stay tuned. By the way, have you talked to Mr. Chen lately?"

"No, not directly" I said "I had been leaving him messages for the past two or three weeks to call me back, but he is not returning my calls."

"Very strange" Drew said "I can always get through to him or he returns my calls usually right away."

"The same with me" I said "he always picked up my calls or returned them very quickly. I wanted to let him know that TTSF is doing a good job for us and make a point to emphasize that we came through for him. But it has been frustrating to be ignored by him."

There was a moment of silence before Drew said "let's both keep trying and if you hear from him, let me know and I will do the same."

I said "will do" and we hung up.

I walked over to Julie's desk and asked her to try calling Mr. Chen for me. She came in a few minutes later and told me she left a message. He was not available.

I continued to try for the next four weeks, but was unable to connect with Mr. Chen.

I was feeling frustrated when Julie came in to tell me that she had left yet another message for Mr. Chen to call me back when Andrew, from HR, came in for his weekly meeting with me.

"Andrew" I asked "do you know Mr. Chen?"

"Yes, of course" Andrew said "I don't know him personally except for the time he was visiting our plant, he said hi to me. But everyone in Tianjin knows who he is. He is a very important man."

"I am a little disturbed" I said "for the past two months, I have been trying to call Mr. Chen, but he does not return my calls. His office only takes messages but no one returns my calls. Do you know what is going on?"

"Do you want to take a walk to the production floor?" Andrew asked.

I was puzzled. It hardly seemed like an appropriate answer to my question, but I decided to go with it.

"Yes" I said "let's go."

We walked down the stairs and out of the building in silence. As we were out of earshot, I asked "what is going on Andrew?"

"I am not comfortable telling you this, but please keep it confidential between us" he said.

"No problem" I said "what is it?"

"Well" he said "it's like this. Mr. Chen was caught accepting a bribe from a foreign company. As a result, he is in jail now and that is why he is not returning your calls."

That hit me like a ton of bricks. Mr. Chen and I had started to develop a friendship and this news made me feel sick to my stomach. I knew that the penalty for a communist party official accepting a bribe was punishable by death. We had heard rumors that there are weekly executions in Tianjin. From what we had heard, those executions are made in public at a local stadium. The way it worked is that the families of those executed have to watch and they even have to pay for the bullet. While we did not know if this is true, I suspected that in any case, the punishment would be quite severe by Western standards.

I finally pulled myself together and turned to Andrew "so, Mr. Chen will be executed?"

Andrew hesitated for a few seconds and then said "not necessarily, it depends."

With all the emotions I was dealing with, I was getting angry and I snapped at Andrew "what do you mean by 'not necessarily and it depends'? Isn't the penalty for a communist party official accepting a bribe a death sentence?"

Andrew said clearly a little intimidated by my reaction and somewhat torn by wanting to explain things but also dealing with the fear of not knowing if he was being a bad Chinese by sharing such information with me.

Finally he said "Yes, it is" and was looking even more uncomfortable than he was before, so I needed to back off and let Andrew know that this confidential conversation was safe with me. I needed to control my emotions.

"Please forgive me for the way I spoke to you a second ago" I said "the news was very unsettling to me, but now I am fine." I continued "I hope you can appreciate that this is very different from the West, so I need to develop my understanding of how things work in China. What I don't understand is the vagueness of 'it depends'. To me, bribery is either punishable by death or it is not, so please explain to me what you mean?"

"You see" Andrew said "in China, the laws are not as black and white as you might think. They are applied with varying degrees of severity depending on the circumstances, who is involved and how much 'guan xi' those involved have with other important people. In other words, it depends on how strong their relationships are."

I gave Andrew an inquisitive look.

"The whole thing depends on who Mr. Chen knows and who his real friends are. If he has very strong relationships with powerful friends who want to save him, then he will be saved" he said.

"And if he doesn't have powerful friends who want to save him?" I asked afraid of what the answer might be.

"In that case" Andrew said eying me with concern "there is no other way to say it, Mr. Chen will be executed."

I was silent for a minute. This was too big a lesson for me about the meaning of what relationships mean in China. I had to let this sink in.

"So" I said to Andrew "what you are telling me is this. Whether, Mr. Chen lives or dies depends on the strength of his relationships?"

"Yes" Andrew said.

We both went back to my office and I decided to wait for some time to pass between my meeting with Andrew and the time I call Drew to inform him. I had promised Andrew to keep our conversation confidential.

I called Drew that evening and was vague about my source. He was equally stunned, but was clear that I need to drop this topic and wait to see what BOLI decides to do about informing us.

Two days later, I received a call from Madam Shen. After some small talk, she informed me that Mr. Chen will be away for some time and that she has been assigned to the position of Chairwoman of the Board of Directors of the JV.

Madam Shen and I became good friends over the next two and a half years. However; we never discussed Mr. Chen again after that telephone call.

I came to find out about two years later that Mr. Chen was still alive. He had just been released from jail and was living in his own home but was under house arrest. I was told that he had asked about me and sent me his regards. I was happy to hear that he was alive and thankful that he had powerful friends that wanted to save him. While I agree that he had done something wrong, I clearly felt the punishment, had it been implemented as it might have been for someone without strong relationships, far outweighed the crime. I inquired discreetly if I will have a chance to see him again, especially after it was announced that I will be returning to the US within two months. I was told no. The only thing I could do was to send him my best wishes and a goodbye before I left China.

Mr. Chen's story took my level of understanding of what relationships mean in the Chinese culture to a whole new level. I have to admit that up to that point, I understood intellectually what relationships meant in China. After all, you can hardly read a book about China without the author mentioning the importance of relationships in the Chinese culture. However; after what happened with Mr. Chen, I came to realize that my understanding was shallow. Relationships can easily turn into a lifeline as we had seen in this case.

I have two other stories that I wish to share with you about relationships (guan xi).

The first was when Toni, one of the Transportation Managers came to review his plans to award a trucking contract for moving raw material shipments from the port of Tianjin to the plant.

Toni walked me through the three bids that he received and concluded by telling me that he had chosen to give the business to the third company. I was pleased with the work he had done and commended him on a good job. That appeared to prompt him to talk some more. In the course of the conversation, I came to find out that the company he was planning to award the business to was nothing more than his cousin who owns a single truck that he planned to run between the port of Tianjin and our Plant. I also found out that his cousin's initial price was not as low as the other two, but Toni announced proudly that he was able to put pressure on him to bring his price below that of the other two competitors.

Naturally, I was horrified to hear those details. I sat Toni down and explained to him that we don't award business to our cousins in this company. I explained the company's policy regarding the bidding process, about conflict of interest and about doing business with relatives. I could see that Toni was very confused and it was clear that he was not quite getting what I was trying to tell him. I finally decided that since Toni worked for James, I will talk this over with James. James will understand what I am talking about and help Toni understand the rules and guidelines. I wrapped up my conversation with Toni by asking him not to award the business until James and I have a chance to discuss it further.

Ten minutes later, James was knocking at my office door. I waved him in.

James explained to me that Toni went to see him as soon as he left my office and was worried because I had said I wanted to talk to James.

I explained to James what I had found out. James's face showed some concern. He explained to me that he did not know that background. It was never mentioned when Toni walked him through the numbers. In fact, based on his review with Toni, James felt that Toni had done a good enough job that he felt comfortable sending him by himself to walk me through his recommendations.

"I understand how this is inconsistent with company policy" James said.

"I know" I said "but I could see that Toni was completely confused by my comments when I walked him through the policy about awarding business and doing business with relatives. Frankly, I was puzzled by his confusion. I know that you had people from the purchasing department train your people about the company's policy and yet, he felt he was doing everything above board."

James was quiet for a second and then he said "the problem is that the company's policy in this area is counter intuitive for anyone raised in our culture."

I looked at James inquisitively and said "I don't quite understand. Can you explain please?"

"In China" James said "people think that doing business with friends and relatives is a good thing. A smart thing to do."

The puzzled look on my face must have prompted James to continue.

"You see. In Toni's example, he was able to get a better price by leaning on his cousin. So in his mind, he has done a good thing for the company."

"I understand the logic" I said "but in reality, I can argue that if we had called any of the other vendors and shared with them their competition's prices, I guarantee you that in 99% of the cases, we will get a lower counter offer. This is exactly what the company tries to avoid with its policy. Vendors get one chance to win the business. If they miss, they have to wait a whole year before having another shot at it."

"So far" I added "I fail to see the advantage."

"Price is only a piece of this" James continued "the other key piece revolves around relationships (guan xi)."

"Continue" I said with renewed interest "how does 'guan xi' play into this? I hope it doesn't involve Toni getting something out of this!"

"That is not what I was referring to. 'Guan xi' gets into this in the form of Toni being able to demand that his cousin provide excellent service to us" James continued "as an example, if there was a problem with a shipment,

Toni can go to his cousin's house, get him out of bed at three in the morning and make him fix the problem. That kind of reasoning applies across the board. As long as his cousin has our business, he will be indebted to Toni for helping him get it and will work very hard to make sure that Toni never loses face with us and the company. He simply can't do that or get that type of leverage with a stranger."

"I think I understand the logic a little better" I said "I still have to say that while I understand that what Toni has done makes sense in the Chinese culture, I cannot support it given how clear our company guidelines are on this topic."

"I understand your position" James said "it took me a while to understand how things worked in Dallas when I was there. What would you like me to do?"

I think that given where we are now, we can meet the spirit of our company's policy by giving the other two vendors a second chance to bid on our business. If one of them comes in lower than his cousin, then we have to grant the business to them, otherwise, I would be fine with granting the business to his cousin. However; for future business, all potential vendors get one chance to bid on our business per cycle and may the vendors who offer us the best value win."

"Consider it done" James said "I will explain to Toni what we had agreed upon and I will take the team through a training refresher on the company's policies."

"Thank you James" I said as we wrapped up our conversation.

The final story I wish to share about the importance of 'guan xi' in the Chinese culture is about the relationship I developed with the Mayor of Tianjin.

As you might imagine, a Mayor of a city with 11 million residents is a very busy man. Tianjin is at least the size of New York City. My first exposure to the Mayor was at the meeting I talked about earlier in this book. During that meeting, the Mayor was looking to get feedback from the General Managers of all the foreign Joint Ventures in Tianjin. As you might recall, I was the only GM that said positive things about Tianjin and who took time to express concerns in a positive way. As it turned out, I was behaving in a way that was building 'guan xi' with the Mayor without even recognizing it for what it turned out to be.

The next morning following this meeting, I had an army of employees from the various bureaus descend upon our plant. They all wanted to know one thing. What can they do to help us?

This was clearly an unexpected surprise and I was quick to accompany them from one department to the next. I made a point to start with the Engineering team. They talked about permitting and got into the specifics of what was needed. I then took them to the logistics department where they discussed delays in clearing our raw materials through customs, and so the morning went.

While the specifics are not important, what essentially was going on was that the Mayor felt that I did him a favor at the meeting by being positive and trying to turn some of the negativity that was taking hold of the participants around. In return, by sending me the army of people from the various bureaus to help us work through their bureaucracy, he was showing his gratitude and reciprocating the favor.

But things did not end there. We quickly noticed that after that meeting, we stopped losing electrical power. Sometimes, when I looked out of my office window, I would see dark offices at other companies that were across the street from us. Sometimes, I would hear from other ex-pats how they lost electricity that week. In contrast, my plant kept running with full power. I did not ask questions, but knew that the Mayor had something to do with it.

In return, without saying it, the Mayor would call me every so often and ask if I would be kind enough to host representatives from US or European companies that are considering setting up Joint Ventures in Tianjin. I would gladly accept.

I made it a point to provide my guests with honest feedback and information about Tianjin and what it's like to do business there. I did not over sell nor trash it. I shared information truthfully and provided both the positives and negatives as I saw them. Some companies chose to set up operations in Tianjin while others did not.

In one particular case, I counseled a company not to set up a JV in Tianjin or anywhere else in China. The basis of that recommendation was based on the fact that the company had proprietary technology that they guarded so tightly that they chose not to even apply for patents for fear of competitors being able to figure out the technology by studying patent applications. After hearing that, I suggested they stay away unless they are willing to risk losing their tight grip on their technology. They listened and stayed out of China.

My relationship with the Mayor was one of convenience and it worked for both of us. We had mutual respect for each other and trusted that the other will be fair and help when they can.

While relationships are important in all cultures, 'Guan xi' in the Chinese culture is like the lubricant that greases all the day to day interactions and touches people's lives in everything they do. It would not be an exaggeration to say that it is always present in the back of people's minds and is part of all interactions.

A final thought for anyone doing business in China and has local Chinese people working for him or her. Be thoughtful in how you approach your Chinese subordinates. Keep in mind that if you ask them to do things that can create ill will with their local contacts, then you are asking them to do things that could hurt them in the long run. By definition, if they do what you want them to do and that creates ill will, they will likely pay a price for it in the future.

If you get frustrated when you feel that your people are stalling or not doing what you need to be done, that will likely mean one of two things.

First, it could mean very simply that they don't understand what you want them to do but are not comfortable asking you for more explanations for fear of appearing ignorant. Alternatively, it could mean that they understand what you need done, but are clueless about how to go about doing it. In those types of situations, the solution is simple …. take the time upfront to explain to them clearly what it is that you want and follow that up with enough questions to satisfy yourself that they know what needs to be done and how to do it.

The second likely reason people may stall is that they may feel that in order to accomplish what you want done, they would have to push government bureaucrats into doing things they don't want to do. Something most Chinese would find intimidating and would be most uncomfortable doing. The reason they would be uncomfortable is that they could be viewed very negatively if they are seen as taking the side of a foreigner versus their own government or people. Remember that, long after you are gone, they will still be there and they will have to deal with those same people. So, if they recklessly ruin their relationships with the local bureaus to satisfy a short term relationship, they would be setting themselves up for long term problems.

My advice is to be mindful of what you ask them to do. Some things, you should lean on your JV partners to do if you have them or do it yourself. But regardless of the approach you decide to take, be sure to take the time to find a win-win approach to getting what you need. You will get more accomplished by investing time to figure out who the key players are and building relationships with them. Just as important as getting things done, by doing this, you will also avoid hurting those who are most loyal to you because they would be the ones who are most likely to do things that can end up hurting their relationships locally.

Always try to find a way to build your own relationships and allow your people to maintain their relationships while moving your business ahead.

If you look hard enough and invest your time, you will always find a win-win approach that allows you to build 'guan xi' with locals and, when you do, things will happen a lot faster.

21

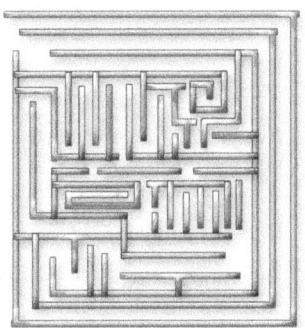

COUNTERFEITING .... WHAT I LEARNED

After our successful launch across China, we started to gain market share at a very fast pace. People loved our products and we were getting hundreds of testimonials from consumers across the country. I started to have Julie translate them for me and occasionally, I would talk about the testimonials during my meetings with the management team. I also would talk about them with the various bureau representatives and our partners with pride since they were almost always very positive and complimentary.

After about six months, something strange started to happen. I saw a shift in the tone and quality of the letters coming in from consumers. More and more of them were complaining about the drop in our quality and about problems they were having including some complaining about rashes, etc. I was very disturbed about this shift and set up a team to review our quality control systems and go over our quality and production records as well as the letters. I asked them to meet weekly and directed them to investigate each and every negative comment that came to us and report back to me during a regular weekly meeting that I had Julie set up. We had to figure out what was happening.

Our records and retained samples confirmed that our quality control and production were being executed exactly by the book. After a lot of discussion, we concluded that the problem was happening outside our plant. After investigating our sub-contractors, the team confirmed that all of them were religiously following procedures and tests run on the retained samples confirmed the same.

To further confirm our findings, we were asking consumers to return the soap they were unhappy with and we would both pay for their postage and give them a present of a basket of our various products to try to salvage their trust in our quality and products.

Those samples tested different than our regular product pointing to counterfeit product. It was clear from those samples that they were missing one of the most expensive ingredients used in our formula. Specifically, the anti-bacterial additive was missing. Lab analysis also told us that inferior oils and pig fat (an ingredient we don't use) were being used; however, the packaging and perfumes were exact duplicates of our own, making it impossible for us to know which was the real product and which was the counterfeit unless we tested the samples in our labs.

I worked with corporate security and we hired a group of people to find out where the counterfeit soap was made.

Within a month, our people identified 5 different small factories that were producing counterfeit soap in various parts of the country and we were able to establish a connection between the locations of those factories and the origin of many of the complaints we were receiving. We tried to work with the local governments to shut down those factories but were not getting much cooperation. After several attempts, we decided to contact people in the Bureau of Light Industry in Beijing that had considerable influence across the country.

With their help, the local governments raided those factories and confiscated their equipment. We were pleased to have stopped the production of counterfeit soap; however, after a couple of months, the letters of complaint resumed. Again, they were concentrated in the same areas as before.

Again, we had our people investigate. Interestingly, we found that there were new factories producing the counterfeit soap. Ironically, they were located in or very near the towns where we found the original factories.

We went through the same procedure as before. Again, the factories were raided by the local authorities and their equipment was again confiscated.

Just around the time we were thinking we may have closed this chapter on counterfeit soap, the letters started to come in again. After doing some research and trying to understand what we were dealing with, things were becoming clearer. The sequence we were going through went something like this.

Keeping in mind that local governments collect tax revenue from factories that are located within their jurisdiction. Those factories also provide employment for local people and when you think about 'guan xi', the people who own and run them very likely are very closely connected to powerful people in their local government.

On the other hand, here we were, a foreign JV that is paying taxes and employing people in another municipality. We come in and demand that they shut their factories down. If they did what we asked of them, they will put friends and relatives out of work not to mention the lost tax revenue for the local government. Net, there is nothing in it for them, and hence their unwillingness to cooperate with us when we first went in and asked them to shut those factories down. If you couple that with the fact that culturally, the Chinese don't have a well-developed system for governing intellectual property and until we showed up at their doors, they did not see anything wrong with copying a product that they think is good ... as a matter of fact, culturally they believe that imitation is the highest form of flattery ... that the biggest compliment that can be given is to copy or emulate something or someone. To the average Chinese, the concept of intellectual property is confusing.

So here is what was really happening. By getting Beijing and the national authorities involved, we forced the hand of the local authorities. In turn, that led to the crackdown and confiscation of the equipment. When that finally happened, we felt accomplished and went home to celebrate what we thought was our victory. In reality and more than likely, while we were still at the pub celebrating our accomplishment, the local government was selling the confiscated equipment at auction to the highest bidder. Chances were that the old owners simply turned around and set up shop in another location in the area using the same equipment.

Life was good again and everyone was happy ... well, that is everyone except the people who own the brand or intellectual property and, of course, their happiness only lasted until we discovered that they were back in business and put pressure to shut them down again.

Armed with that understanding, I sent our purchasing people to the next auction and we bought the equipment which we subsequently arranged to have destroyed. Destroying it was the only 'bullet proof' option since it guaranteed that it will not be bought back by the same people or others for very little money and be set up once again to make counterfeit product. To be absolutely sure that the people who are hired to destroy the equipment do not themselves turn around a resell it after collecting their fees from us, we had our people present while the equipment was destroyed and rendered completely unrecoverable.

While that did not get the problem to go away completely, it considerably slowed it down since new equipment was more expensive and had a wait time while it was being manufactured and delivered. Unfortunately, after a while, our objectives became more modest. Our hope was that by staying diligent and persisting in our approach to find the counterfeiters, shut them down and ensure that their equipment is destroyed after we purchase it, we will make counterfeiting our brands less attractive than the possibility of pursuing other more legitimate businesses. Sadly, we were never able to completely stop the counterfeiters; however, we were able to keep them in check which kept the amount of counterfeit soap in distribution relatively small. In some ways, we were victims of our own success. Our brand had become the most popular in China with the largest market share and, therefore, the most desirable and lucrative to counterfeiters.

A particularly troubling problem surfaced at one point when we received a letter of complaint. In the course of our investigation, we discovered that the counterfeit product was actually purchased from a reputable department store that was a very good customer of ours. We were able to trace the soap all the way to a completely legitimate shipment with our own bills and the proper paper trail. On the surface, everything looked completely legitimate with the soap coming from one of our own factories; however, there was only one problem. The soap was counterfeit. Our own retained samples from that shipment met our product specifications and appeared to be legitimate yet the product at the store was counterfeit. Again, this was puzzling and nothing appeared to add up.

After a lot of poking around, we eventually decided to have our next shipment to this client from the same factory followed. Here is what we found out. The truck arrived at the factory as scheduled. The driver picked up the load with all the proper paperwork. He left for the customer's warehouse. Everything looked normal until the driver made an unscheduled stop at a warehouse located a few miles from the client's warehouse. The legitimate soap was unloaded and replaced with identical boxes of counterfeit soap. The driver then continued his journey and delivered the counterfeit soap along with all the legitimate paperwork to the client. The motivation to do this is simple. Authentic soap fetches a higher price from shopkeepers than does counterfeit soap.

Counterfeiting is a major problem in China. As intimated above, the country still has not figured out how to deal with it and frankly, it is not a high priority. The problem is only complicated by the fact that, for the most part, culturally, the Chinese don't believe they are doing something wrong by counterfeiting. As a general rule, people genuinely believe that it is ridiculous to pay a premium for a name brand if you can get a knockoff for a fraction of the price. As an example, the average person would brag about what a good deal they might have gotten from a street vendor when they buy say a Ralph

Lauren Polo shirt pointing out that you can't tell the difference between the counterfeit and an original one.

Suffice it to say that when one adds up the local interests and benefits that can be derived by local governments, the personal relationships at stake, the money to be made by copying successful products and the cultural belief that there is nothing wrong with counterfeiting and you have a practically insurmountable problem. Add to that the fact that even if the central government in Beijing wanted to crackdown on this problem, it has huge obstacles to overcome in dealing with thousands upon thousands of local government officials. The same people they have 'guan xi' with and, in the normal course of business, have to count on to keep the masses employed and local economies going.

While there are ongoing efforts to rein this problem in, given that their view of intellectual property is very different from ours, I would not count on this problem to be resolved any time soon.

If you are planning to do business in China, you would be wise to both expect and plan for how you would want to deal with counterfeit product.

22

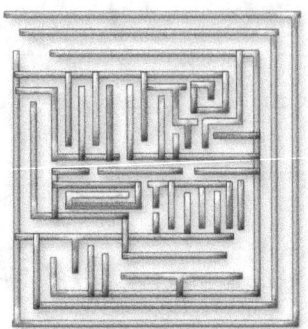

MANAGERS DEVELOPING INTO LEADERS

After about six months, it was becoming obvious that things were different at the plant. The supply situation was stable. The plants I had contracted out were doing well and have learned to adhere to our company's strict guidelines. Joe had visited Tianjin and toured the plants we contracted and was satisfied that we had everything under control.

Best of all, our primary competitor was scrambling. As it turned out, they had been "sleeping on the job". They were taken by complete surprise when we rolled out our soap across China. They had been working on the assumption that they had between eighteen months and two years before we would be ready to supply on a national scale. They had mistakenly assumed that we would not be in a position to supply the market until we finish building and modernizing the Tianjin plant.

When our product became available nationally within two months, they were completely unprepared. Our market share was now in the mid twenties and climbing while theirs was shrinking. Not a bad place to be. While they were trying to figure out how to respond, Drew, Daniel and I were exploring introducing liquid gel products into China. They have been wildly popular in Hong Kong and Taiwan and all indications were that they would do well on the Mainland.

The construction project was progressing well. The building that will house the glycerin refinery was already up and a significant amount of the bracing was already done on the older buildings to make them earthquake ready and prepare them to accept the equipment once it arrives from Italy.

I decided to buy some locally made equipment because it can be delivered fast. I felt the risk was low since it cost $1/10^{th}$ the price I had to pay my Italian suppliers. The continuous soap making unit was operational and it was producing six tons per day. Way below what we needed, but exactly what it was designed to do.

In short, things were coming together nicely and the strategy was working well. People had learned how to use the strategy deployment process. Monthly and quarterly reviews were in place. In fact, the second quarterly review is scheduled for this afternoon. The first quarterly review generated a lot of ideas. Most teams were on track. The few that were not, heard a consistent message from me that they needed to revise their plans to get back on track. Today I will find out how they are all doing against their plans.

This morning, I had a meeting with Ralph, the head of our company's China HR, and Robert, who has responsibility for training and development for the China organization. They both were separately visiting Tianjin and I wanted to take some time to talk to both about management retention planning and development plans. I had asked James and Gaston to tour them through the plant before my meeting with them.

Several of my ex-pat friends, working for other companies, were complaining constantly about being raided for management talent. It appeared that there was a pattern that developed whereby foreign JV's were constantly raiding each other for 'trained' management talent. As soon as a manager is ready to assume broader responsibilities, he or she would be hired away by another JV. There was no shortage of new companies that were setting up shop in town and they all wanted trained and experienced managers. They would pay a significant premium, sometimes doubling and tripling salaries in order to lure them away.

I had not yet lost any significant talent, but knew that my people were coming along very nicely and would make serious targets for other employers. I wanted us to be proactive and put in place preventive measures.

As I was deep in thought, I heard a knock on the door. I waived James, Gaston, Ralph and Robert in.

"How was your tour?" I asked.

"I hardly recognized the place" Ralph said.

"I assume you meant that in a positive way" I said laughing.

"Absolutely, in the most positive way possible" Ralph said.

This was Robert's first visit to Tianjin.

"I am relieved" I said "do either of you have any questions for James or Gaston before they get back to their busy schedules?"

"They did a great job touring us. I think we have already asked all the questions we have for now" Robert said.

"Thank you" I said to Gaston and James "I will see you both this afternoon."

"What did you guys think of James?" I asked as soon as the door was closed.

"Very strong" Ralph said "he is one of our star managers. Gaston is also coming along well. I have known him since he came from France for this assignment. He has grown a lot and should be an asset to the French organization when he goes back."

"I agree with your assessment" I said "which is precisely why I am concerned about developing a solid retention plan for our management team. We have a lot of stars and I want to make sure we only lose the managers we want to lose and keep the rest."

"We all agree on the objective" Ralph said "the thing we have been struggling with is how to provide a long term link between the local managers and the company."

"That is the million dollar question" I said "is there anything we can learn from how we are able to retain managers in the US? I know so many long term employees. Our attrition rate is so low there that I know of very few people who have left the company. Why don't we examine what made the three of us stay with the company for so long. Robert has been with the company the longest, then me and I am assuming you have been with the company the shortest Ralph."

Ralph said he had been with the company fifteen years, Robert said he was on his thirty first year and I was on my nineteenth year.

"The question" I asked "what has kept us with the company for so long? Why are we still here?"

We talked for a while and I decided that we better start to put the key points down. Robert went to the white board and started to write down the key bullets:-

1. Company treated us well and is principled.

2. In every assignment, we always felt that we have someone who cared about us and looked out for our careers – Mentorship.

3. Company offered good benefits. We did not have to be concerned about our family's wellbeing.

4. We were paid well. Our overall compensation package was competitive ... felt just right.

5. We always felt that if we had any concerns we had a way to air them and we would be heard.

6. The company contributed shares of its stock to a profit sharing plan. This meant that if the company continued to do well and its stock price continued to increase, we all do well.

7. Stock ownership was encouraged and, as managers moved up, they were granted stock options. Those typically provided an opportunity to reward good results and more deeply linked us to the company's wellbeing. Another link that aligned our interests with those of the Company. If the company did well, we did well. Otherwise, both the company and employee suffered.

"I think this covers the key ingredients" I said "of course there are also the intangibles. The company picnics and various family events that allowed us to all feel like we belonged."

While the company in the past few years has started to shift away from its paternal heritage, the culture of caring and belonging played a role in keeping us from looking for outside positions. In some ways, I felt, some guilt in considering outside positions when headhunters called.

Ralph said that we already had all of those elements at play with our local managers. There were limitations however that were imposed by local laws. For example, local employees were not allowed to own stock in foreign owned corporations. As such, stock ownership was more limited as a tool. He went on to say that our attorneys were looking for alternatives and that we are looking at granting stock appreciation rights. Those would work the same way as stock options work except, the local managers cannot receive stock at exercise. They can only receive cash equivalent to the growth in the value of the stock between the time of grant and the time of exercise.

"This should work" I said. Are we limiting the grants to managers at third level and above?" I asked

"That would be consistent with how we treat managers across the globe" Ralph offered.

Julie walked in and asked if she should order lunch for us and reminded me that I was scheduled to sit in on the quarterly reviews. I asked her to go ahead and order lunch. After she walked out, I said "I hope you guys don't mind McDonald's food. I prefer it to the mystery meals they serve in the cafeteria."

"McDonald's is fine" Robert said and Ralph nodded his agreement.

Back to our discussion, I said "I think it would be a mistake to adhere to our traditional approach of making grants to managers at level three and above only. Going by those criteria, I will only be able to retain James. All the other managers will be recruited away long before I can promote them. I understand that the company needs to be fair to all of its managers across the globe, but we need to do something to make sure we can retain our local managers, at least until we get to the point where we have multiple levels of local management. I am thinking aggressively and I see it taking at least 5 years."

"I agree" Ralph said "we need to do something for the short term."

"Maybe we can offer Stock Appreciation Rights to all managers. I would say that instead of them vesting in one year, like we do in other countries, we make them vest after five years. We can reassess this plan every year. Once we have filled our management pipeline and people have developed a sense of loyalty to the company, then we can move towards the normal company plans. Over five years, this approach will allow us to get people wanting to stay for at least ten years because the grant they receive five years from now will have a five year vesting period. If we make the offer significant enough, we should be able to retain most managers."

"That sounds like a good plan" Ralph said "we had been thinking about it for all the operations in China. I like your idea of an annual grant which can be reassessed every year. This will help us manage expectations and work through the transition period."

"There is one other area that we should consider" I said "people have grown up with the idea that their employer or the Chinese government would provide them with their housing. As you know, we are tearing down the dormitories to put production facilities in their place. We are giving people a housing allowance which we plan to incorporate into their salaries and they seem to accept this as being fair."

"I know" Ralph said "I am not hearing any negative feedback about it. What are you thinking?" he asked.

"I would like to see us provide interest free home loans to our star managers" I said "possibly loans that do not have to be paid back unless the employee leaves the company. Maybe having a time limit of say 15 years."

"Say more" Ralph said.

"We give them enough money to buy a nice apartment. They don't have to pay us back unless they leave the company. At that time, they will owe the full amount. The caveat would be that if they stay for say fifteen years, the loan would be forgiven and they will owe nothing back."

"That is creative" Robert said.

"It may not stop people from leaving" Ralph said "I am sure a prospective employer who really wants to hire someone can float them the funds to pay us or even buy the loan outright for them.

"I agree" I said "but it may stop them from being tempted to look outside the company in the first place. I believe that it has to be cumulative. When you think about why we stayed with the company for all those years, it would not be one thing, but the collection of things that the company did to retain us that synergistically worked together. The housing loans would give something for the younger managers to look forward to. If we grant say four or five loans per year, people will have something to aspire to and work towards."

"I agree" Ralph said "I will take those ideas up with management and see what I can do."

"Excellent" I said to Ralph and turned to Robert "I know you have only been in China for about two months. What are your thoughts about management development?"

Robert pulled out an outline from his folder and gave me a copy. In it he had a detailed outline. He went on to explain that he was thinking of doing three weeks of intensive training. This would involve key managers as trainers and would be attended by our identified star managers for the first round with subsequent sessions that would allow us to cover all managers in our Chinese operations over a period of 12 months.

"This sounds like an excellent idea" I said "it will give management exposure to the local managers from all the plants and JV's across China."

"It was part of the plan" Robert said "and, if we are to accomplish this much training, we need to have all the leaders involved."

"You can count me in" I said.

"I was counting on you" Robert said "I heard that you had been an instructor in the corporate university program in Cincinnati."

"Guilty as charged" I said "I was also Dean of the company's College One program. Overall, I was deeply involved for two years in a row. It was a lot of fun, but it certainly was very demanding while it lasted. You could say that my family missed me while I tried to do my day job on top of overseeing the program."

"It is a lot of work" Robert said "but we have found it to be the most efficient way to bring a lot of people along and make sure we provide consistent quality training at the same time.   By making sure Senior Management is involved in teaching, we can be sure that the benefits from those programs are maximized."

"Again" I said "you can count on me. Since I have done this before, I can be flexible on topics, although, I have a passion for Strategy Development and Deployment. It gives me a chance to drive home the need for discipline in execution which is the single most critical element for successfully delivering a strategy and is what separates strategies that come alive from strategies that end up being words on paper. "

"Funny you should say that" Robert said "if you look on page 3, you will see that I had your name against that module."

I flipped through the pages and could see that Robert had done a good job lining up the presenters with their areas of expertise. I looked up at Robert and said "I can see that I don't have to worry about you. You have done your homework. Good to see."

Julie walked in with three boxes of pizza that said Pizza Hut on them. I was surprised. I did not even know that there was a Pizza Hut in Tianjin.

"Julie" I said "you are full of surprises today. I did not even know that there was a Pizza Hut in Tianjin."

"Yes, I thought I would surprise you" she said with a big smile "they just had a grand opening ceremony over the weekend. I went and even though I don't like the taste of cheese, I thought it tasted ok. I hope you like it."

"I am sure we will enjoy this" I said "help yourself to some before you leave."

We wrapped up our meeting fifteen minutes later and Robert and Ralph left for the airport.

The quarterly reviews went better than I expected. All the teams had drilled down into the details and had action plans that were meaningful. I was very pleased with how far they had come in the past six months. It was clear that implementing systems in China was easier than implementing systems in the West. People tended to simply do what they were told and implemented plans without trying to change them and put their personal stamp on them.

While I wouldn't have thought so a year ago, now I realize that having people blindly follow orders or directives to the letter can present its own set of challenges when trying to run a business. I reflected back on my first few weeks in China. Whenever, I took a walk through the plant, managers would rush over to escort me through their areas. I would ask a lot of questions hoping to stimulate thought and help them develop by making them think through questions and come to their own conclusions; however, it did not always work well. More often than not, my questions or comments would be interpreted by the local managers as me telling them they needed to do the things I was asking about.

Ironically, instead of stimulating intellectual thought, my conversations resulted in people automatically executing against anything I asked questions about. People thought that if I mentioned it, they needed to do it. I quickly learned the importance of being careful about what I said. I had to make sure I clarified what things I wanted executed right away. Without that distinction, the default was to execute anything I talked about.

I explained my concern on several occasions at my weekly management meetings. People were starting to get the hang of it, although, in some instances, I found that some things that I had intended for people to do right away were not done. As I probed those instances, I found out that after I explained my concern to people a couple of times, some got a little confused and went a little too far the other way.

The key to successfully developing people anywhere is to have clear expectations, thoughtful delegation of responsibilities, a supportive environment that allowed people to seek help when they needed it and finally, a feedback loop or a system that tracked progress and measured results. It always came down to taking the time to communicate clearly. At the end of the day, regardless of where you are, people are people and they all want to do a good job and be recognized for it. Clear expectations and targets make it easier to know when things are going well and when they are not. After all, you get what you measure!

I will close this chapter with a story that happened when Peter, my US boss and mentor came to visit China. He had a very tight schedule and the only time available was during one evening while he was in Beijing. By the time of Peter's visit, it was becoming clear to me which managers had the potential to grow and eventually become senior executives within the Company either within the China organization or outside China.

As part of the process of developing people and getting them ready for promotion, it is usual to give them exposure to senior management and, in turn, give senior management exposure to those individuals. Particularly in a big company, senior management needs to know the people who are being recommended for promotions.

To facilitate this process, I asked James to make arrangements to have both of us and eight other managers travel to Beijing to meet Peter over dinner. I gave James complete freedom to pick the location and make all the necessary arrangements for a private room and dinner.

As we all met, before Peter and I sat next to each other, we went around the table and I introduced Peter to each of the mangers. As we sat down, I asked them to go around the table and tell Peter a little about their background. As they were telling Peter their backgrounds, the waitress came in and took our drink orders.

Peter and I ordered a local beer. The Chinese managers ordered a variety of drinks but bai jiu shots were also served to every one as I have come to accept as typical in Chinese tradition.

As the managers were still giving Peter their backgrounds, a man carrying a live snake that was about six or seven feet long came in. He was holding the snakes head in one hand and the tail in another while the snake moved around his neck and shoulders. He walked around slowly as he ceremonially displayed the live snake to us. I have to admit, I don't know much about snakes, but was certainly uneasy about being this close to a live one. I was trying to stay cool as he passed by me and had the snake's hear only a few inches away from my head.

After he finished displaying the snake, he moved over towards the table on the opposite side and cut the snakes head off and proceeded to drain the blood into a container. I was horrified, but had to appear cool in front of my subordinates. Later on Peter, confessed the same to me.

Next, the snake's blood was poured into shot glasses and each of us was served one.

Peter and I looked at each other. He asked "what is the tradition in those types of situations?"

"This is a first for me" I said "I have to drink it because I have to work with everyone around the table for the next two or three years, but you don't have to, you will be on a plane to Cincinnati in the morning."

Peter said "No, if you do it, I will also do it."

With that, I raised the shot of blood which was still warm and said cheers as I drank it as everyone else downed theirs. A big gulp of beer, to wash it down, followed as quickly as I humanly could grab my mug. Peter did the same and this part of the evening was thankfully over.

At this point the man took the headless snake and soon returned with a bowl of snake bone soup and a platter of stir-fried snake with mixed vegetable. If one did not think about snakes, the food was tasty; it tasted a little bit like chicken with some fishiness to it but had a chewier texture to it like beef.

As unusual as the evening was, it served its purpose. My managers had exposure to Peter and he to them and I would venture to say that it is highly unlikely that Peter will ever forget them or this evening. When their names are offered up for promotion, he will definitely know who they are.

23

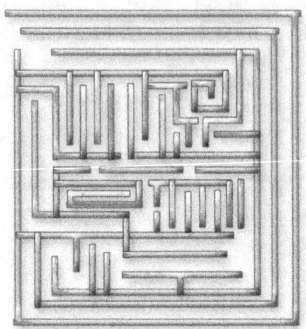

MARIE SUN AND THE CHINESE WEDDINGS

It was late on Wednesday afternoon. I had already completed my usual walk through the plant and was almost finished with my e-mails. I was looking forward to being able to finish work 'early' today. I had to chuckle to myself. "These days, 'early' meant before eight PM" I thought to myself "Nancy will be surprised to see me before eight thirty or so. Today I am on a roll and, at this rate, I might even be out before seven."

I heard a light knock on my door. I looked up and Julie was there with one of the local managers. Her English name is Kaitlin. Kaitlin had joined the company about 9 months ago and she worked in the technical organization.

"Kaitlin wants to talk to you" Julie said "do you have a few minutes?"

"I always have a few minutes for Kaitlin. Please come in and sit down" I said pointing to a chair across from my desk.

Kaitlin walked in very hesitantly and remained standing by the chair.

"Please Kaitlin" I said "have a seat and tell me what's on your mind."

Kaitlin was very flustered and though I knew that her English was not bad, she seemed to have trouble speaking. So before Julie can leave, I said "maybe Julie can translate, would that be helpful?"

"Yes" Kaitlin said.

"Ok, good" I said "tell me what's on your mind?"

Julie translated that Kaitlin wanted to invite me to her wedding this weekend and was wondering if I can attend.

"I would be honored" I said "this is very exciting" I added "I have never been to a Chinese wedding. Tell Kaitlin that I would be very happy to attend."

Kaitlin's face was all smiles now and it seemed that she found her English again.

"Thank you; thank you" she said "I am very happy that you can come."

"It would be my pleasure" I said "thank you for inviting me. Please give Julie the details of where the wedding will be and the time and I will see you there."

"I will give the information to Julie" she said and left saying "thank you."

I was excited. I thought this will be a good opportunity to see an authentic Chinese wedding and in some ways, while I did not know Kaitlin very well, I felt as if I am about to attend a wedding of a family member.

On Saturday, I put on my suit and Nancy put on a formal dress. Mr. Li picked us up and drove us to the wedding. The wedding was being held in a nice hall near Tianjin's Ancient Culture Street. We arrived about half an hour early and decided that we would wander around and look at a few shops and kiosks. There was the usual Chinese sword and calligraphy stalls. Both play an important part in the country's artistic history. The Chinese swords on display on one stall were works of art, I thought. The Chinese people view swords as valued symbols of legends; of Emperors and Kung Fu Warriors.

Nancy went across the street from where I was to the shops that sell Chinese paintings displaying a variety of water color landscapes in the ancient styles. Next to that was the kiosk of the artist who made our name scrolls in Chinese calligraphy. He made four scrolls. Each displaying one of our names alongside the animal from the Chinese almanac that represented the year in which we were born.

When I crossed over to join Nancy, the artist waved to me and walked over. He remembered us. He only spoke a few words of English but they were enough for us to have a brief conversation. His English was better than my Mandarin, I thought, yet he kept apologizing for his poor English.

I checked the time and it was about ten minutes before the wedding is scheduled to start, so I said to Nancy we needed to get there. As we walked, I was starting to wonder if I made a mistake by not asking Julie to join us.

When we arrived there, out of nowhere, Kaitlin appeared next to us just before we could go in.

"I was worried you had changed your mind" Kaitlin said.

"Absolutely not" I said "I would not miss your wedding for any reason."

"I am glad" she said "we are about to start the ceremonies" she then turned to the two men on her side and introduced them to us. The first was the groom, who did not speak any English. The other was her cousin who spoke some English, although he struggled with it. She told us that her cousin will be staying with us to translate during the ceremonies. His English name was Tony.

Tony walked us to the very front and soon it was obvious that we were seated at the table of honor. He introduced us to her parents and other guests seated at the same table none of whom spoke any English.

As we looked around the hall, it was obvious that red was "the color" in Chinese weddings. It was everywhere you looked. Before we could settle in our chairs, we heard some firecrackers outside the hall. With that, everyone got up and walked towards the hall entrance.

Tony led us and, as we stepped out, we saw Kaitlin and the groom coming out of a red sedan. As they walked in, a lot more firecrackers were set off. There was a lot of clapping and cheering.

Soon, we were all seated back at our assigned tables. Kaitlin was wearing a white dress and looked beautiful. The bride and groom walked into the hall. There was a heart shaped arch that was erected and they walked through it as they walked toward the front.

At the table, the bride and groom had laid out an assortment of goodies for the guests. There were licorice flavored pumpkin seeds, cigarettes, an assortment of juices and alcoholic beverages. A woman (I wasn't sure if it was the Bride or Groom's relative) went around and placed a red pin in every woman's hair. It made a great souvenir.

The bride and groom walked down the aisle, between the tables. A grade 10 student was the flower girl, a grade 8 student the ring bearer. As they passed our table, indoor fireworks went off which took us by complete surprise.

As I was talking to Tony, I learned that couples get married before they arrive at the ceremony. Sometimes, they are married a few days before. The wedding ceremony is only a formality. The couple has to file an application with a government bureau. Once their application is approved, a marriage certificate is issued to the couple. Without the government issued certificate, there is no marriage in China.

Next the MC took over the mike. He introduced the family first and then I heard my name. I looked at Tony inquisitively; he told me that I was just being introduced.

Shortly after that, Tony turned to me and said, please come with me. I was clueless, but followed him. He walked me to the front where the bride and groom were standing next to the MC. People clapped and the MC handed me the microphone. I did not know what was going on. I asked Tony "what should I be doing?" He told me that I will be presenting the wedding certificate to the couple. Later, Tony told me that I am supposed to say a few words.

I had to think quickly on my feet. I knew Kaitlin, but not very well, but I knew enough to say a few words about her, but did not know the groom or anything about him. So I decided to use generalities. Fortunately, very few people spoke or understood English. I hoped Tony will have enough sense to sensor what I say to make it appropriate for a local wedding.

I presented the wedding certificates wishing the happy couple a long, prosperous and fruitful life together and went on to say a lot of nice things about Kaitlin and how successful she is and tried to make as many general statements about the groom. Judging by the faces after Tony translated, I was feeling that this might be going ok, or put another way, I did not think I was screwing up too badly. I concluded with again wishing the happy couple, their friends and families a lot of happiness.

After the speeches were over, we got down to the meal. It was an incredible assortment of dishes to choose from. I tried some fish, which although I didn't know what it is; I knew for certain that I had never had it before. It was really good, and very fresh. Whenever we thought that surely they are done, more dishes of food came. It was a very generous spread of food. Even if you didn't like everything, there was more than enough food and choices to satisfy everyone's taste.

The bride and groom disappeared at the beginning of the meal, but then reemerged, this time with Kaitlin in a beautiful traditional red dress. During the meal, the bride and groom came around and took a drink with each table. We just had wine, but they were drinking, bai jiu; their traditional potent rice wine. They snuck off again and emerged a third time, this time she was wearing a gorgeous turquoise colored dress. Changing dresses several times is part of the traditions in a Chinese wedding.

We went back to the hotel and rested before meeting with our friends Craig and Shelly that evening for a drink. Nancy and I recollected our experience at the wedding and we laughed about how often we find ourselves surprised in our day to day life in China.

On Monday, back at the office, I had a busy morning. At 3:00 PM, Marie came in for our weekly meeting. After settling in her usual spot across from me, she said "I heard that you went to Kaitlin's wedding over the weekend."

"Yes, I did" I said "it was quite an event. This was my first Chinese wedding and I was pleased that Kaitlin invited me."

"What did you think of Chinese weddings and how do they compare with weddings in the US?" she asked.

"In many ways, they are very similar" I said "brides in the US usually wear a white dress whereas here they wear a white dress at first, but quickly change to a red dress. I thought Kaitlin looked radiant and beautiful, just like brides look on their wedding day in the US or anywhere else in the world."

"I was a little surprised when I discovered that I was giving Kaitlin away or presenting the wedding certificate to the bride and groom."

"In China" Marie said "many times the guest of honor is asked to do that."

"That is what I found out" I said "it was a little awkward because I did not even know that and 'I' was 'the guest of honor'. I had to think fast on my feet. Fortunately, Kaitlin's cousin spoke some English. He was assigned to accompany me and do the translation."

"Julie did not accompany you?" Marie asked.

"No, I did not know the customs, so I thought I would be sitting in the back and just observing the proceedings" I said "so I did not ask her to accompany me."

Marie was trying hard not to laugh. She thought it was funny as she imagined what I must have gone through.

"Marie, it was not that funny" I said even though I could see how she and all the people at the wedding might have thought so.

"Yes, you are right" she said "it is not funny" as she broke into a loud laugh, apparently unable to control herself.

"Ok" I said "it was very funny. I had no idea what I was doing and Kaitlin's cousin was not the most detailed person in the world. He kept assuming that I should know what to do and would only tell me when I was failing to do something."

"Someone gave me the Wedding certificate" I said laughing "I had no idea what it was or what to do with it. After I had it in my hand and everyone was looking at me wondering what I was waiting for, he finally whispered to me that I am supposed to present the certificate to them and say a few words.

No wait, he did not even tell me I am supposed to say a few words until later. So I presented the certificate after he prompted me and stood there waiting for further instructions. I can only imagine what all the guests must have been thinking during the long silence."

By now, Marie was almost on the floor, she was laughing so hard.

I continued "then he told me that I am supposed to say a few words. I knew nothing about the groom, so I had to think fast to make comments in generalities about the happy couple. Fortunately, I was able to sing Kaitlin's praises because I remembered quite a bit about her from when I interviewed her. I hope the groom did not feel slighted."

"I did not know that in China the wedding ceremony is only a formality. The actual official marriage happens by applying for a license to get married and a couple is married only when the government approves the application and grants them the license" I said "in the US and most Western countries, the couple is actually married at the actual ceremony. Their marriage is registered with the church, state or a government agency after the ceremony takes place."

By now, Marie had gotten her laughter under control and she said "not this week end, but the weekend after, there is a group wedding. If you are available, I would like to take you to the wedding. Twelve couples are getting married at the same ceremony and since I will be with you, I will explain all the details to you."

"Will I have to give away any brides?" I asked.

"Not this time" she said.

"Ok" I said "if you promise that I will not have to participate in any part of the ceremony, I will plan on it."

"I promise" she said.

"Ok" I said "we have a deal."

The group wedding was a little different but essentially the same. Marie helped me better understand the different steps in a Chinese wedding, but since this was a group wedding, the ceremony was much more spectacular with a lot more fanfare and the MC was a famous DJ. There was more competition amongst the brides I thought when it came to changing dresses and with each bride trying to look even prettier than the others.

I enjoyed the event and appreciated Marie's continued effort to educate me on Chinese culture. The following week, Marie brought me a gift in her quest to continue to educate me. It consisted of 12 pictures that were made in

Yunnan Province from butterfly wings. Each picture represented one of the ladies from the story book 'A Dream of Red Mansions'. A massive, sprawling classic novel about China that was written in the mid-eighteenth century, during the Ching Dynasty, and has been widely read during the past two hundred years. It is considered to be the greatest work of Chinese fiction and is a brilliant achievement and a marvelous read.

Metaphysical, allegorical, and vividly realistic, the immense scope of Dream of Red Mansions touches on the lives of over 400 characters and provides something for everyone. A rich family saga, a tragic love story, and a philosophical meditation. It is one of those rare huge books in which one can lose oneself completely.

The author, Tsao Hsueh-chin, was born and raised in an aristocratic family, but died in misery and isolation. From his own bitter, personal experiences, Tsao created a tragic love story between a young man, Chia Pao-yu, and a young woman, Lin Tai-yu, and, along with their love story, he described in careful detail the ups and downs of four leading aristocratic families: Chia, Shih, Wang, and Hsueh. It is through his precise description of the decline of these four families that the reader gets a deep and careful analysis and criticism of the Ching Dynasty's economics, politics, culture, education, law, ethics, religion, and marriage, focusing in particular on the social superstructure of the Ching Dynasty, China's last feudal dynasty.

Clearly, this novel is, like life itself, extraordinarily rich. It depicts with artistic appeal and succinctness the hidden crises and various kinds of intricate social conflicts of the declining feudal society, while offering many different characteristics of different kind of people. The novel has profound social significance and a high historical value.

Ever since that day, Marie's gift, the pictures of the twelve ladies from 'A Dream of Red Mansions', has sat on display in my office.

24

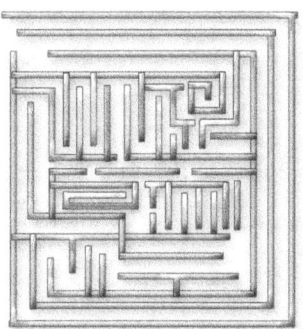

HOLDING ON TO PRINCIPLES.
A LESSON FROM A JAPANESE CAR MANUFACTURER.

I had met my friend Koby about one year ago. He and his family lived at the Sheraton Hotel as well. Koby worked for a top Japanese auto manufacturer. I came to find out that Koby had also attended MIT, my Alma Mata. Although he and I attended at different times and had different majors. We instantly had a common link when we met.

I introduced his daughter, who had recently graduated from a Japanese University with a marketing major, to a key contact at my company's Japanese headquarters which led to her being offered and accepting a job after successfully interviewing for an opening there. To show her gratitude before leaving Tianjin to start her new job, she invited Nancy and me to their home. When we arrived, she was dressed in traditional Japanese dress ready to treat us to a Japanese tea ceremony. Something that neither Nancy nor I had experienced before.

Yuka explained that there were some variations of the ceremony. She said "what I am about to perform is called a Chaji, which means a full tea presentation with a meal. However, since we were not at their home in Japan, she will not be able to carry on the ceremony exactly as she would have done in Japan."

"My mother will explain every step of the way as I am doing it and she will also tell you what would be more typical of a tea ceremony in Japan."

"That would be perfect" I said and thought this must have taken a great deal of planning.

"We appreciate you doing this" Nancy said and turned to Tanabi, Yuka's mother, adding "we really appreciate you explaining things to us and telling us what may be different."

Tanabi started "as in virtually every tea ceremony, the hostess may spend days going over details to insure that the ceremony will be perfect."

It was obvious that Yuka was feeling a little nervous and had already spent a lot of time preparing for this evening.

"Through tea" Tanabi went on "recognition is given that every human encounter is a singular occasion which can, and will, never recur again exactly. So in Japanese culture, every aspect of tea must be savored for what it gives the participants."

"Typically, the ceremony takes place in a room designed and designated for tea. It is called the chashitsu. Usually this room is within the tea house, located away from the residence, in the garden" she said commenting that "however, since we are all living at the Sheraton Hotel in Tianjin, Yuka has to make accommodations and perform the ceremony in our living room."

"The guests (four is the preferred number) are shown into the machiai (waiting room)" she continued. "Here, the hanto (assistant to the host) offers them sayu (the hot water which will be used to make tea). While here, the guests choose one from their group to act as the main guest. The hanto then leads the guests with the main guest directly behind, to a water sprinkled garden devoid of flowers. It is called roji (dew ground). Here the guests rid themselves of the dust of the world. They then seat themselves on the koshikake machiai (waiting bench), anticipating the approach of the host who has the official title teishu (house master)."

"Just before receiving the guests" she continued "the teishu fills the tsukubai (stone basin), which is set among low stones with fresh water. Taking a ladle of water, the teishu purifies his hands and mouth then proceeds through the chumon (middle gate) to welcome his guests with a bow. No words are spoken. The teishu leads the hanto, the main guest and the others (in that order) through the chumon which symbolizes a door between the coarse physical world and the spiritual world of tea."

"The guests and hanto purify themselves at the tsukubai and enter the teahouse. The sliding door is only thirty six inches high. Thus all who enter must bow their heads and crouch. This door size points to the reality that all are equal in tea, irrespective of status or social position. The last person in, latches the door."

"Of course" Tanabi said "clearly, everything I have described until now is missing from this tea ceremony. Unfortunately, until you come to visit us in Japan, you have to imagine all of those steps."

"Inside the Teahouse" she continued "the room is devoid of any decoration except for an alcove called a tokonoma. Hanging in the alcove is a kakemono (scroll painting), carefully selected by the host, which reveals the theme of the ceremony. The Buddhist scripture on the scroll is by a master and is called bokuseki (ink traces). Each guest admires the scroll in turn, then examines the kama (kettle) and hearth (furo for the portable type and ro for the type set into the floor in winter to provide warmth), which were laid just before they were greeted by the host."

"At this point, the guests are seated according to their respective positions in the ceremony." As Tanabi was saying this, Yuka motioned me to sit on a pillow on the floor next to a small and low table and then motioned Nancy to sit right next to me while she sat across from us.

"Welcome" Yuka said looking at me.

"Thank you for inviting us" I said.

Then Yuka turned to Nancy and said "welcome, I am glad you can come."

"It is our pleasure" Nancy said "thank you for inviting us."

"At this point" Tanabi said as she and Koby joined us at the table "a charcoal fire is then built if it is ro season and after the meal if it is furo season. In ro season kneaded incense is put in the fire and sandalwood incense in the furo season."

"Each guest is served a meal called chakaiseki. The meal consists of three courses" Tanabi continued as Yuka stood up, bowed to us and walked backwards still facing us. Yuka came back with individual trays each contained fresh cedar chopsticks, cooked white rice in a ceramic bowl, miso soup in covered lacquer bowls and raw fish in a ceramic dish. Sake was also served.

We all enjoyed our food. I do not mind raw fish, so I ate my portion. Nancy, on the other hand, will not eat raw fish. So she moved it to the side. Yuka noticed that Nancy was not eating her raw fish, so she backed away again facing us and returned with pickled vegetables in a ceramic dish and placed it on Nancy's tray as she removed the raw fish dish saying "please try the pickled vegetables. Not everyone likes raw fish. I am not crazy about it either and prefer pickled vegetables instead."

I noticed that Yuka was not eating with us. I asked "am I allowed to ask a question?"

Yuka and Tanabi said simultaneously "Of course."

Looking at Yuka I asked "why are you not eating with us?"

Tanabi answered "the host does not eat during this portion of the ceremony."

Yuka added "I will join you during the first course in a minute."

"Great" I said.

Tanabi continued "The first course is called hashiarai (rinsing the chopsticks)". Nimono (foods simmered in broth) are served in separate covered lacquer dishes. Yakimono (grilled foods) are served in individual portions on ceramic plates. Additional rice and soup is offered each guest and the plate is then cleared with kosuimono, a simple clear broth served in covered lacquer bowls."

Again, we continued to enjoy our meal. This was a lot of food I was thinking when Tanabi said "the next course derives its name from the Shinto reverence of nature. It is called hassun which is also the name for the simple wooden tray that is used to serve this course. This course consists of uminomono and yamanomono (seafood and mountain food respectively) which signify the abundance of the sea and land. The host eats during this course, and is served sake by each guest. The position of server is considered a higher position and, to insure equality of all in the tea room, each acts as host if only momentarily."

This was my cue to fill the sake glasses. I decided to play it safe and served the sake by age starting with Koby, then Tanabi, Yuka, Nancy and then my glass. Shortly after that, Nancy offered more rice and each of us in turn fulfilled the role of servers.

Tanabi continued 'konomono (fragrant things) are served in small ceramic bowls, and browned rice is served in salted water in a lacquer pitcher, representing the last of the rice. Each guest cleans the utensils they have used with soft paper which they bring." At this point, Tanabi pulled a piece of tissue paper and wiped her chop sticks. We all followed suit.

Next Yuka presented us with a small plate of sugary candy. It looked like there were 5 pieces, one for each of us. While she was serving us Tanabi continued "an omogashi (principal sweet) is served to conclude the meal."

As we ate our candy, Tanabi went on "at this point, the host invites the guests to retire to the garden or waiting room while preparing for the tea. Once the guests have departed, the host removes the scroll and replaces it with flowers. The room is swept and the utensils for preparing koi cha are arranged. Over thirteen individual items are used. Each is costly and considered an art object."

"Maybe we can retire to the living room while Yuka gets ready for the tea ceremony" Tanabi said. We all got up and walked to the next room.

"In Japan, we talk about the Spiritual World of Tea" Tanabi continued "in the tea ceremony; water represents yin and fire in the hearth yang. The water is held in a jar called the mizusashi. This stoneware jar contains fresh water symbolizing purity, and is touched only by the host. Matcha is kept in a small ceramic container called a chaire which is in turn covered in a shifuku (fine silk pouch) which is set in front of the mizusashi. The occasion will dictate the type of tana (stand) used to display the chosen utensils.

If tea is served during the day a gong is sounded, in the evening a bell. Usually struck or rung five to seven times, it summons the guests back to the tea house. They purify hands and mouth once again and re-enter as before. They admire the flowers, kettle and hearth and seat themselves."

Almost on cue, a bell sounded in the next room. We all stood up and went back to the next room. The table had been cleared and the utensils were all neatly arranged. I could not believe the amount of detail involved.

Tanabi continued as we sat down again in our assigned spots and went on to describe each step as Yuka was doing it "the host then enters with the chawan (tea bowl) which holds the chasen (tea whisk), chakin (the tea cloth) which is a bleached white linen cloth used to dry the bowl, and the chashaku (tea scoop), a slender bamboo scoop used to dispense the matcha, which rests across it. These are arranged next to the water jar which represents the sun (symbolic of yang); the bowl is the moon (yin)."

As Yuka left the room Tanabi continued "retiring to the preparation room, the host returns with the kensui (waste water bowl), the hishaku (bamboo water ladle) and futaoki (a green bamboo rest for the kettle lid) and then closes the door to the preparation room."

"Using a fukusa (fine silk cloth), which represents the spirit of the host, the host purifies the tea container and scoop. Deep significance is found in the host's careful inspection, folding and handling of the fukusa, for his level of concentration and state of meditation are being intensified. Hot water is ladled into the tea bowl, the whisk is rinsed, and the tea bowl is emptied and wiped with the chakin" she continued as Yuka was doing each step "lifting the tea scoop and tea container, the host places three scoops of tea per guest into the tea bowl. Hot water is ladled from the kettle into the tea bowl in a quantity sufficient to create a thin paste with the whisk. Additional water is then added so the paste can be whisked into a thick liquid consistent with pea soup. Unused water in the ladle is returned to the kettle."

As Yuka was handing me a tea bowl, Tanabi said "the host passes the tea bowl to the main guest who bows in accepting it. The bowl is raised and rotated in the hand to be admired."

On cue, I bowed, raised the tea bowl, rotated it and looked at it with admiration. Interestingly, I was genuinely impressed when I saw what a beautiful piece of fine China was being used and knowing the amount of detail involved not to mention the effort that Yuka has put into this event.

"The guest then drinks some of the tea" Tanabi continued "wipes the rim of the bowl, and passes the bowl to the next guest who does the same as the main guest."

I took a sip, wiped the rim and passed the bowl to Nancy who did the same and passed the bowl to Tanabi and then on to Koby who returned it to Yuka after taking his sip.

Tanabi continued "when the guests have all tasted the tea, the bowl is returned to the host who rinses it. The whisk is rinsed and the tea scoop and the tea container cleaned. The scoop and tea container are offered to the guests for examination. A discussion of the objects, presentation and other appropriate topics takes place."

Tanabi continued "the final stage of the ceremony is to prepare for departure. The fire is rebuilt for usa cha (thin tea). This tea will rinse the palate and symbolically prepares the guests for leaving the spiritual world of tea and re-entering the physical world."

"Smoking articles are offered, but rarely does smoking take place in a tearoom" Tanabi said "this is a signal for relaxation. zabuton (cushions) and teaburi (hand warmers) are offered. To compliment usa cha, higashi (dry sweets) are served. Usa cha and koi cha are made in the same manner, except that less tea powder of a lesser quality is used, and it is dispensed from a date-shaped wooden container called natsume. The tea bowl is more decorative in style; and guests are individually served a bowl of this frothy brew."

"At the conclusion" Tanabi wrapped up saying "the guests express their appreciation for the tea and admiration for the art of the host. They leave as the host watches from the door of the teahouse."

I clapped and Nancy joined me as we profusely thanked Yuka for the ceremony and told her how impressed we were that she is able to do such an elegant and elaborate ceremony. Then we thanked Tanabi for beautifully explaining each step to us.

"This was such a special event for us" Nancy said looking at Yuka and then turning to Tanabi she said "without the explanation of the different steps, we would not have understood their significance. Thank you so much."

Koby and I retired to a corner of their living room to chat over sake.

"How are things going with you?" I asked.

"I am going a little crazy" Koby replied.

"What is going on?" I asked "you sound so serious."

"How do you deal with people asking you for things?" Koby asked.

"I don't" I said "what is going on?"

"When we first arrived in Tianjin" he said "as a token of our appreciation, we presented a mid sized sedan as a gift to the head of the bureau that helped us get established."

"Ouch" I said.

"Yes, 'ouch' is right" Koby said "ever since then, we have had people from every possible bureau asking us to extend to them the same courtesy. They all feel that their help to us should be rewarded in the same way. The problem is that when we say that we are unable to do it, people take it the wrong way. People seem to feel slighted because they read into it that we don't value their help and contribution enough. Otherwise, we would give them a mid size car like we did with the other bureau."

"I see" I said deeply understanding the predicament Koby was in but totally seeing how others will feel slighted when they don't get their own gift of a midsized car.

"Of course" Koby continued "once people feel slighted, they lose face and then all of a sudden, they provide zero cooperation."

"I can see that" I said "it becomes a downward spiral that feeds on itself."

"Exactly" Koby said "I don't know how to break through this problem and get to the point where I can run a normal business. How did you manage this issue?"

"The way I dealt with it" I said "will not work for you at this point. You need to think of a different approach."

"So how did you deal with it?" Koby persisted.

"Well" I said "when I first arrived in Tianjin, an official from the customs bureau insisted that my people give him 20 cases of soap. Nothing overly expensive compared to your mid size car, but that made me upset enough that I went to our JV partner and insisted that he deliver a message to this official for me. My partner denied he knew this person and claimed he could not deliver any messages, so I threatened to get in my car if another request comes in and drive straight to the mayor's office to file an official complaint.

I used the word bribery in describing this and explained that I understood the severity of the punishment for any official that requests or receives bribes."

"Wow" Koby said "that was very bold."

"Yes, it was" I said "but I was determined not to allow myself to get into this game and I was confident that my senior management would have backed me. Although in retrospect, I should have at least checked before doing it. At the time, I was very angry that this man felt free to intimidate my managers and I felt so strongly about it that I just acted on my instincts without hesitation."

"In any case" I added "I never had anyone else make other requests. At least, none that I know of, or that were brought to my attention after that."

"You are right" Koby said "that will not work for me right now. Unfortunately, we had set the precedent by giving away the first car. Do you have any ideas or suggestions?"

"The only thing I can think of right now is to find a way to get the message out that you are not being disrespectful to the various bureaus" I said "let's think this through. There has to be a way to do this."

"I don't know if the same is true in Japan, but in the US, it is illegal to give bribes to government officials. This applies to all US company dealings anywhere in the world. Basically, it is illegal to give gifts with the objective of securing business or getting an unfair advantage."

"We have similar laws in Japan" Koby said.

"There you go" I said "you need to put yourself on the same side as them. While they all would like a mid-size car, I am sure they can all relate to a well-meaning foreigner who does not want to be punished or lose his job."

"I am all ears" Koby said "I have been trying to figure this out for a long time with no luck so far."

"I think you have a lot of work to do but you have to do it in multiple steps" I said "the first step is to let everyone know that there will not be any more cars given out as presents followed quickly by a series of deliberate steps to build good relationships with officials from the various bureaus."

"One possible way to approach this" I continued "is to see if you can enlist the help of the bureau that received the car as a gift."

"What do you mean? He asked.

"I am assuming you have a good relationship with the head of the bureau you gave the mid-size car to" I said "so, when you talk to him, and I would suggest you do that over dinner in a relaxed setting, you should try to achieve two objectives. The first is to explain to him that, when you gave his bureau the mid-size car as a token of your appreciation for his bureaus help, you did not realize that you were breaking your own company policies. Share with him, in confidence of course, that you actually got yourself in trouble with your company's senior executives. After that, explain to him that if it was left up to you, you would have liked to make similar gifts to the other bureaus that have been helping you; however, unfortunately, if you were to do that, you will lose your job and, most definitely, be replaced by someone else to head your business in Tianjin."

"Once you establish this information, ask him for his thoughts on how you can deal with his peers to make sure they don't feel slighted" I continued adding "keep in mind that he would not want to be directly involved in doing anything that involves his peers. After all, he has his own relationships with them that he has to worry about ... so don't expect much more than very basic advise from him that will likely be given in a roundabout way. But, I suspect that once you finish talking to him, the word will be out that you are not in a position to give away any more cars."

"That is good" Koby said "you mentioned a few steps. What else did you have in mind?"

"Please keep in mind that I don't know if this will work, but I believe it is worth a shot" I said "the second step is for you to buy a lot of dinners. You have to separately invite the officials who are feeling slighted and start the process of building your relationships with them. You need to be saying that you appreciate their help and support. Explain to them what kind of trouble you will be getting into if you were to give any of them a car, etc. You get the idea. After a few dinners, you will be less of a bad guy and they will start to accept that giving them cars is beyond your ability to deliver."

"I can do that" Koby said.

"The key is to work hard at building relationships with the various bureaus. Once they start to view you as their friend and someone they have a relationship with, then you will be able to get past the stalemate that I think you are in right now."

"Finally" I said "lean on your JV partners, they already have a relationship with the bureaus and they can play a very important role in getting the word out that you are not in a position to give away any more cars. Don't allow them to be bystanders, they have a role to play and should be able to help you through this."

It was getting late and I could see from the corner of my eye that Nancy was ready to call it a night, so I closed with Koby by wishing him the best of luck and letting him know that he can call me if he wants to discuss other ideas.

We thanked Yuka, Tanabi and Koby for a lovely evening and a unique experience as we said goodnight.

25

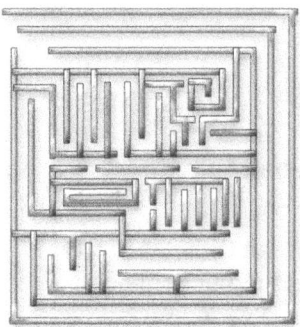

SOMETIMES, THINGS ARE EXACTLY AS THEY SEEM AND SOMETIMES THEY'RE NOT. STILL, LIFE GOES ON!

Living in China can be very exciting and rewarding as a life experience. It can also be very trying and difficult at times. How difficult or rewarding depends on one's outlook on life and how one chooses to adapt to unfamiliar situations. In some situations, things will rub people, especially those entrenched in the Western Culture, absolutely the wrong way.

It is not a question of 'if' you face situations that are difficult for you to accept. It is rather a question of 'when' you face such situations, how will you react. If nothing else, I learned that, in life, people face many situations that they cannot control. The thing that distinguishes one human being from another is how they respond when faced with such situations. One can try to pretend it is not happening, it will go away, or maybe get angry and try to control it and fight while others simply choose to go with the flow.

To illustrate my point, I will share with you three different stories.

I will start with what I refer to as my 'FAX' story.

Shortly after I started my job in Tianjin, I tried to fax some documents to some colleagues in Cincinnati. Since I had been told about the importance of securing information, I stood by Julie while she made 4 or 5 attempts to transmit a simple fax. I noted her frustrations.

"Do you always have trouble with this fax machine?" I asked.

"Yes" she answered. It is over five years old. It jams, it sends faxes with poor quality and most of the time, we have a hard time reading faxes that come in because of the poor quality and, worst of all, it is very slow to transmit and receive faxes. It certainly tests one's patience." she answered.

"I can see that it is a very old model" I said "why are we not replacing it with a newer and faster model?"

Julie hesitated for a minute before answering but simply said, "I don't know."

To my relief, as if the machine heard our complaints, all of a sudden it started to feed the first page. This gave me the opportunity to observe how slow it was.

"Why don't you tell Sampson to buy us a new machine tomorrow" I said as the first page finished transmitting "tell him I want him to buy the fastest and highest quality fax machine he can find on the market."

"Ok" Julie said absently "I will get the purchase order ready for you to sign."

"After watching you struggle with this fax, I will happily sign it" I said.

The next morning, Sampson knocked on my office door and asked "would you like to see the new fax machine?"

"Absolutely" I said as I stood up and walked with Sampson to the fax and copier room.

The machine was what you might expect, brand new and looked like it had all the bells and whistles.

Sampson is taller than average and always dressed very nicely. He usually wore a suit jacket and looked very dapper. During my meetings with him, he was usually very intense and typically perspired when he talked to me with beads of perspiration forming on his forehead and upper lips. While he spoke good English, his accent got thicker when he was nervous to the point where it was difficult for me to understand what he was saying. I had learned to speak to him in English but to have Julie close by to translate as needed.

Later in my assignment, Sampson and I developed a friendship and he became much more relaxed around me. It was amazing how much easier it became for me to understand his English when he was relaxed.

"Now we need a training course to teach people how to use the new fax machine" I said in jest, however, Sampson, with his usual intensity, started to talk about contacting the vendor to arrange for training sessions, etc.

I had to put him at ease and told him I was kidding. "We should be able to figure it out" I said as we both headed back towards my office. I thanked

Sampson for picking such an excellent machine and doing it so fast."

"I went to the vendor's warehouse and picked it up myself" he informed me.

It was going to take 3 days for them to deliver it."

"Was it very far?" I asked.

"Only one hour in the company van" he said.

"Good" I said "Again, thank you and I really appreciate your initiative and hard work."

"My pleasure" he said as we parted company.

A few days passed and by then so many other things had happened that the fax machine was a distant memory when I heard a knock on the door and Julie walked in. Behind her was a man she introduced as Mr. Chen from the Security Bureau.

I shook hands with Mr. Chen. He did not speak any English.

I ushered Mr. Chen to the adjacent conference room and told Julie to ask him if he would like tea or something else to drink.

Mr. Chen said he was in a hurry but appreciated the offer.

"Very well then" I said as we sat down turning to Julie and asking "to what do we owe the honor of Mr. Chen's visit today?"

Julie translated and then translated back.

"Mr. Chen wants us to remove our new fax machine and put back the old one" she told me.

"Interesting" I said "I don't understand why?"

"Those are my orders" Mr. Chen explained.

"Please explain to Mr. Chen that the old machine was very old and did not work very well. Maybe you can explain all the difficulties you had in trying to fax just the other day" I said.

Julie appeared uncomfortable but proceeded to explain to Mr. Chen about our problems with the old fax machine.

"I understand" Mr. Chen responded "but I have to insist that you put back the old machine."

"I still don't understand" I persisted "why would Mr. Chen or the Security Bureau want us to use antiquated technology."

Mr. Chen was silent for a moment then moved closer to Julie as he responded.

"If you must know" Mr. Chen explained "the reason for this request is because our monitoring equipment is too slow to be able to monitor faxes sent from the new machine. It works well with the old machine which is why we must insist on you putting your old machine back."

"I think I understand" I said "Maybe Mr. Chen can provide us with a list of models that his equipment is capable of monitoring and we can replace the old machine with a newer one that works better for us."

Mr. Chen said he will work with Julie to make sure we get a newer fax machine that works for us and is compatible with their equipment."

With that, Mr. Chen stood up and we said goodbye.

The second story involves an evening when Nancy and I met our friends Craig and Shelly for a drink and I was still in a state of disbelief about my conversation with Mr. Chen. As I replayed my conversation to them, I was still having a difficult time believing that Mr. Chen did not try to hide the fact that someone in the Security Bureau actually reads every fax we send or receive.

While I was in the middle of describing my experience, Tyler and his wife Sue walked in and we invited them to join us for a drink. Tyler and Sue are from Australia. Tyler is a medium built man with a full head of light brown hair and a very bubbly personality, especially after he has a few beers. Sue had black hair and blue eyes. She is very outgoing and also enjoys a good cocktail or two.

Tyler was one of very few foreigners who worked at the hotel where we all lived. We had all become friendly and on occasion socialized together.

I started telling the story over again and Tyler seemed to be looking at me as if he was wondering "why that was a surprise to me?"

I decided to press him for information.

"So Tyler" I said only half joking "I understand there are video cameras in our rooms at the hotel."

Tyler appeared very uncomfortable as he said "I don't know anything about that."

"Come on Tyler" I persisted "you are the deputy general manager, you must know something."

"No, really, I don't" he said still looking uncomfortable.

I looked at him and waited.

"Even if I knew something" he continued "I would not be able to tell you."

At this point, Nancy and Shelly piped in with a lot of anxiety saying if that was the case, we had to move out of the hotel. They were getting panicked. I decided that this was not the smartest way to have introduced the subject. In the span of about thirty minutes, I went from being concerned about faxes being read by people at the security bureau to now having gotten everyone panicked over video surveillance in our rooms. Thankfully, the waitress stopped by to see if we needed anything else, so I ordered another round of drinks for everyone.

I whispered to Nancy to see if she can take the girls to the ladies room or away from the table for a few minutes. Soon, the girls were gone and Tyler, Craig and I stayed behind. While Tyler and I had become friends, Craig and Tyler were closer friends and they played tennis together. I felt we had a better chance of being able to lean on Tyler and get some information if the ladies were not there.

"I understand you cannot say anything" I started again "how about you nod if I say something that is true."

Tyler took a big sip from his drink and said he would, so I persisted.

"Are there video cameras in our rooms?" I asked.

Tyler shook his head sideways. Craig and I were relieved.

I looked at Tyler again, but noticed that he was still waiting for us to ask him more questions.

"Are there microphones in our rooms?" I asked.

He nodded up and down.

"In every room?" I asked again.

Tyler nodded again and now looked like he was finished and was not expecting any more questions.

The waitress came with our drinks and a couple of minutes later, the ladies came back and the band was back and started playing again.

We all danced to the music and had a round of Cointreau while Craig, Tyler and I smoked Cuban cigars.

When it was time to say goodnight, Tyler whispered to me to make sure I kept our conversation confidential or he will lose his job. I assured him it was safe with us.

Nancy and I decided to go for a short walk before going up to our place. As we walked back, I explained to Nancy that there were no video cameras in our rooms, but that there were microphones and let her know that we cannot discuss it with anyone. All expats speculated about such a possibility and we can only discuss this as speculation with others. I explained that Tyler would lose his job if word got out that he talked about the microphones.

Nancy was spooked and frankly so was I. While we suspected that this may be a real possibility, somehow, knowing for sure made it worse. Neither one of us wanted to go back to our place but we knew we must.

"I don't know if I can take this" Nancy said "maybe we should consider packing up and going home."

"It creeps me out too" I said "first the conversation with Mr. Chen and the fax machine and now this."

"What do you think?" Nancy persisted "should we be seriously thinking about going home?"

"We will have to think this through" I said.

"What's to think about?" Nancy persisted "you have people listening to every conversation you have. We already know that the phones are tapped. The people who are listening in on the phones don't even try to hide it. Sometimes you hear them coughing or chewing on food and if that is not bad enough, we now know that there are microphones in every room with people listening to everything we say and do."

"I know this is creepy" I said again "I am feeling angry and yet none of this should be a surprise to us. With everything we heard and read before taking the assignment, this all was to be expected."

"That is true enough" she said "maybe we heard it before, but somehow it wasn't until now that it actually sank in."

"That has to be it" I said "I guess more than anything, I am angry with myself. Intellectually, I knew all this stuff from the books I read and my conversation with the head of corporate security before leaving Cincinnati. Everything suggested that those types of things were considered a normal part of everyday life here. Ironically, at the time, I was a little skeptical of what I was hearing. I guess, after this episode, I am not skeptical any more."

"You are right" she said "I guess it feels much worse when you know for sure." She looked at her watch and said "we better get back, it is getting late and we should make sure the kids are in bed."

"Ok" I said "let's head back although, if we are going to stay sane, we have to find a silver lining in this."

"Good luck" Nancy said with a note of skepticism and continued "what are we going to do about telling the kids?"

"We have to tell them so that they can be aware" I said "it's not like any of us is doing anything bad or illegal that we need to be hiding anything."

"I know there is nothing for us to be seriously concerned about in that sense "she said "but I can't help but feel violated."

"I share your concern and feelings" I said "we need to tell the kids. We can't tell them how we found out and we need to ask them to keep it to themselves. Tyler can easily get in major trouble and possibly lose his job for this."

"I agree" she said "we can't tell them how we found out. Maybe all we tell them is that we heard rumors and that we all need to be careful because someone may be listening all the time. We still need to figure out how are we going to discuss things that we want to keep confidential?" she added.

"Why don't we go for a walk" I said "that seems to be what my Chinese managers suggest we do when they want to talk about stuff that is sensitive."

"That sounds like a plan" she said as we arrived at the hotel's main entrance.

The next evening I noticed that a light bulb was burnt in one of the bathrooms. Instead of calling the maintenance department, I decided to put the microphones to good use.

I turned to Nancy and asked "did you know that the light bulb in the master bedroom is burnt?"

"No, I did not know that" she said "I am surprised the cleaning staff did not notice that."

About 10 minutes later, there was a knock on the door. I opened the door and the maintenance man was there with a ladder and a light bulb in hand. I simply ushered him to the bathroom.

While I did not expect to ever come to accept that it is ok to have our privacy so blatantly and seriously violated, we had to make a choice in order to maintain our sanity. The choice we made was to 'live with it' and try to make the best out of a bad situation.

Knowing that it was happening gave us the ability to work around it and manage or control what we kept private and what was intentionally shared. In a way, once we decided to have fun with it rather than allow it to consume us, it became a bit of a game for us which helped us maintain a sense of humor about things and possibly our sanity.

Two days later, the Herald Tribune, which is normally slipped under our door around 5:00 PM every day, was late. I asked Nancy if she had seen it yet. Five minutes later, my copy of the Herald Tribune was slipped under the door.

Such is life I thought to myself as I picked up my copy of the Herald Tribune with a little chuckle.

My third story involves Mr. Tian, the Deputy General Manager, who was assigned to my JV by BOLI. I learned this information only one month before I concluded my assignment in China.

My management team had worked very hard and made significant progress towards achieving the company's growth objectives during the past three years. We had grown the business from $40 million to a little over $500 million in sales and were on track to achieve our cost and profit objectives. I decided that it would be appropriate to treat all of them to a week end in Beijing that included a trip to the Great Wall.

To help prepare the team for my pending departure, I decided to have a session on Friday morning aimed at team building before the non-business portion of the weekend started.

As part of the agenda, we used some team building exercises to help break the ice. One of those exercises was to have everyone around the table tell the team two things about themselves that the team could not possibly know about them. During the exercise, we learned a lot of interesting information about all the players since we did not let anyone get away with shallow or superficial input.

The big surprise to me was when Mr. Tian shared his two things. The first was that he had shared an office with Jiang Zemin, China's Paramount Leader, when they both worked for the Shanghai Soap Factory. He also knew China's Gang of Four.

I was stunned to learn this information. To me, Mr. Tian came across as a very nice and unusually quiet man, despite the fact that he was overly verbose when he had a point to make. I saw him as someone with very little influence both inside and outside the JV. He often indicated there is not much he could do when there were issues that could have benefited from an insider's intervention. As a result, I naively concluded that he was merely a bureaucrat assigned by BOLI to keep an eye on how things ran inside the JV.

Obviously, things were not as they seemed in this case.

Mr. Tian had considerable influence. The mere fact that he was connected to Jiang Zemin would give him almost unlimited capability to get minor things like permits approved, and government agencies to deliver. He chose not to use his influence to help the JV.

Why would he not use his influence one might ask?

The answer is very simple. 'Guan xi'. He saw us as transients and the people he may have to push to get things done were his friends and people he had spent a lifetime building relationships with. If he pushes them to change their decisions, they will lose face and that would be bad for their relationships. He would save the 'guan xi' and the goodwill that goes along with it for times when he may really need a favor. Then he will ask and get what he asks for.

By staying on the fringe, he was able to get the best of all worlds. On the one hand, he gets a JV salary and benefits which would be a big plus compared to the benefits he would get as a regular employee of BOLI. On the other hand, by refraining from being involved when needed, he gets to keep and grow his local relationships which he expects to outlast any relationships he develops with the foreign JV partners.

As the title of this chapter says, sometimes, things are as they seem and sometimes, they're not …. Still, life goes on.

26

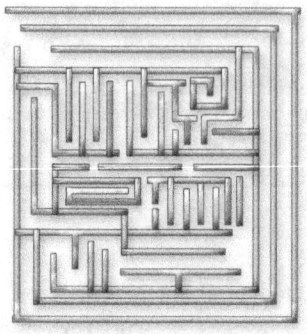

SAYING GOODBYE TO ALL MY NEW FRIENDS.
GOING HOME.

When my three year mark was approaching, the Company asked me if I would consider another assignment in Asia. The company was expanding in Korea and Malaysia and they wanted me to take a position in one of those countries.

I was flattered because the company appreciated my contributions and wanted me to take another very challenging assignment; however, as Nancy and I talked about it, we both agreed that we needed to get back. By now, both John and Elizabeth were attending private boarding schools in Connecticut. We were concerned about them being so far away from us. Holidays were tough for everyone. The flights took 16 to 18 hours and were simply too long. Nancy and I decided that it was time for us to go back to the US.

On top of that, my responsibilities had me traveling between two and three weeks a month. With the kids away and me traveling, Nancy was spending a lot of time in China by herself. She is a good sport which helped, but with the kids and me away, it was a bit much to ask of her.

I informed the company that I had decided not to extend my assignment in China or take another assignment in Asia. At the time, I was told that there were very few openings in the US which led me to believe it will be a long time before something desirable opened up.

With that background, Peter's call was a surprise. He informed me that there was an opening coming up in Sacramento, California that he thought was a perfect fit for me.

"The good news" he said "is that this position has just become available. The bad news is that for it to work, you need to be able to make the move in the next four to six weeks."

"Boy, that is fast" I said "my replacement still needs work and there is so much to do before I can move. I thought I would have three to six months to transition everything."

"I understand" Peter said "we can pass up this opportunity and take our chances to see what comes up in the next little while. But, unfortunately, the fellow you would be replacing has to assume his new responsibilities for a project that is on the CEO's top priority list. He needs to be moving to the UK and they want him there yesterday which means that both of you will have almost no time to transition responsibilities."

"I can tell you that I did not make any friends when I insisted on four to six weeks" Peter continued "If you think that you would be putting the China business in jeopardy by moving this quickly, I would not have any problem continuing to look for other key opportunities for you. Although, I would hate to see you miss this one. It is an excellent fit."

"I agree" I said "This is a great opportunity. I will find a way to make the transition happen successfully."

While I was happy to hear about my new assignment, I was panicked since there was so much to do yet. So much for having a minimum of three months to transition and get my replacement ready. Under the circumstances, I simply have to find a way to make things happen and happen fast.

Leland, the young Chinese Manager who was identified as my replacement is not ready yet. I have been working with him for the past couple of months to get him ready. Jack and I decided that he would report to me while he trained and then after I left, we would have him report to another ex-pat manager to make sure he gets enough support until he is more comfortable in his new role.

Unfortunately, Leland's selection for the role meant that we were bypassing James, a decision that I had difficulty supporting. Leland was the choice of our Chinese partners and, as a company; we had a number of issues we were working on, including negotiations to buy back BOLI's share of the JV partnership.

Much to my dismay, as we looked at all the issues at hand, I had to concede that it would be prudent for us to go along with our partner's recommendation to promote Leland instead of James.

As a result, I had to spend some time with James. I had to explain to him that he was very highly regarded and that his future with the company is bright. I could see his dissatisfaction with my explanations but he was too polite to show his anger. I concluded our conversation with me promising him that I would do anything within my power to make sure he stayed on track for a promotion in the not too distant future. Unfortunately, this turned out to be a promise that was not kept by my successors. A few months later, James left the company to work for another major US company in the area. James and I have continued to stay in touch and I always felt that his departure was a loss for our company.

Nancy and I recognized that for the next month, I will be working nonstop. We agreed that it made sense for us to have the movers pack our belongings and ship them. We were told that our belongings will take between four and six weeks to arrive in California. During that time, Nancy would travel ahead of me and visit each of the kids for a few days before going to Sacramento to start looking for a house.

The movers were coming in two days and today the inspectors from the Bureau of Antiquities will be coming in to verify that we were not taking any valuable Chinese treasures with us. I spent some time talking to the inspectors and we became fast friends. I invited them to have lunch with us in the main restaurant but they said they had too much work, so we ordered some food and beverages to be brought upstairs. About an hour later they gave us the formal ok to ship all of our belongings, we bid them goodbye and I went back to the office.

Before we knew it, our belongings were packed and were en route to California.

Nancy had already packed her suitcases and was ready to go. Today, the International Women's Club members were holding a goodbye luncheon for her.

She had mixed emotions but she was mostly happy and excited to be moving to California. She had always wanted to live in California ever since she visited a friend of hers when she was 12 years old. Her friend had moved from Massachusetts to California. During that visit, she fell in love with California but had never thought she would end up there.

While she was sad to be saying goodbye to all the friends she made in the past three years, her sadness was tempered by her excitement that her dream of living in California was about to come true.

The next day, I accompanied her to the Beijing airport and we said goodbye. I waited for her plane to takeoff before walking out to Mr. Li and the long drive back to Tianjin.

The next few weeks were nonstop work as I had originally expected. Time was too precious to waste and I was feeling better about Leland and my concerns that he may not be quite ready to continue the journey the JV was on were diminishing as I was spending more time with him.

I had to wonder how much of that concern was subconsciously clouded by me not wanting to take any chances with a business that I presided over as it grew twelve fold. I was able to develop and execute the strategies that allowed us to grow our revenue from $40 million to over $500 million in the past three years. In order to accomplish all this, it took a lot of hard work and a great deal of personal sacrifice.

As I reflected on my feelings, I was starting to realize that this may not have anything to do with Leland. It is probably more likely that, subconsciously, I was thinking that no one can be good enough. Maybe this is what it would be like to be the father of the bride. I decided that I needed to give Leland a chance and make sure I did everything possible to ensure he can successfully lead this organization to the next level.

During my last week, I was running on fumes. I was exhausted and have been getting very little sleep as I worried about every little detail. On Wednesday, a goodbye party was planned in my honor. On Thursday, I will travel to Hong Kong to close my bank accounts there and take care of a few other financial transactions before leaving the region. On Thursday night, I fly back to Guangzhou where another goodbye party was planned and finally, on Friday, I will board an Asiana Airlines flight from Guangzhou to Seoul, South Korea and connect to a flight to San Francisco.

I woke up the next morning with a stiff neck and a lot of pain whenever I tried to move my neck. To look in any direction, I had to turn my whole body and the pain was worse than anything I had experienced at any other time in my life. It may have been the way I slept the night before, but most likely it was stress related. Simple pain killers did not do anything to relieve the pain. I struggled in the shower and made my way to the first floor where Mr. Li was waiting for me and, as usual, efficiently drove me to the office.

At 9:00 am, I had my weekly meeting with my direct reports. Julie was very concerned about me coming to work in my condition, but I assured her that I was fine. Besides, what am I going to do sitting in my hotel room all by myself? Being busy will keep my mind off the pain, I had told her as I headed for the big conference room.

I had Leland run the meeting. He was doing well although he kept looking at me to confirm I approved. About 20 minutes into the meeting, Julie knocked on the door and asked me to come out. I excused myself and told Leland to continue the meeting. She escorted me to my office where a man was standing. Next to him were several needles lined up on my desk.

I looked at Julie inquisitively.

She explained that he was one of the top acupuncturists in the city and that she took the liberty to call him over to treat me.

"But I don't believe in acupuncture" I said.

"I would encourage you to try it unless you have a better idea" she said.

As I was listening to her, I could feel the weight of the pain in my neck and decided to give acupuncture a try even though I was convinced it would be a waste of time.

I sat down and he proceeded to put needles in my neck, in my cheeks next to my ear, slightly above my jaws and between my thumbs and index fingers. I have to admit for someone as skeptical as I am about acupuncture; I felt instant relief as he inserted the needles. Even though I still felt pain, I was now able to move my head without having to turn my whole body.

He asked Julie to tell me that I can now go back to my meeting. I was puzzled, the needles were still stuck in me, but neither he nor Julie appeared to think it was strange. Being pressed for time, I decided to go ahead and return to my meeting. Julie said she will get me when it is time to remove them.

As I entered the meeting room, I was looking to see how people would react to me walking in with needles sticking out of me. The reaction was split by cultural background. The Chinese managers were not fazed and carried on as if all was normal. The ex-pats were clearly amused. As for me, I did not care. I was feeling less pain and that was all that mattered.

Twenty minutes later, Julie walked in and escorted me back to my office. As it turned out, it was not time yet to remove the needles. Instead, he turned and adjusted the needles and sent me back to my meeting. Another twenty minutes passed before Julie came back to get me and the needles were removed. That was my first experience with acupuncture and I was impressed by the results.

The next two days went by very fast and before I knew it, I was at my goodbye party. As it turned out, there were over 100 guests. All the ex-pat and Chinese managers were there. Most of the JV General Managers that I had become friends with as well as many heads of local bureaus were there. I was touched to see how many people were there to say goodbye.

I was presented with a sixteen inch ceramic statue of myself as a reminder of my time in China. I finally understood what happened about a month ago when a man came by my office and kept staring at me from different angles. One of my managers had accompanied him and since I was getting irritated, he asked me to please be patient and not ask any questions.

As it turned out, the man was a famous local artist who sculpted the statue. He had been given pictures of me, but he still felt he needed to see me in person. During the presentation, they told me that he needed to see me in three dimensions because it was more difficult for him to get the features of foreigners accurately. I was thrilled with the statue and most grateful to receive such a unique gift. It meant a lot to me. It has always occupied a prominent spot in all my offices ever since that day.

I finally went back to my room, finished packing my bags to make sure I was ready for my departure flight to Hong Kong in the morning.

The next morning, I went down to the hotel restaurant for a quick breakfast. After finishing, I went around to say goodbye to as many of the hotel staff as I could find. They took good care of us for the past three years and they always did it with a smile.

The trip to Hong Kong was a short one. I simply had to go to the bank and close my accounts there and wire money to my Bank back home. I took an hour to visit the office there and say goodbye to people who supported me for my Hong Kong and Taiwan responsibilities and then I caught the next flight to Guangzhou where I had a leadership meeting and needed to say goodbye to folks there as well.

After the meetings, Jack had arranged for a dinner with the leadership team and several of my direct reports and others that I worked with closely. Once again, I was very touched by how sincere people were and by how close I had gotten to so many people. The group presented me with an antique map of China that was over 100 years old. It was very interesting because it showed different boundaries than those that define China today. Everyone pitched in to purchase it from one of the largest antique dealers in Hong Kong. It was framed in a very fine, hand carved wooden frame and every one had signed their names on the matting surrounding the map. A very fitting goodbye gift I thought. Ever since then, I have hung the map in my office right above the statue that my friends in Tianjin gave me.

The flight home departed on time. I was very close to missing it because of a traffic jam due to an accident. The cab driver got us lost when he tried to go around the area to find an alternate route. However; he eventually got me to the airport about 25 minutes before departure. This appeared to irritate the immigration officials who assumed I was simply tardy and did not respect the expectation that one must be at the airport two hours prior to departure.

After giving me a small lecture, fortunately one that I did not understand since it was delivered in Cantonese, they let me through and I made my flight to Seoul where I connected to my flight to San Francisco.

As the flight took off, I could not help but start to reflect on my three years in China.

I have to admit that I felt very proud of what I was able to accomplish there during my three years and, most of all, I was proud of the organization that I left behind and the managers I helped develop. They have become serious business men and women with the skills to develop and execute a well thought out and aggressive business strategy.

It was with a mixture of pride and sadness that I finally conceded to myself that they did not need me anymore in Tianjin .... I have succeeded in my mission, they are now self-sufficient.

As I was thinking about the various managers and how far they have come, I dozed off. I woke up when the Captain announced that we have started our final descent into San Francisco. I put my seat belt on and realized that I was dreaming. It took a second but it finally hit me .... I was not dreaming about the past, but rather about the future .... I had already moved forward. In my dream, I was very happy and excited about my new life and feeling very lucky to be moving to sunny California where once again Nancy, John, Elizabeth and I will be reunited as a family.

THE END.

About the Author

Saba Joseph has a Master's Degree in Chemical Engineering from M.I.T. and has participated in a wide range of Executive training programs at Harvard Law School, Harvard Business School, University of Tennessee , University of Massachusetts, Lowell and Northwestern University's Kellogg School of Management.

He is married. His wife of 33 years, Nancy, and his two adult Children, John and Elizabeth moved with him to China and helped shape the personal experiences described in this book.

His career included 24 years with a top rated Fortune 500 consumer products company, 7 years with a direct mail marketing company and 4 years to date running his own consulting firm, The Joseph Group. He has and continues to consult for a broad range of clients including China JV's, Manufacturing arms of small to mid-size businesses and Venture Capital firms where he specializes in turnaround situations for new acquisitions.

He enjoys teaching and sharing his knowledge, developing management talent, coaching executives and helping people succeed and achieve their best. He has unique and interesting perspectives and an uncanny ability to work effectively with people. He is just as much "at home" at the factory floor as he is in the Board Room.

E-mail the Author - saba.joseph@yahoo.com
http://www.linkedin.com/in/sabajoseph